THE LAST GODFATHER

THE LAST GODFATHER

THE LIFE AND CRIMES
OF ARTHUR THOMPSON

REG McKAY

BLACK & WHITE PUBLISHING

First published 2004
This revised and updated edition
first published 2006
by Black & White Publishing Ltd
99 Giles Street, Edinburgh EH6 6BZ

ISBN 13 978 1 84502 086 6
ISBN 10 1 84502 086 3

A CIP catalogue record for this book
is available from The British Library.

Cover photograph courtesy of
Newsquest (Herald & Times) Ltd

Typeset by RefineCatch Limited, Bungay, Suffolk
Printed and bound by Nørhaven Paperback A/S

THANK YOU

Thanks to all the other scribblers who have written a little about Arthur Thompson, leaving me with an itch that needed scratching – the question of what else was there to know.

To The Fox, for his selfless sharing of contacts and his wise old eye for a story.

To those who helped but didn't want to be named.

To those who helped but didn't know it.

You all know who you are.

I know who you are.

Arthur Thompson knew you fine well.

You knew him better.

Reg McKay
Paisley

DEDICATED TO . . .

My partner in crime.

The one who helped me break out of wage slavery. Who didn't grumble when the loot ran out and the family silver was flogged. Who stayed in my team when the flak started flying. Who has humoured my craziness and tolerated my weaknesses beyond any measure of sanity. The one who has had more faith in me than I deserve.

To my blue-eyed green-eyed Gerry.

My partner in life.

CONTENTS

INTRODUCTION

'You don't know me but I know all about you,' said the voice of the nameless man down the phone. 'And all about that old bastard.' It was one of the less polite contacts I had about Arthur Thompson yet still one I was grateful for. Since the book hit the shelves, I've become accustomed to being approached by people who claim to have the in on whatever or whoever I've written about. With *The Last Godfather* those contacts almost took over my life. For months, I couldn't go to the pub but some old geezer sidled up to me with some story about Arthur. Then there was this one, the undercover cop. Now that was a surprise. The cops don't talk to me – they get rapped on the knuckles if they do.

This cop had been on surveillance of The Ponderosa, Thompson's house, on the night Bobby Glover and Joe Hanlon were shot dead, the night before Fatboy Thompson's funeral.

'We saw him seven or eight times that night through his window,' the cop said. 'He even came out to talk to us once. He couldn't have slipped away to be involved in Bobby and Joe's shooting.'

Couldn't have walked through the secret tunnel under the house to Fatboy's place, out the back window, over the wall and down the back lane to a waiting car? Like he'd done hundreds of times before? Then driven to a spot five minutes away, done the deadly deed and come back the same route to give the cops a wee wave from his front room? Couldn't he?

But I'm grateful to that cop. He did give me useful information that I didn't have before and it tied in with what this other fella told me in yet another bar when I was in search of nothing but a quiet drink.

Then you've got the blokes the same age as The Godfather, who grew up with him and grew away from him for very good reasons.

The straight businessmen came out of the woodwork in droves. Funny that a book should shake them out when they've been keeping their heads down for years. The kind of shenanigans they got up to with Thompson makes you wonder if the world is full of crooks – the only difference being that some admit it while others hide it.

Then there was the paperwork that people passed to me – usually anonymously. Copies of letters from Chief Constables, official reports, death certificates, reports on unsolved murders, notes about caches of illegal shooters, murder scenes and a whole heap more.

All of it helped me fill in some of the missing pieces in Arthur Thompson's jigsaw of a life. For a life that was so long spent at the top of organised crime, there is so much to discover. For a life spent trying to keep out of the public eye there are secrets by the wagonload. And with so many other folk in the know about his deadly doings still terrified of the spectre of Arthur Thompson, their snippets of info will only slowly dribble out over time – but not until they feel the way is safe. There are inevitably new tales.

Some new tales they are – torture, kidnap, concrete boots, Scots running crime abroad . . . and a whole heap more. There's more than enough of them to fill a book on their own but they're included here in this revised edition.

Will the story of Arthur Thompson ever be complete? Who knows? After all, he was The Last Godfather.

1

THE BLEEDING BUSINESS

The car snaked slowly along deserted streets shining dark and greasy after a day of rain. It was a cloudy winter evening, black as blood in the night and a time for the safety of your own fireside – but not for the three grim-faced men in the car. They had business to attend to.

Down from the north of the city, they travelled past the glowering Victorian bulk of the Royal Infirmary, a symbol of pain and hope to all who lived in their neighbourhood – a place they preferred not to have to visit. An ambulance, lights blazing and siren blaring, overtook them as they passed the Cathedral. Grotesque profiles of the monumental gravestones in the ancient burial ground of the Necropolis sneaked a look at them as they sped on their way. This was old Glasgow. Theirs but not theirs. There was no money to be made in history. These were modern times and they were men of their time.

On to the toll at Trongate and the lights of pubs, chip shops, cafes and Argyle Street. Groups of young men with greased-back hair, in the long jackets and drainpipe trousers of Teddy boys, strolled the pavements and whistled at pairs of young women in beehive hairdos and too much make up. Most would be going in the same direction as the men – east for the dancing at the Barrowland Ballroom. In a few years, it would become synonymous with death in the most unexpected of guises. A bible-quoting, neatly dressed, polite young man called John, the type you could take home to your parents, would pick up girls there, only to leave them dead by morning. In a few years, the name Bible John would define the face of uncaught serial killers – but not yet. John had not started stalking the city streets yet. Now they were safe. Or so people thought.

To the south was the High Court and Glasgow Green where throngs of thousands had regularly gathered to gloat at the unfortunates who were hanged in public. The car turned left through The Barras market, stalls now deserted and ghostly, sodden litter shifting in the wind.

'Pull in here,' the front passenger ordered.

'Want us to come in with ye?' the driver asked, receiving a scowl for his trouble.

'Just keep the motor running.'

On the pavement, the front passenger straightened his collar while casually looking this way and that. He felt into one coat pocket and weighed something, then slipped a hand into the inside of his jacket. It was a routine he carried out as regularly as most men checking they had their wallet and their car keys. Satisfied, with one quick glance across the street, he strode confidently through a pub's doors.

'He's a careful one, that,' offered the rear seat passenger.

'He is that,' agreed the driver, pulling a ten-packet of Bristol from his pocket and offering one to his colleague.

'He's no' expecting trouble, is he?'

'Naw, it's just his way. The man doesn't miss a beat.' The two men nodded agreement, smoked and stared through the rain-speckled car windows, idly watching an old man with booze-wobbly legs trying to make some progress up the pavement. One step forward, two to the side. Another step forward, two to the side. He kept straying on to the road then stopping, a surprised expression on his face. Taking off his cap, rubbing his bald skull, he'd set off, determined to get back on to the pavement. By the time the pub's doors swung open, the old drunk boy was heading back on to the street again.

'Any luck?' asked the driver.

'Nah, no show,' replied the front seat passenger.

'The stupid bastard.'

'Aye, stupid, right enough.'

'His place?'

'Aye, Duke Street.'

The long, unbroken rows of Duke Street tenements held a slice of Glasgow's street history that the men were all too familiar with. The packed population displayed a capacity for murder and mayhem that, to Glasgow dwellers, was more frightening than the violent reputation the outside world attributed to Gorbals. It was an old part of the city and it stank of blood.

There was the slaughterhouse where every day hundreds of cattle were corralled to their deaths, the moans and stench of their terror drifting miles across the rooftops. The site of old Duke Street Prison where executions took place when the public were first denied the spectacle of corpses swinging in the open air. Further up the way was the back close of 652 Duke Street where Susan Newell had dumped the body of John Johnston, only thirteen. In her Coatbridge flat, Newell had killed the young paperboy for reasons no one could fathom. She set off walking the twelve miles to Duke Street, which was alive with people, chaos and squalor and would be ideal for disposing of a corpse. Susan Newell didn't have to walk to Duke Street since she was given a lift by a thoughtful lorry driver. However, she did have to walk on 10 October 1923 when hangman John Ellis sent her to her maker in Duke Street Prison, the last woman hanged in Scotland. That was Duke Street – a brutal, unforgiving place, just like Glasgow itself.

The car rumbled down the street, the driver alert for potholes.

'Nutters. You're all of ye crazy!' The man in the back seat had rolled his window down and was shouting at the yellow squares of light that were the windows in the local psychiatric hospital. The other two men sniggered and grinned.

'It's no' them that's mental,' said the front seat passenger. 'Who's howling at a building?'

'Aye, well, ye know what they say about walls?' replied the back seat man without missing a beat. 'Walls have ears.'

His two colleagues guffawed at his persistence till the front seat passenger hit back, 'That one might be stone deaf, but.'

'Stone deaf? Ha, that's a bloody good one. Stone deaf, eh?'

'Pull up a couple of closes short,' ordered the front passenger. 'Don't want them seeing us coming, eh?'

As the car pulled in to the kerb, the two men were still enjoying the quips. 'And that means no laughing, ye fucking idiots, ye,' growled the front seat man, now deadly serious as he picked up a tool bag from the footwell. The men went silent quickly and effortlessly as if someone had switched off their humour buttons. It was almost that. It was fear of their young boss.

The tenement close smelled damp, mildew sweet, and halfway up to the first floor someone had urinated against the wall. There was the unmistakable stench of beer-riddled urine hanging near the door the front seat man rattled at while his two associates stood a little back in the shadows.

'He's no' in.' No 'Hello' or 'Can I help you?' from the small woman who opened the door. Obviously, she was expecting the visit and knew who they were. Bottle blonde hair fell across her face from too few loose clasps. Her face was streaked with last night's powder and faint red lipstick smeared her upper lip. She was thirty years old going on fifty. For the area, she was wearing well.

'I'll come in,' said the front seat man, moving towards the doorway.

4

The woman didn't budge. Looking down on her from up close, he could see the fear in her eyes but not hear it in her voice.

'No ye'll no'.' Placing her hands on her hips and shoving her elbows out she barred the doorway. As she moved the thick checked dressing gown she was wearing fell open, showing her naked breasts. The front seat man smiled, gently but firmly pushed her aside. The three men walked into the flat and shut the door behind them.

An hour later they emerged to strains of accordion-driven reels playing loudly on the wireless in the living room they had just left.

'He's got shite taste in music, eh?' said the driver wanting to talk, to break the silence and the tension of what they had just done.

'I don't know,' replied the front seat man, 'I like a bit of a dance.'

'Aye, he'll be dancing in there right enough,' said the driver and the three men laughed loud, skipping their way down the steps and out to the car. It had been a good night's work.

Driving back down Duke Street, the front seat man was lost in his thoughts. It hadn't been a huge debt. Just two hundred borrowed and fifty paid back. A fair bit of dough but not the biggest he'd lent, not by a long shot. He'd had his doubts though.

The borrower was just a two-bit pimp with one whore, his own wife. She was working as hard as she could and barely keeping the pair of them in drink. Besides, that type of work and the bevvy had stolen her youth, ruined her health. She would be getting paid less and less and probably forced to work the dodgy end of the Green. Her man swore he was going to retire her, start up a flat and get a few younger lassies in. Low wages and high prices, he'd pay off the debt in no time. But he'd been told in no uncertain terms that two hundred borrowed meant three hundred repaid at fifty a week and he'd better not miss one. Now he hadn't paid a dime for three weeks. Worse, he'd started hiding. That wasn't just bad business – that sent messages out to the streets. Bad messages that couldn't be allowed. Soon every bastard would be reneging on their loans. No chance.

Behind him, in that flat in Duke Street, there was a woman crying real tears of fear and hurt for the first time in a long, long time. At her feet was her man, lying in a pool of his own urine, faeces and vomit. Not that he could be blamed. When the first nail went through his hand, the pain must have been excruciating. With both mitts pinned the pain would have left him and terror would have taken over as he wondered what was going to happen next. Was he going to be killed? No wonder his body just let go and he messed where he lay. But who crucifies people these days? Well, he did.

The car headed north through the city, up the Garngad, now known as Royston, and on to Provanmill where it pulled in.

'You know ye'll no' see any of your money,' said the driver to the front seat man as he lifted his tool bag and opened the door.

'Aside from the twelve pounds I got the night – aye, I know that.'

'That pair will be oot o' Glesca first chance.'

'Aye, but have ye no' forgotten something?'

'Whit?'

'A small matter of four seven-inch nails.'

The three men giggled, remembering how the man had writhed and the more he'd struggled, the more he'd hurt.

'Aye, right enough,' conceded the driver once the mirth had died down. 'But do ye no' think ye were a wee bit too hard on them?'

'Hard? My arse? I left her the claw hammer to get the nails out.'

No humour now, just silence as the men pictured the distraught woman weeping as she tried to prise the nails from the floor and found it impossible to do so without hurting her man.

'See me, I'm a soft touch.' The front seat man stepped out of the car and stood on the pavement outside his home. He leaned down to the open car door. 'The sooner they two vamoose from my city, the better I'll like it.' With that, he slammed the door shut and strode away.

The two men drove towards their home patch of Springburn without their usual chatter.

'That big yin is some man, eh?' said the driver.

'Fucking right. He'll rule Glasgow one day.'

It was the 1950s and Arthur Thompson was beginning to make his name. If the world had only known what was to come next.

2

WELCOME TO HELL

1930s

The early life of Arthur Thompson was as typical as it was extraordinary. He came howling and kicking into the world in September 1931, right into the middle of hard times.

The economy was knackered and unemployment rife with the big industrial cities like Glasgow the worst hit of all. It was the days of cod liver oil and orange juice as mothers force-fed the supplements to their babies in a desperate effort to fend off disease and early death. For many, it didn't work. Too many died. Most suffered debilitating illness. The survivors were so small they had to change the rules for admission to the armed forces. As an infant, Arthur Thompson was a success story against the odds.

The shortbread box version of history would have Glasgow as the second city of the Empire. Tobacco, sugar, tea, coffee and anything else worth a farthing were imported to the city and, from there, they were traded on. A place where big ships were built by couthy, working-class men in mufflers and bonnets just content to do a good job, their job for life, building the best seagoing vessels in the world. A warm place where the idealism of Socialism caught the imagination as nowhere else in the country. Where football and religion made a heady cocktail that produced some of the best players the world had seen. A hard-working place, a hard-playing place. Mostly true, of course, but not even half the story.

Ireland and Scotland are linked on so many levels – not least their people. A question we hear today is why Glasgow has never become a violent melting pot like Belfast. It has teetered on the edge so often like a clown on a high rope, never more so than in the 1920s and 1930s. A few years before Arthur's birth, the streets of Glasgow were alive with open warfare. Forerunners of the IRA, the Fenian Brotherhood, bombed power-supply lines in the city's Darnley scheme in an effort to cut off contact between Glasgow and Ireland. But worse was to happen.

In 1921, two prisoners were being escorted to Duke Street Prison in the back of a cop van. One of the cons was facing charges of indecent assault but the other was in a different league altogether. Frank J. Carty aka Somers was a commander in the Sligo branch of the IRA. He was a difficult customer to hold and had already slipped jail twice in Ireland. Now the Glasgow cops had him and they intended to keep him.

These days there would be outriders on motorbikes, a cavalcade of police cars, a bulletproof armed response vehicle or two and at least one helicopter. Back then, there were two cops, carrying out routine tasks and issued with handguns.

It was a ten-minute journey from the High Court to the jail and no effort was made to take a different route. The van and its officers were sitting targets. At a junction into Duke Street, three groups of armed IRA men stormed out on to the street, surrounding the van and shooting without warning. Within a minute, one cop was dead and the van had been halted. But the ambush team had a problem breaking into the van. They even fired into the lock, only succeeding in sending bullets whizzing round the tin can inside. For the schoolchildren and passers-by running for cover in the busy city centre streets, it must have seemed that gun battle lasted for an eternity. In fact, it was over in minutes and had failed.

Later, it would be discovered that the lock to the rear doors to the van was damaged and specialist tools had to be used to free the prisoners. That night, the general populace took to the streets rioting and mobbing and fighting the cops. Throughout the media, there was shock and outrage that such an incident had taken place. But no one from the tenements was that surprised. Ireland and Scotland were too close together in almost every respect and Glasgow ran the perpetual risk of becoming another Belfast. It still does.

Sectarianism was evident in other ways – or so the pop historians would have you believe. A couple of years before Arthur Thompson was born, an eighteen-year-old youth was participating in the sport the city loved – football. He played well. By all accounts, if he had kept working hard at the game, he could have made it as a professional – that was one of the routes out of the slums, the other being boxing. He had played too well. On his way home, some irate supporters of the opposition team jumped him, thumping him with hammers and kicking him with their metal-capped boots. That was the day Billy Fullerton decided to fight back and it led to the formation of the notorious Billy Boys.

Named Billy not after their founder but after William of Orange, the symbolic leader of the Protestant faith in Britain and Ireland, the Boys were organised. They marched to fights, often behind flute bands, contributed regular funds to the gang to pay off fines or help members in need, appointed officers and turned out smartly dressed.

Their great adversaries were the Norman Conks, led by Bill Bowman. The Conks originated from Norman Street near Celtic Park and were, by repute, Catholic. Sectarian pressures had boiled on the city streets before but, for the first time, Glasgow had two large organised gangs fronting the strains between the religions – major fighting teams with membership numbers just short of a thousand men, all intent on violence.

The authorities' response was to bring in a hard copper, Sir Percy Sillitoe, who vowed to be the hammer of the gangs. To start with, his tactics had little effect. Then he decided to play hardball. Sillitoe started recruiting from the north of Scotland, an area hit as badly by unemployment as the cities of the south. He wanted the sons of the land, big strapping men with enough brawn to see them through any tussle. Once recruited, they were sent out with a simple order – beat hell out of the gangs. They obliged.

When alerted of a gang fight, the police would rush to the scene and then do . . . nothing. These men only fought with each other so why should the police bother while they were doing just that? Once the battle was finished, the cops sprang into action, picking off the victors and walking wounded and giving them a kicking from hell.

Later, police tactics were refined a little further. The highly visible police vans were dropped and replaced by nondescript vehicles. Thus, at all times, the uniformed boys had the upper hand of surprise. These vehicles soon became known as the Batter Wagons for less than subtle reasons. One way or another, police tactics in Glasgow didn't change for the next fifty years, except that the unmarked transport became known as the Meat Wagons. While public opinion and the media were on the side of the police, they didn't have much of an effect on street violence. Sir Percy, rightly heralded as one of the founders of modern policing, won plenty of street battles but never the war.

Violence on the street continued as per usual but all was not as it seemed in terms of the perceived religious divide. Fullerton was a Protestant all right but his mother was a Roman Catholic – as was his wife, Nan. He never attempted to conceal the links and, as a result, he was frequently subjected to harassment by Protestants because of his Catholic wife and mother. At that time, he was also refused membership of the Orange Lodge. But that was during his young adulthood and all that changed after he formed the Billy Boys. In spite of being refused membership, he was often invited to lead

Orange Walks during the marching season each July as the symbol of strong Protestantism and for other, more practical reasons. These walks and the Catholic equivalent, Hibs Walks, had long been a source of bloody violence between ghettoised communities along the religious divide. Billy Fullerton never refused an opportunity to participate or to fight.

The easy split between the Billy Boys and Norman Conks – between Protestant and Catholic – however, was not so simple. Both gangs took care of their own and often locals in need, regardless of religion, had reason to be grateful to them. It was a point of honour – a code found in similar forms among street players the world over. You didn't harm non-combatants, you didn't cooperate with the cops, you settled your own problems. These were the rules of the street the year Arthur Thompson was born. These rules were Arthur Thompson's heritage.

3

TRAINING FOR WAR
1939–45

Forget the mythology of bad seed begetting bad brood. Arthur Thompson came from a good family. His parents, Catherine and Edward, were decent, law-abiding working-class folk who wanted the best for their children. Edward was a steelworker and, like all his colleagues, especially in the 1930s, he was a tough cookie who was capable of labouring in the most inhospitable environment, six days a week.

The Thompsons lived in Springburn, then a highly industrialised area in the north west of Glasgow. There were steel mills and railway engineering works as big as towns and they manufactured steam locomotives to be sent all over the world. In some countries, the engines are still in daily use. The grey tenements were black coated with the smoke and filth pouring from the engineering works twenty-four hours a day. It was a hard, violent place with poverty everyone's neighbour, if not a permanent resident. The Thompsons kept penury at bay with hard work and thrift. But that wasn't good enough for young Arthur. He looked around himself and saw daily grind, alcoholism, wife beating, disease and misery. From an early age he knew he wasn't going to succumb to that. He was going to be a fighter.

At primary school, he had a knuckle fight almost daily and, by the age of twelve, he had graduated to boots, clubs and a 'Malky Fraser', as open razors were called. No Queensbury

Rules for him. Jumped by other guys and beaten up a couple of times, he learned and learned fast. At the first hint of a threat, he would hit out with whatever weapon he had at hand, no warning or quarter given. It was the way of the street.

The Second World War put the lights out in our cities to protect against enemy bombers. Yet the blackout had an unwanted side effect – a boom in crime. Arthur, now eight years old, and his young cronies took to thieving from shops and factories, seldom getting caught. With Springburn an industrial hot spot and near the flight path to top target Clydebank, bombing was common. Folk had more serious threats to worry about than a bunch of kids stealing. When he did get caught, most often he received a slap on the earhole or a swift kick up the backside before being marched home to face the wrath of his parents.

But the war had brought many changes, some invisible to the eye. For many folk, already struggling to get by in peacetime, the realisation that they might not be alive tomorrow brought a fine edge to their existence. The normal mores of right and wrong were quietly, imperceptibly eroded and, for some, permanently suspended. When bombs are raining down on you and your loved ones are risking their lives fighting abroad, it is easy to become bewildered. Forget the Dunkirk Spirit, wartime is always crimetime. This was not a polite war for the folk of urban Glasgow.

Then there came the shortages and rationing. To start with, people applied their initiative to producing more grub. Spending hours in an allotment growing vegetables wasn't young Arthur Thompson's scene. Stealing the produce was. He soon found more exciting ways to pass the time and earn a few quid. Some local men decided that their country cousins had an unfair bonus in being able to hunt extra food. Springburn, as with many areas of Glasgow, is only a few miles from the rolling green fields and the Campsie Hills. All that fresh air supported a mass of rabbits, deer and game – just the ticket for a decent meal. They were going on a killing trip.

The men gathered together a motley collection of old shotguns and First World War arms. One bloke who was in Dad's Army somehow managed to smuggle out a rifle and a few rounds of ammunition. At first glance, it looked the best weapon in their armoury and, after all, it was army issue. But, on closer inspection, it was a decrepit affair with a tendency to seize at random. The rifle probably offered more of a risk to the guy shooting than the target. God save the souls of Springburn if the Germans ever invaded.

Somehow young Arthur got himself invited along on the hunting trip. He was known as a handy lad locally and did favours for a lot of the men – running their lines to the illegal bookies and fetching another screw-top bottle of beer from their homes so they could continue their game of pitch-and-toss on the street corner. Late one Sunday afternoon, they all set off in a borrowed van. In its prime, the vehicle had seen service in the Royal Mail and the faint etching of the letters was still visible on the side panels, now scarred with rust and a patchwork quilt of lumps and bumps.

By the time the party reached the countryside, they must have been stiff and bruised from sitting in the back of the van with its non-existent suspension and bare metal floor. A few hundred yards off the main road and the first rabbits popped their heads up. With no game plan or experience the men started firing wildly – at least those with guns that actually worked did. One bloke with a shotgun was knocked on to his back by the recoil firing uselessly into the air. 'Fuck that,' he muttered, throwing the gun to one side, 'that bloody hurt.'

Without hesitating, Arthur reached down and scooped the gun into his arms. 'Can I have a go?' he asked the man who was now rubbing his aching shoulder and trying to shake the buzz out of his ears.

'Please yersel',' he replied. 'Buggered if I want to try again.'

Young as he was, Arthur had no problem in handling the recoil from the gun as he fired his first shot. It's not known if he actually managed to kill any rabbits. The total haul on that first expedition didn't amount to much anyway, so it's unlikely. What is known, however, is that this was the first time Arthur Thompson fired a gun. Unlike his older colleagues, in his case, it wasn't to be his last.

As soon as rationing was introduced, the wide guys in Glasgow spotted an opening. Limiting the amount of food, drink or petrol anyone could buy simply created an unmet need. It's good business to meet that need – at a price of course – and the idea that there might be cash to be made attracted people from both sides of the track. Some black market dealers had been street players, involved in armed robberies and protection rackets. But there was less money around and the war had resulted in the authorities being perpetually armed – not a good risk factor for an armed robber. Other black market traders were those operating at the edge of crime – the illegal bookies, club owners and gambling den patrons. Those guys could sniff out an opportunity to make money at a hundred miles.

Glasgow was a good city for trading in illicit goods. The river, shipbuilding and major railway junction meant that all sorts of produce passed through and was there for the nabbing. Often, the staff running the show or even guarding the goods were on the payroll of the traders, whispering what was coming in and when. Though the hunting party was amateur, they had the right idea in that the countryside was rich in food, now an extremely valuable commodity. But the traders didn't do anything so laborious as hunt or cultivate the illicit food. They simply made contact with the right farmers, struck a deal and smuggled the goods into the city after dark. Before long, Glasgow's black market was thriving.

Just entering his teen years, young Arthur was recruited to help out from time to time. He delivered the orders to the customers, picked up payments and generally kept the bosses in touch with what people wanted. Thompson learned that there was profit to be made in formerly everyday produce like fresh eggs and rashers of bacon – something he never forgot. While he was making himself a few pounds, usually paid in kind, he was learning important lessons in making money. In his adult years, those lessons would serve him well and mark him out as different from all his peers. There were men as fierce as Arthur Thompson – some even fiercer – but none had the kind of business sense that made him top man, The Godfather.

The Thompsons were a strong breed and Arthur was no exception. By the end of the war he was fourteen years old, strong-limbed and muscular. He had reached his full height of five feet ten inches – something of a giant by the standards of that time. He wasted no time in putting that physical power to use in the place he was most familiar with – the street.

Even at that tender age, growing up during the war years had given him a reputation as a hard man already involved in the business of crime. The teenage Thompson had the typical cockiness of youth and thought he knew it all. But he didn't know he was about to meet the men who would change his life and put him on the road to wealth and notoriety.

4

BOBBING AND BOUNCING

1945–53

Glasgow has a tradition of admiring fighters rather than gangsters. Money and fancy cars were something but, to win real respect, there was only one place and one way – on the street with your knuckles and boots. The heroes were the street fighters of the day.

Young Arthur Thompson was no different from anyone else. Raised a strict Protestant, one of his youthful heroes was the legendary leader of the Billy Boys, Billy Fullerton. But Fullerton had had his day. During the 1930s, some of the Billy Boys had established a brigade of Oswald Mosley's Blackshirts with fascist overtones, marching and violence. But there was no disloyalty intended by this action – at least not from Fullerton himself who was deeply patriotic. Mosley was slung into internment for the duration of the war and the brigades broke up. For Fullerton, there was only one option – to volunteer for service. He joined the Royal Navy and spent several years on active service in the Far East. When he returned to Glasgow, he retired from his role as gang leader, going on to play security-guard-cum-bouncer at the boisterous boxing bouts then common in the city. Though he never lost the respect of the legions of street fighters, Fullerton was no longer a major force.

There were those who didn't serve in the forces through avoidance, desertion or rejection. It is ironic that one Patrick

'Carry' Carraher was deemed unfit for the army, due to a bad stomach and a weak chest, yet he had the strength and the callousness to wreak terror and death on Glasgow streets for several decades. Originally from the Gorbals, Carraher's life of strife started in the early 1920s. By the age of sixteen, he was deemed so violent his own father and stepmother kicked him out. He led a fearless band of thugs who terrorised all they came across, dishing out frequent, often random, slashings and kickings. Between spells in jail, Carraher and his team led an orgy of mobbing and rioting, serious assaults, attempted murder and eventually murder. This was one of the guys youthful Arthur Thompson aspired to be like.

Juries in Glasgow had a well-established dislike of the death penalty – amazing for a city with such a violent reputation and record. That served Carraher well when, in 1938, he stabbed and murdered soldier James Shaw near Gorbals Cross. Arrested and tried for murder, Carraher seemed destined for the gallows – something everyone had been predicting ever since he first wore long trousers. A brilliant defence lawyer established that, in the seconds before the fatal blade struck into Shaw's jugular vein, none of the witnesses had actually been looking at the victim or the alleged culprit. Carraher, however, was still deemed to have been responsible for the man's death. He was found guilty of culpable homicide and sentenced to only three years in prison – and some believe that sentencing is lax these days.

But Carraher's luck was running out. In 1945, a man called John Lyon was hanged in Glasgow for his part in the murder of one John Brady who had, a few days before his death, been discharged from the navy. Lyon was the first person to be hanged in Glasgow in eighteen years and every street player took notice – except, of course, Carry Carraher.

Released following his three years for the culpable homicide, in 1943, Carraher was then convicted of slashing a bloke in a melee in a pub and got another three years.

Violence was his life and he just didn't stop. No sooner was he released than he was in trouble again.

John Gordon was a hero of the war. The ex-Seaforth Highlander had been captured at Dunkirk and spent years in prisoner-of-war camps. Released at the end of the war, he was entitled to a quiet, fulfilling life. Instead, he bumped into Carraher. Mistaking Gordon for one of a group of men who had attacked his brother, Carraher slashed him deeply behind the ear. It sounds petty by the standards of Hollywood Technicolor gore but it was a lethal blow and Gordon died a short time later. This time Carraher's luck had run out. Glasgow juries had found their way back to the death penalty and he was to be next. On 6 April 1946, he walked the walk to the gallows – except he didn't walk. Carraher fought, punched, screamed and bit every step of the way. He died as he lived, cursing and swearing and drawing the blood of anyone close.

Patrick Carraher has faded in the mists of time. Who wants to remember a man whose life was full of vicious petty violence? But, while he lived, he was the talk of the town for players like young Arthur Thompson. To Thompson and his like, he was a kind of living legend who was scared of nothing and no one. It helped that Carraher reflected the 'mad psycho' role model. There was nothing to admire in why he fought and hurt others. The fact that he did was the point.

Consider, then, a fifteen-year-old Arthur Thompson at the end of 1946. The most pre-eminent street fighter in Glasgow had just swung by his neck and young Thompson also learned that, in Leeds in January of the previous year, his namesake had also been hanged for a murder committed during a robbery. Pub fights and robberies were meat and veg for street players. To participate was to run the risk of fatalities and, therefore, a one-way trip to the gallows.

When Arthur Thompson opted for a life of crime, rather than following his father into the steel mills, as was common then, he knew he was likely to face death either at the hands of an adversary or at the end of the state's rope. It wasn't a call to be made lightly. We may wonder why the street players of his generation seem to be a different class from today's drug traffickers and smart-suited con men. The constant threat of death was one reason but it was not the only one.

The truth was that Arthur Thompson wasn't a great fighter – or, to put it in the words of his peer Walter Norval, then running the streets of Maryhill, 'Thompson couldn't fight.' This has to be put in context. Norval and his ilk were hard men extraordinaire. They would carry out feats of brutality and bravery that would be dropped from a film script as being too fantastic to be real. Compared to your ordinary Joe Soap, Thompson could fight all right and proved it often enough. He just didn't make the top league. But, then, few did and most of those died in the gutter as a result of a battle over nothing more lucrative than honour or territory.

Arthur had learned a lot by now, though. As far as he could see, there was no point in involving yourself in crime and the violence that went with it, like fish goes with chips, unless you made a profit. Young Arthur had other heroes besides the street fighters. Most prominent were those who made the bucks – the bank robbers, heist merchants and the protection racketeers. From an early age, Thompson aspired to be with the guys involved in organised crime rather than organised violence. Men like Bobby Campbell who, though only slightly older than Thompson, was already a legend on the street for his audacious robberies. Campbell came from polite Protestant stock. His father owned stacks of properties around the city and he expected his son to follow. Well educated and with every chance in life, Bobby Campbell chose to earn his living on the other side of the tracks. Some say this decision was underlined when he married a young Catholic woman – she was the love of his life and worth the sacrifice.

Campbell's speciality was ingenious armed robbery. He applied great thought and preparation to the jobs, always trying to outwit the law with maximum gain and minimum fuss. And these operations were armed because that was the name of the game in those days. In the pre-sophisticated security system age, banks were lucrative targets. But if you tried robbing one without a shooter, how would you cope with the have-a-go merchants and, worse, the armed coppers that would come on your tail? The cops simply assumed that bank robbers were carrying weapons and so bank robbers had to carry weapons. A vicious cycle leading to many a shoot-out on the streets of Glasgow.

Some credit Bobby Campbell with inventing the good-thief/bad-thief routine. A small gang would hit the bank during office hours when it was full of the public. Most would be carrying pistols but Bad Thief would have a big, nasty looking shotgun and he would make sure all the staff and the punters saw it. As the real leader of the gang politely, but firmly, took control of the situation, Bad Thief would start ranting, rushing around threatening people and brandishing his gun. If he reckoned there were too many nervous folk in the room or someone was at risk of having a go, he'd up the tempo and blast off one shot with a deafening noise and the smell of cordite – but always through the ceiling, always safe. Bad Thief was under strict orders not to hurt anyone. Persuasion was his game. It was all an act to ensure maximum cooperation and it usually worked.

A more sophisticated ruse, invented by Bobby Campbell, took a great deal more planning and effort. Post Second World War, large quantities of valuable goods like alcohol or tobacco were being moved by road. Even when the long haul was by train, they had to go that final stage of their journey in a large lorry. It was too good an opportunity to miss.

Campbell got all the signs of the day for road closures and diversions made professionally but entirely unofficially.

He'd find out which lorries had to travel down quiet country roads – often the source of information was the drivers themselves – and set traps for them. The lorry driver would encounter the signs and a group of workmen signalling him into the side, friendly like. Once he'd been stopped, he'd find himself looking down the barrel of a pistol, before being ordered to open up the back. Goods would then be quickly transferred to another wagon, which would be driven over the horizon at double-quick speed.

This method was to be further refined and used to tackle targets more heavily laden with riches, like security vans. In the sweatshops of the east end, realistic police uniforms were tailored for all the gang. Then one, or sometimes two, cars were totally transformed to look like cop cars. The security driver and his mate – the vans were not very secure in those early days – would be driving along, minding their own business, chatting about the football or whatever, when they'd see the blue light of the cop car behind them.

The bogus cops would signal to the target to pull in which they promptly did. Well, you would, wouldn't you? They didn't realise that the spot of the pull-over had been carefully researched beforehand and they were about to go on a major diversion. Once the 'cops' had taken control of the wagon, it would be driven to another predetermined spot well off the beaten track. There the gang could work in privacy, ensuring all the goods or the cash were taken. Then they'd drive off, leaving the drivers tied up and gagged. Once back in the city, with the loot stashed and the tools of their trade well concealed, a call would be made from a phone box, telling the police where to find the hijacked lorry and the men.

This type of hit worked very effectively for a number of years and had the added bonus of being of minimal risk to the gang and to the drivers. No wonder Bobby Campbell spent some time in jail under what was called Preventive Detention.

This was a kind of internment introduced during the war to take dangerous gangsters off the street.

But it was Bobby Campbell and his mates who gave Arthur Thompson his first step up. As soon as he could, young Arthur started working as a bouncer on the doors of local pubs. His brother, Robert, also worked at this trade which, at the time, entailed a lot more than peacekeeping. In the hard drinking all-male pubs of Glasgow, there was the potential for trouble to flare up at any second. All it took was someone to look the wrong way or just have the wrong look and it kicked off. 'Are you lookin' at ma beer?' wasn't a question but a preamble to a bloodletting. You can imagine what happened when someone actually did accidentally spill another's pint. It was the bouncer's job to end any such battle, throw all combatants out on the street and then follow through with a good beating to all concerned. The rights and wrongs of the dispute didn't matter to them. You could be sitting quietly, supping your drink, when a gang of thugs might pounce on you. If you decided to fight back to save your life, that would also have qualified you for a good kicking from the bouncers. Scrapping in their boozer was breaching their rules – full stop.

Working the doors wasn't for the faint-hearted but there were perks. Moneylenders recruited Thompson to collect their debts – not an unusual move for a bouncer. Standing on the door, watching the passers-by as well as the incoming customers, was an ideal position for a moneylender's heavy. If you were fearsome enough to take on all comers in the pub, the ordinary citizen who had borrowed a few pounds to get through hard times wasn't going to scare you. And Arthur Thompson didn't scare easily anyway.

Thompson was already beginning to show how he was different from his peers. Most equalisers would work for one moneylender only but Thompson worked for several. Normally, the bosses wouldn't have stood for this. They would want the world to know who was their man in case a dispute arose between them and a competitor. But Thompson saw no conflict of interest. As long as he collected in the money for everyone, they would all be happy, he reasoned, and he was right. Because he always delivered, the older heads let him off with his split loyalties. Of course, it also meant that he was collecting cuts from several sources rather than one. The young Arthur Thompson was a grafter and no doubt.

The moneylending business shouldn't be underestimated. At a time when credit facilities were far from being as accessible as they are now and most of the population was one short step away from dire poverty, moneylending was huge. It was one of the central planks of organised crime in Glasgow – the other being protection rackets, a game Thompson also entered at an early stage.

Some of the less scrupulous bar owners employed heavies to put pressure on competitors. The men would go to the bar, order drinks and then start a rammy, causing as much chaos and damage as possible. This would be repeated at regular intervals. If a pub became renowned for fights, the average punter would take their custom and cash elsewhere. That's why it was so important for pubs to hire the meanest bouncers. Thompson extended this little rigmarole on his own initiative. He would eye up the pubs around the east of the city, decide on the ones that were vulnerable and make them an offer they couldn't refuse. Their pub was at risk from the heavy-handed treatment but he would save them that grief – at a price. It was a crude and basic version of the protection racket but it worked for him and paid well.

But the work required a sting in its tail. When someone didn't pay up, they had to be taught a lesson that everyone could see. Thompson carried out these 'just business' assaults hundreds of times. Usually, the victims would be in such fear of further violence that no one approached the police. One time, Thompson went too far or maybe chose the wrong target to be heavy-handed with. The result was his first adult prison sentence when, in 1953, he was jailed for eighteen months for extortion. It was a short sentence but enough to tell Arthur Thompson that he didn't like jail – a formative experience that was to help make him the type of man he became in years to come.

Barely into his twenties, something good was happening for Arthur Thompson. Word had spread among the serious street players that there was a new, young talent on the block. Already, Arthur Thompson was someone to watch out for.

Those older and more established faces spotted Thompson's potential. One was a straight Joe or so his lack of criminal record indicated. Mendel Morris was one of the richest, most powerful men in Glasgow. Officially, he ran pubs, clubs, casinos and bookmakers, veritable gold mines, and he was also a very successful gambler. But, in common with so many entertainment entrepreneurs of his period, Morris also toiled on the wild side with moneylending and brothels. But Morris didn't lend a few pounds at a time – he dealt in large sums, usually to other businessmen or street players needing to finance a job. Whatever the outcome of the borrowers' ventures, the debt and substantial interest had to be repaid and that's where Thompson came in.

Women managers – madams, to you and me – ran the brothels for him. Reputedly, there were as many as ten at any one time with over one hundred working girls. They were based in the old part of the city centre, the west end and in a couple of big houses in the classier quarter of the Gorbals.

The problems with that game were manifold. Often a husband or boyfriend would take exception to his woman's occupation, cause a rumpus and have to be put in his place. Sometimes a woman had previously worked on the street and her pimp would try and force her back to his stable. The incoming Chinese population were congregating around the Garnethill area of Glasgow and some set up their own brothels. These provided so-called exotic fare of Chinese women and drew customers away from Morris's houses of ill repute. All this had to be sorted out with muscle, strength and tact – and without contaminating any of Morris's legitimate enterprises. That's where young Arthur Thompson came in. He quickly learned a great deal from Mendel Morris on how to ride two horses at the same time – legitimate and illegitimate, that was the way forward.

Bobby Campbell and his associates were persuaded by Thompson that he was just what they needed as a junior apprentice. He was big, fierce and ruthless but he also had a brain and knew how to use it – perfect for Campbell's mob. So Arthur Thompson sallied out on a number of bank robberies with the older team, playing the Bad Thief to a T. Banks were taken in Renfrewshire, Lanarkshire, one in Dundee and another in Stirling. Lesson number one – avoid your own backyard where you are known and you'll make money and stay free. Thompson had just turned twenty and was a skilled armed robber. But he had a lesson to teach his older counterparts about their stashes of money from the banks. What they didn't spend on drink, they kept under the floorboards. But Arthur was slowly investing his cash in businesses. It was a small start but it was an approach he would perfect and it would help make him the most powerful player in Glasgow.

Arthur Thompson must have felt very satisfied with how his life was going – and not just professionally. He had married his sweetheart, Rita, and life must have felt good. He was a young man on the up and up and the future looked like plain sailing. He could do anything – even tackle Scotland's harshest jail. Or could he?

5

WHO CAN'T?

EARLY 1950s

The Thompson Family had moved to the Provanmill, an area of the city already familiar to Arthur and his brother Robert through working as bouncers in the local Provanmill Inn. To outsiders, Provanmill appeared to be a quiet little council estate. At that time, it was practically brand new with the local corporation building houses to clear its citizens out of the terrible deprivation of run-down tenement slums. Moving to the area and homes with several bedrooms and inside toilets gave folk new hope. But it was short-lived.

The planners of the 1950s had built decent enough houses but had forgotten to provide access to shops, doctors, public transport and other essential amenities. The people realised that new jewels had been given with one hand but old familiar ones had been snatched away with the other. Across the road from Provanmill was the newly developed area of Blackhill. There, the council leaders decided in their wisdom to parachute in several families who had been causing grief in their former areas. It was a recipe for anarchy. In double-quick time, that scheme became synonymous with poverty and crime. It was a lawless no-man's-land for strangers, officials, workmen and even the cops. Arthur Thompson felt very much at home.

Among the players of his own age, Thompson chose his associates carefully. He was interested in those with skills and

28

ambitions. Even by this time, many of the hard youths who had ruled the streets were dead, jailed long term or so disabled as to be out of the game. Most street players of his generation had a short career but not Thompson – or Teddy Martin.

At the time, Martin was the major player from the Gorbals, then still a heavily populated area that was rife with every form of corruption. Being top man there was no mean accolade. Dark haired, sallow skinned and handsome, Martin had a taste for well-tailored, expensive suits and it was no surprise that, at any one time, he had several lady friends. Like Thompson, Teddy Martin had developed his own business of protection rackets with pubs and bookmakers as his main targets. They had the money – often hot money, to boot – which meant that any scam or robbery wouldn't be reported to the police.

Thompson and Martin were well suited. It was an alliance that crossed the River Clyde from north to south, breaking through the territorial disputes that seemed to obsess the hard men of the streets. This was business and both were out to make as much dough as possible. There was just one weakness that everyone was aware of – Martin had a violent and unpredictable temper. Arthur Thompson knew fine well that it wasn't acceptable to give in to irritability when there were cold calculated crimes to be executed. That temper of Martin's could get in the way of successfully completing their business.

Thompson's other associate was a different type altogether. Paddy Meehan was not an easy man to get on with. Dour, serious with a nasty tongue, Meehan couldn't stand fools. If you crossed him, you never forgot. All very nasty except for one small point – Paddy Meehan was bright and highly skilled – he was the best safe cracker, also known as peterman, of his generation. Glasgow had a long reputation of producing the best crackers but Meehan got a hand up by the best of the best. During spells inside, he had met a man who was a legend and deservedly so – 'Gentle' Johnny Ramensky.

By the 1950s, Ramensky was in his fifties, in failing health and his best days were over. But he knew the business of safe cracking and cat burglary better than anyone around. He was also a hard man to hold, having escaped more often from jail than anyone else. Ramensky was nicknamed 'Gentle' because he never offered violence and, when cornered by the cops, went with them without a struggle – if only to escape again a short time later.

Such was Ramensky's notoriety that he was freed from jail during the Second World War and recruited as a spy. On many occasions, he was parachuted behind enemy lines with orders to break into specified German command buildings and steal top-secret documents. This was not a unique move. Another peterman freed from jail to carry out espionage was Londoner Eddie Chapman, who became a close colleague of gang leader Billy Hill – rated by some old faces as the hardest man on those streets. Ramensky was undoubtedly the best safe cracker, though, and he took a shine to the young Paddy Meehan, teaching him everything he knew. The gift of that knowledge was worth more than money. It was a career.

The three-man gang of Thompson, Martin and Meehan was made in heaven. Martin was renowned as a lethal hard man but also a smooth talker capable of carrying off a con in the most unlikely of situations. Meehan could break into any building, dispose of any security system, crack any safe and, if the going got rough, would hold his own. Thompson, himself, was no pushover but he was the quiet thinker with plans in progress for crimes anew constantly bubbling under his calm exterior. They were going to go to town.

Well, they would have except Martin got a prison term. He was already known as a dangerous man so it was no ordinary jail for Teddy Martin but the infamous Peterhead. This prison was built as a penal colony in the nineteenth century because too many Scots, sent south for dispatch to Australia, were escaping en route and terrifying the locals. Back then, Peterhead's guards had carried cutlasses and rifles and a shoot-to-kill policy for any would-be escapees was in place. The order of the day was hard labour and men were set to smashing granite out of the local quarries, an arduous and extremely dangerous task. Stuck in an isolated corner on the coast of the grey and stormy North Sea, those crazy enough to try to escape were then left with a problem of where to go. Most of the few nearby houses were occupied by the families of prison staff who were all on the alert to report anything suspicious. When Martin arrived there, the cutlasses and rifles were gone but Peterhead hadn't changed much.

The only other man to have escaped from Peterhead was Johnny Ramensky who went on to complete the feat at least five times – though he never got far. Everyone knew Ramensky was different class. Even the authorities that considered Peterhead as the most secure jail in the country admired Gentle Johnny.

It was 1954 and it is perhaps no accident that Meehan's mentor, Johnny Ramensky, was also serving time in Peterhead. It would have been Gentle Johnny's style to help anyone intent on escape and Martin's links with Meehan would have been a further incentive for Ramensky to offer him aid. It was a well-orchestrated job that was planned months in advance. Somehow, Teddy Martin scaled the prison walls, dead on time, to be met by Meehan and another associate, John Harvey, in a car. As the car sped him away from Peterhead, Martin, in the back seat, quickly changed into a set of his own clothes brought by Meehan.

A few days later, the cops received an anonymous tip-off that Martin was hiding out in the loft of a tenement flat in the Blackhill scheme of Glasgow. It made so much sense to them since they were well aware of his association with Arthur Thompson and Blackhill was his neighbourhood.

Immediately, several cars were dispatched to the address above an otherwise empty flat and, sure enough, officers found regulation prison gear with Martin's number. It was immediately assumed that Teddy Martin had travelled from Peterhead to Glasgow, changed into civvies and slipped away, probably with Thompson's help. But someone was keeping an eye on the cops' search of the flat.

That same night, Arthur Thompson made a phone call to a hotel, only ten miles from Peterhead Prison, and spoke with Paddy Meehan. Replacing the receiver, Meehan strolled into the hotel bar and told Teddy Martin the good news – he could now head home. The police roadblocks on the road south to Glasgow would have been lifted as they concentrated their search on the city. Martin had been holed up right under the authorities' noses since he jumped the wall and he went on to get well way from the prison before eventually being recaptured. It was the most successful escape from Peterhead Prison during those dark days of the regime.

The brains behind this escape belonged to Arthur Thompson. He didn't know much about clambering over prison walls but he did know how to feint and lay misleading booby trails. What is more, he had increasing contacts and influence.

Thompson's house was a two-minute drive from Glasgow's infamous Barlinnie Prison. Known as the BarL, it was almost a local home from home for Glasgow street players and Thompson himself was no exception. Early in his adulthood, he realised how useful it might be to have some warders on his payroll. Fronting pubs and clubs as well as his association with Mendel Morris's brothels proved to be very useful indeed in this regard – especially since the majority of BarL staff lived locally.

In the pubs he could befriend the BarL staff, treat them with respect and make sure they had free drinks. Gaining their trust and friendship, he'd then move in to propose a wee arrangement of mutual benefit – money, of course, in return for favours within the jail when called on to deliver.

The working girls at the brothels were all instructed to advise Thompson if any of their punters were BarL warders and, of course, there were plenty . . . as well as cops, lawyers and judges. But, with these guys, the approach was different. He'd let them know he knew all about their visits and then he'd reassure them that their secret was safe with him, making a point to show his knowledge of their home addresses, wives' names and other personal details. Then he had them where he wanted them. They stood to lose their jobs, their marriages and probably a lot more. As they say in Glasgow, he grabbed them by the short and curlies, where it hurts. But Thompson did offer regular small payments for their cooperation. While he was never slow to impose his will with the most extreme violence, he needed these guys to stay in the job where they were useful to him. Besides, with every payment they took, he gained greater control as they dug themselves deeper and deeper into a compromised hole of their own making. During his lifetime, Arthur Thompson helped scores of BarL staff excavate.

So one of his earliest prison officer recruits was called on to help out with Teddy Martin's escape from Peterhead. All the warder knew was that Arthur wanted a regulation prison uniform and that's what he got. Thompson then had a local seamstress add Martin's number so that it looked authentic, planted it in the Blackhill loft and made the phone call. It was an approach that would not be sophisticated enough today with all the developments in forensics and DNA. But, for the circumstances of the early 1950s, it showed cunning and intelligence and more – the arrogance to take on the cops and Scotland's harshest jail and win.

Another lifelong trait of Arthur Thompson's emerged after this episode. When Teddy Martin was eventually caught and returned to prison, Paddy Meehan was duly charged, found guilty and sentenced to eighteen months in jail for helping him escape. But Arthur Thompson was never even charged, let alone convicted. He had already begun to develop the Houdini touch for escaping from the most incriminating circumstances. But it wasn't going to last forever – as he was about to discover.

6

A WEE TRIP IN
THE COUNTRY
1954

The road seemed to go on forever. It had been at Arthur's
insistence that they had set off from Glasgow early that day
and to cover the distance in one go.

'Christ Almighty, Arthur,' said Paddy, when they had
planned the job two weeks before, 'it's in the middle of
nowhere.'

'It'll cut down our chances of being spotted,' Arthur
Thompson replied.

'There's more sheep than humans that far north,' Paddy
Meehan insisted.

'Still . . .'

'And the folk that *are* there are too busy shagging the
sheep.' Meehan wouldn't let go when he thought he was right.

'They'll notice any strangers, Paddy – that's how they are
in they wee places.'

'Either that or fucking their sisters.'

'With our accents we'll stick out like sore thumbs,' insisted
Thompson, determined that he was right.

Meehan wasn't listening.

'. . . or their mothers.'

'This is too good a chance to miss, Paddy – we agreed.'

'Aye, no arguments there.'

'So let's no' take any risks, eh?'

Meehan looked at Thompson with an expression he often

used – one most folk interpreted as a prelude to a fight. Thompson knew better. Meehan was very shrewd but liked to get his own way. All his expression indicated was that he was deciding whether to concede to a fair point or continue with the argument. His associate decided to help him along, 'There's a bundle in this one, Paddy. Stake money to get us out of this game.' He wasn't telling Meehan anything they hadn't discussed before. 'It's no' worth taking any . . .'

'Risks, aye, I know. We'll do it your way.'

Meehan was a bright man and highly thought of by other players but he felt somehow that he was never in command – too often he was a second-league player. This rightly irritated him since many of the jobs depended on his skills in safe breaking. His partnership with Thompson and Martin was hard on him since those two carried leadership status on the street. Meehan knew his own worth and thought he should be the one who was calling the shots – if only now and then.

Thompson, on the other hand, thought he was handling relations between the men with some delicacy. It would have been even more sensitive if Teddy Martin had not been in jail and was along for the job. With that temper of Martin, Thompson had to be really careful. Meehan's griping was no problem by comparison. He had a sharp tongue, end of story. Martin, on the other hand, could explode without warning. Still it was Thompson and Meehan on this job and, if they pulled it off, maybe Martin wouldn't be an issue for much longer.

Two weeks later, they found themselves car-weary and driving through the night, along country roads, to Beauly, north of Inverness. They had been there before, of course, casing the bank. The target had been Arthur Thompson's idea. Those early years with Bobby Campbell and his crew meant he kept a sharp eye open for new opportunities in out-of-the-way places. He told Meehan he had read something in a newspaper about the world's richest man Andrew Carnegie and all sorts of other billionaires having an interest in this beautiful rural corner of Scotland. The broadsheets were a good guide as to where the cash could be found. There were Carnegie's Skibo Castle and his best friend, Henry Phipps, who had a particular interest in Beaufort Castle near Beauly. That got him thinking . . .

Thompson wasn't so naive as to think the area only housed mega-rich outsiders and nor did he assume that the area's wealthy folk would necessarily use the local bank. But it was an area of hunting estates and farmers and, with a city dweller's bias he shared with many people, he had never heard of a poor farmer. During the war, wasn't it farmers who had been sitting comfortably thank you very much?

Meehan didn't argue with that but he did want to know about the bank to be hit, the local police force numbers and all those other practical issues. A short recce to the town and they thought they were in dreamland. A couple of police officers walked about a lot but looked as if they were more prepared for giving directions to lost tourists than stopping crime. Even better, the Commercial Bank was being refurbished so business had been moved temporarily to the local Institute, a kind of cultural centre to the town with a library, community hall and the like. When Thompson found out that the real name of the place was the Phipps Institute, because Henry Phipps had put up the cash, he took it all as a good omen. Hard-headed Meehan just smiled. They'd waltz into the place.

Beauly was deserted – as they knew it would be. They parked the car round the corner from the Institute and set to work. Five minutes later they were standing in the temporary bank looking at the safe. Except they weren't. There were five safes and no clue as to which one held the most money. It was a minor complication for a man with Paddy Meehan's skills. He swiftly set to work opening the first safe. There, they found only a few pounds and a stack of documents. The second safe didn't hold much more. One safe was entirely empty. Another safe held nothing but another safe. Now that looked promising. Why go to all that bother unless the big money was stashed there? Except it was as lacking in funds as the others.

Hours later, Thompson and Meehan emerged on to the Beauly streets with little more than £400 to show for their troubles. While it was the equivalent of many months' wages for the average worker at that time, it was well short of the expected haul.

'Rich pickings, my arse,' Meehan griped, as soon as they were in the car.

'OK, Paddy, we're both disappointed,' Thompson replied, deeply downhearted but trying to keep a lid on things till they were safely away from the place.

But Meehan wasn't for shutting up, 'All this fucking way for four hundred nicker. We would have been better off betting at one of Mendel's joints.'

'Aw right, Paddy, aw right.' Thompson was angry at his friend's sniping. Besides, this was all about the money and he had plans that would now have to be postponed. He was going to buy into a few lucrative businesses . . . a couple of pubs and a casino – money-spinners that would get him away from this risky game. He steered his car, a flashy Humber Snipe, down the country road towards Inverness, the gateway to the south, home and safety.

'A dead cert, you said. Some fucking dead cert. Ye were half right – it was dead.'

'Paddy . . .' Thompson's temper was rising. This was not a good sign.

'Petrol money. That's what we got and maybe some loose change.'

'Paddy . . .'

'Instead we're hours from the city and . . .'

'Shut the FUCK UP!' It started as a low, almost inaudible

38

growl and quickly rose to a full-blown bawl. That was a sure sign that Arthur Thompson was one short step away from losing his temper. Not a desirable set of circumstances for anyone in his company – not even a friend. Meehan knew that Thompson had taken to carrying a loaded Beretta on him most of the time and certainly would have had it on this job. Unlike other Glasgow players, who preferred to stick their pistols in the waistband of their trousers at the back, he carried his in a shoulder holster. Thompson confided in his friend that the holster made it easier to draw quickly and, besides, it didn't ruin the cut of the expensive suits he had taken to wearing. What a waste that would have been and Thompson hated waste. That night it wasn't Thompson's suit Meehan was worried about.

The two men drove on in a strained silence. Such occasions weren't common between them but they weren't unheard of either. These were two men used to asserting their will. Hardly a surprise then that they occasionally rubbed each other up the wrong way. With others, both would go the whole road if necessary. But with each other they always stopped short of the mark. There was a growing bond between Meehan and Thompson that would last as long as they did.

In the powerful Humber Snipe, they made good time on the road to Glasgow with only one stopover for petrol as the car guzzled fuel. As the men got closer to Glasgow, they started talking to each other again, tentatively to start with and gradually back to full flow. Their spat hadn't lasted long and soon they were consoling each other that at least they were £400 better off. It could have been worse. In the robbery business they had to expect some failures before they hit the big one. It was all part of the life they had chosen. As the men chatted away, they didn't realise they were about to face another professional risk.

The garage attendant who had served them petrol didn't like the cut of their jib. He reckoned the car was far too flash for those rural parts and the men too sharply dressed. The world, even Scotland, was a much bigger place in the 1950s. Strangers were spotted and levels of wealth were noted – and the broad Glaswegian accents of Thompson and Meehan hadn't tied in with the petrol pump attendant's notion of folk who had money. Nor had the few but obvious facial scars both men carried from past spats. The garage man noted the car's registration number and called the cops with a very good description of Thompson and Meehan. Pretty soon, they had confirmed a link with Thompson. As if that wasn't bad enough, by the next day, the robbery in Beauly had been sussed and the local cops were searching for clues and they weren't as sleepy as Thompson and Meehan had made out. One eagle-eyed copper spotted a set of keys lying in the town square, close to the bank's temporary home in the Institute. Thompson was hauled in for formal questioning about the robbery.

'Can you explain these, Arthur?' one of the investigating cops asked, dangling keys in front of Thompson.

'They're devices for opening doors,' quipped Thompson, as fast as you like, with only a glimmer of humour showing in his eyes. 'Least that's what I use them for.'

'And do you recognise them?' The policeman hadn't had a humour bypass – he was just fed up of Thompson's wisecracks intermingled with his refusal to answer most questions.

No reply.

'They are for your house and they were found in Beauly on the ground near the bank.' None of this came as a surprise to Thompson who knew he had lost the keys but not where. Also, he was well aware the cops had been at his home trying the keys. 'How did they get there, Arthur?'

'Must have lost them when I went on that wee trip to the country.' Thompson knew they had him but, true to form, wasn't going to give the cops any help at all.

His wee trip was to lead to another place – jail for three years. His co-accused, Meehan, got six. So it was back to that place he hated with plenty of time to think – no more rural shots in the dark for Arthur Thompson. He was heading south to the big smoke.

7

KISS MY ARSE

MID 1950s–1960s

Mendel Morris proved to be useful to Arthur Thompson in so many ways. Not only did the entrepreneur give him his first proper job but also contacts that any other young street player would have struggled to make on his own. Around Glasgow, Thompson was known as Mendel's man, a very useful tag when he was just starting out. Now it would be his passport to where the real money was – London.

Thompson had travelled south a few times with Mendel to meet with club and casino owners there. This wasn't unusual. The entertainment players had many reasons to meet up for mutual benefit – some legal, some not so clean. For them it was all about money. Cheap booze sources were a major issue. People in the alcohol industry were often only too keen to come to arrangements to distribute labelled goods by-passing the duty men. But strictly for cash.

Stealing the booze was also common, as was hijacking lorries stuffed full of the commodity. With the massive whisky industry in Scotland, much of this cut-price drink came from there. Often the loads were too hot and too large to sell in Scottish pubs. But London was another story. Thus, the young Thompson would be the face of many of these deals with the London pub and club owners. Like Mendel Morris, of course, they also associated with a few street players and often the official owners were simply the legitimate faces of businesses owned by the gangs. The big London teams were always happy to do a bit of business for profit.

From early on, Thompson was meeting London faces. Among them were: the Butler Family, who commandeered much of the work around London Docks; Bert Rossi, who ran a few clubs; and the Mills Family, who would go on to control the streets of the West End. Around Canning Town, he also had some dealings with a group nicknamed The Brown Boot Gang, a large group of individual players from the East End who grouped together in a syndicate in order to prosper better. These guys were all smart dressers, favouring Savile Row suits well beyond the average budget, but they had a habit of spoiling the effect by wearing brown boots and white socks with them. Apparently, it was a fashion fad in the East End at the time but one that wasn't shared by all – thus, the rather derisory nickname. It's maybe no accident that most of this group would eventually move out to Essex.

None of these people should be underestimated. Though hardly household names now, they were powerful and important in their own sphere and time and, besides, they avoided publicity, a habit most crime factions follow for obvious reasons.

All of these people contributed in a vital manner to Thompson's links with London though he also made more famous associates in those early days. The Richardson Gang from the south east of the city, led by Eddie and Charlie. Billy Hill, deemed by many to be the hardest of all London's players, was probably the lead player at that time. 'Mad' Frankie Fraser, also known as The Dentist for his routine of torturing people by removing their teeth with pliers without anaesthetic. No surprise that Fraser and Thompson found they had a lot in common and became lifelong friends. If Mendel Morris was the passport, these people were the ticket to work in London and Thompson quite deliberately fostered good relations with them.

This marked Arthur Thompson out as a bit different from other Glasgow career criminals. There was a tendency then to stick to your own home patch, concentrating on the protection rackets and robberies in a familiar landscape. Thompson did all these things in Glasgow, of course, but saw no reason why he shouldn't do a bit of trade elsewhere and nowhere was more lucrative than London.

At first, Thompson stuck to wheeling and dealing particularly around Soho. Back then, it was the hot spot for London nightlife and was controlled by Billy Hill and Jack Spot. In return for booze, there were often trade-offs rather than cash. The London Docks were a rich source of almost anything you fancied. High value, small bulk items like expensive Ronson cigarette lighters, then a must-have item, were commonly traded. The London gangs were also into long firm scams and often would allow trusted associates to benefit from whatever goods the bogus company was meant to be trading in. Thompson also became involved in the horse-racing circuit and illegal gambling. The scale of Ascot and the number of punters far outweighed the courses in Scotland so that was one thing he was quite happy to leave to others back home. But the south of England was a different matter and that's where his expertise as a bagman, the heavy who carried the loot, came into play.

Some of the teams would pitch in and try to rob each other, particularly when the takings from a big day at the racing were available. Given that the loot was illegal in the first place, these were robberies that would never be reported. But, if the identities of the robbers were known, then they would have a highly lethal, armed-to-the-teeth squad on their tails. Not good. One trick they deployed was to hire people from outside the city – unknown faces from Newcastle or Liverpool. That's where Thompson came in. Not, as you might expect, committing the robberies but carrying the payroll from the races, greyhound tracks or one of the big clubs that made a packet at illegal gambling, with a sideline making and selling blue movies. Whereas the usual routine was to go team-handed, he worked alone – and very successfully.

He would be given precise details on where the money was, what it would be in, who was passing it on and where to take it. Usually, he was told to travel by bus or tube. This seems an unnecessary risk but the robbers would suss out the team's cars and wait for any movement. Also, taxi drivers very often worked for the gangs or were paid for reporting any suspicious comings and goings from certain locations.

Often the money was in an ex-serviceman's kit bag or in a khaki gas mask bag, commonly used by the public at the time – certainly never a briefcase or anything that looked expensive or secure. Sometimes the money would be quadruple wrapped in thick brown paper and tied with string. Hardly the Hollywood image of a bagman for a top firm of London gangsters but then this was real life and that was the whole point – not to be noticed. Already, in Glasgow, Arthur Thompson would be spotted by some street player wherever he went but, in London, he was just another man catching the bus home.

There were eyes on Thompson, of course. The team who had hired him didn't make a secret of their intention to have him tailed at a discreet distance. Usually, it was explained as an insurance policy in case he was ambushed. Maybe, but Thompson knew fine well that they were also watching in case he decided to do a runner with their money. Never told who his shadow was, Thompson knew it was essential to follow his travel instructions precisely. Go to the wrong bus stop, turn left instead of right and he could find himself at the end of a bullet. But this pressure didn't bother Arthur Thompson who would have been disappointed if the gang hadn't taken such precautions. It was only being professional and, during his jail time, Thompson had not only planned to go south for work but had also decided he was finished working with amateurs.

Part of the game plan required that Arthur Thompson didn't advertise who he was, where he was from or what he was up to – not even to his close confidants back in Scotland. All they knew was that Big Arthur was often away in London. Even then, loose talk, in the windowless, dead-eyed bars of Glasgow, led to all sorts of fantasies being passed off as gospel. Over time, they have become old urban myths, long accepted as fact. Hit jobs, threateners, running with well-known gangs that are now completely entrenched in the history of true crime. All that was to be true but just not back then.

The young Arthur Thompson was a careful man. He laid each brick with calm professionalism and the firm knowledge that he would lay another and another. He kept it all to himself, almost, knowing that, if word of what he was really up to got round, some bad bastard would come along and kick the bricks over before the cement had set. Thompson planned his career like a miser saves his money, in secrecy, savouring every successful move. He would count and recount what was in the kitty as he planned to go out and steal or earn some more.

The new bagman's success rate was one hundred per cent and that was being noticed. Soon, Thompson was invited to take part in jobs, along with various players. That meant he couldn't play the role of undercover bagman any more. It also meant his reputation would spread in the big city and, if all went well, it could lead to more lucrative business. This was what he had been hoping for all along.

In those days, London was buzzing with robberies and heists and, while there are very good records and accounts of some of them, little is known about the majority for one excellent reason – they remain unsolved. Old players who survive today aren't keen to talk about what they have never been convicted of. There are too many examples of careless talk on TV interviews and in the pages of biographies that have resulted in police investigations being reopened. Also, in London, Thompson was a team member, recruited to carry out a particular role under someone else's leadership. Thus, it's difficult to pin down exactly which London jobs Thompson was involved in early in his career but we have a good idea of the type of crime he committed – bank robberies, raids on warehouses and heavy arm action on pub landlords refusing to pay up their protection money. There are also many reports agreeing that he tackled a Chinese group who were muscling in on the prostitution racket around Euston Station – something that reminded him of protecting Mendel Morris's brothels back in Glasgow, which must have made him homesick.

All was working well for those first few years. Thompson was making his links and forming alliances that would see him in good stead over the years. He was also becoming familiar with the massive city of London, which was no mean feat for an outsider just popping down there for a day or two's business at any time. It wasn't just the Knowledge that Thompson was acquiring but also the politics of the street – which team ruled which area, old squabbles, scores to settle and all that goes with human social behaviour.

The organised crime scene in London was complicated but Thompson was taking his time, listening all the time and being careful not to be seen as asking too many questions. Nothing makes a player paranoid more than someone constantly wanting to know more. His approach was as disciplined as a young politician, merchant banker or whatever other legitimate career you care to consider. This was a bloke destined for the top. Not of Glasgow or Scotland but the UK and farther afield. Then he got greedy.

With his licence to work in London well earned, Thompson carried out a few more independent jobs in the city. They were successful big earners till an old partnership got back together. Teddy Martin and Paddy Meehan had been very busy in their own right but there was still an allegiance between them and Thompson. When a London contact of Thompson's suggested a night-time raid on the Westminster Bank on City Road, he got in touch with his old partners. The London contact was carrying out a lucrative role. For certain information, details and the idea, he'd get a cut of any proceeds without taking a risk and without even having to fund the job. It's a role that's very common these days and would come to underpin why infamous robber gangs, like the BarL Team, were never caught. But, back then, Arthur Thompson was once again decades ahead of his time.

Meehan, Martin and Thompson met in a pub to put their money up to cover the expenses of the heist. There was dynamite to buy – as well as clothes and guns that could be safely disposed of later. The kitty was £300 and Teddy Martin was to purchase the goods. When Thompson produced a very rare £100 banknote as his payment, Martin went ballistic, almost starting bloodshed in the pub. All such robberies were planned with great care to avoid attracting any sort of attention. Yet here was Thompson, who knew that fine well, flashing a rare note that could easily be traced and it was to be Martin's task to cash it. Thompson was doing very well at that time – he felt like London was his second home and might have been trying to show off a bit, though that was not his usual style. But, the longer Martin thought about it, the more he concluded that Thompson was trying to set him up.

By the time they went back to Meehan's flat, Martin was in full flow. In that state, he was likely to cause somebody severe injury – as he had proven in innumerable similar incidents throughout his life. This was well known to Thompson who simply drew his Beretta and shot his pal Teddy Martin. This might sound cold and callous but Martin was a very dangerous man when his temper was aroused – even more lethal than Thompson, according to their peers. Thompson left the flat immediately and Meehan and his wife drove the badly bleeding Martin to hospital.

The wound was superficial and, next day, Martin insisted the job go ahead as planned – though obviously without Arthur Thompson. It was a disaster and Martin was caught red-handed when an office worker heard the explosion of the dynamite packed in the safe door.

Meehan escaped and he was keen to make up his losses. Thompson's London contact, the very guy who had proposed the bank robbery in the first instance, suggested a large Co-op store in Edmonton was just the ticket. It has to be remembered that the Co-op was then one of the country's biggest retailers and the amount of money taken by the larger stores would be massive. But it was another balls-up. This time Meehan was caught red-handed and was jailed for eight years.

What was Arthur Thompson's role in this? At the time, folk assumed it was just one of those things and he grieved just as much as anyone when he learned of his friend Paddy Meehan's misfortune. But there was a growing feeling that Thompson was escaping from too many jobs without any convictions. His success rate was just too high and his escape-rate even higher. Like every other major player, he owned a few cops, paying them regular stipends to turn a blind eye and warn him of any interest in his activities. But he never went down – others did.

So far, most folk didn't question Thompson's relationship with the cops. Teddy Martin asked that question. Officially, his murder by a gunman on 25 March 1962 remains unsolved. Unofficially, even the dogs in the street knew that Arthur Thompson had Martin killed. He didn't pull the trigger himself but he ordered it. Given how nasty and violent Teddy Martin could be and how he'd look for revenge on Thompson at some point, there was a lot of sympathy in Glasgow for Arthur Thompson.

But the same couldn't be said in the south. Billy Hill passed a message to Thompson that word was going round in certain London quarters about 'the Jock who was trying to take over a slice of the action'. It wasn't complimentary. Worse still, it was emanating from the boys least likely to hold with outsiders – the Kray Twins.

Trouble was brewing and it was all Thompson's fault. London's potential for earning some crooked money had fazed him into working more and more with his own people, rather than the local teams. It seemed to him that, as long as someone wasn't planning to rob a certain bank, say, what was the problem with someone else doing it? That 'someone else' being him. And that's where he had overstepped the mark. Sooner or later, it was going to happen that he became embroiled in the politics of the London streets and now that time had arrived. No matter how careful he was, he couldn't keep in everyone's good books. That's not how it worked.

'Who the fuck's this Jock?' That's what they were asking, according to the word. It wasn't so much a question as a warning signal that said, 'STAY OUT!'

Thompson had a few choices, none of them palatable. He could heed the warning and stick to his own city of Glasgow – after all, he had made a good few quid in London already and, week by week, he was growing in his home base. But sticking to Glasgow would wipe out all the careful work he had built up over a few years and mean he would have to forgo the rich pickings London had to offer – bugger that. Or he could ignore the warning and just slow down his action for a while. But that would mean losing face and it would be back to square one when he next dropped into the capital. Then again, he could gather together a bunch of his troops, head south and link up with the Richardsons who were increasingly lining up against the Krays. Maybe they fancied joining in and dealing with the twins? But that would result in Thompson having to take sides, which would gain him as many enemies as allies. Besides, he might be strong in Glasgow but he wasn't sure he was ready for all-out war with the London mobs. None of those options would do so he had only one choice remaining.

The hackney cab drove slowly through the early evening London streets, carrying the silent grim-faced passenger. All the taxi driver knew was that the Scot had asked to be taken to the Double R club where the Krays hung out. Everyone knew that place was trouble, especially the taxi drivers. But one look at the passenger warned the driver to keep schtum. This guy looked like he was more trouble than even that club could handle.

The taxi pulled up to the kerb. 'Wait for me – I'll no' be long,' said the passenger, stepping out on to the wet pavement. He pulled his coat straight and, without waiting for an answer, strode into the club. The place was full of stars like Judy Garland, Sonny Liston and Diana Dors, as it was most nights. And there were the faces too – Jack 'The Hat' McVitie was there, the Dixon Brothers and George Cornell. They would all come to a sticky end – McVitie and Cornell at the hands of the Krays – but, at that time, they were well in, part of The Firm.

The man in the short checked raincoat looked out of place. Smartly dressed as he was, he had a different style, an awkwardness that didn't match the glitz and glamour of the city lights. 'Are the twins in?' he asked a white-jacketed barman.

The twins were in every night, he was advised politely but in a patronising tone.

'I want to see them.'

A waiter disappeared into the club to pass the message on.

A few awkward minutes later one of the Kray Twins arrived. No one can remember which one – or maybe they choose not to.

'Can I help you?' the twin asked, all polite and smiling. What did he have to worry about? This was his territory, his place. He was surrounded by some of the fiercest street players in London and they were on his side. The man in the raincoat looked up to respond and saw the other twin approach, more slowly, smiling, stopping and chatting to guests in the club. He paused till the both twins were close by within hearing.

'Aye, you can,' the stranger said quietly as he put one mitt into his coat and smoothly pulled out a sawn-off shotgun. Both twins stood gaping, dumbfounded. 'You . . .' the stranger jabbed the barrel at one twin, 'you kiss his arse.'

That particular Kray twitched, looked furious and his hand jerked towards his waistband. He looked at the stranger's unblinking face and the gun held firmly in his grip and just knew he wouldn't hesitate to pull the trigger. He had to be some kind of crazy to try to pull off that type of stunt right there, in their own backyard – the kind of crazy who would start blasting without hesitation. The twin slowly dropped to his knees behind his brother, his face white with fury.

'My name is Arthur Thompson from Glasgow,' said the stranger. 'You'll no' forget me.'

Holding the gun at the twins till he backed off to the door of the club, Thompson turned and walked swiftly to the waiting cab. As the driver steered through the city traffic to the station, Arthur Thompson sat in the back and said nothing. He would have been deep in his own thoughts. He'd done it now. Either the twins were going to come after him or that was the matter settled. Whatever was going to happen, his life would never be the same after that night. But isn't that the way progress is made – by embracing change and taking a few risks? He was the man for that routine.

At Euston Station, he paid off the taxi driver and walked straight into the concourse, then all the way along the front of the platforms and out an exit at the other side of the station. He walked a few blocks more until he found his car exactly where he had left it. If the cab driver was in the pay of the twins they would be sending a team to the station or to points farther up the railway line to Glasgow. That was fine by Thompson who was going south then heading homewards up the east-coast route. It added hours on to his journey but at least he would return home alive.

The tale of the confrontation with the Krays has clearly been augmented over time – mainly in the pubs of Glasgow where everyone is a self-proclaimed expert on Arthur Thompson. The incident did happen, though it is very much in doubt that he made one twin kiss the other's arse. More likely this is an embellishment reflecting Thompson's strongman reputation and alluding to Ron Kray's homosexuality. Players who knew Thompson well say that he definitely pulled the shotgun but reckon what he said to the Krays was 'Kiss my arse!' – a good old Scottish way of telling someone that you'll be doing exactly what you want to do, no matter what they think. Either way, it was an enormous risk that could have cost Thompson his life, if not that night then very soon.

While Arthur Thompson had many special qualities that led him to the position of Godfather, it must never be forgotten that he was an extremely hard man capable of cold, calculated and extreme violence. And he was going to need to be hard. Major trouble was waiting for him at home.

8

NEIGHBOURS FROM HELL

EARLY 1960s

The Provanmill area of Glasgow is small, insignificant and famous for nothing. Yet that's where Arthur Thompson and his family lived though many mistakenly believe it was in Blackhill only a few steps away across Provanmill Road. Comparing the quiet scheme of Provanmill to the rowdy deprivation and squalor of the Blackhill scheme was like comparing chalk and cheese. Yet, a few blocks away from Thompson, in the same scheme, lived a danger he was about to confront – the Welsh Family.

The Welshes were a huge tribe. The matriarch, Maggie Welsh, owned and ran a couple of fruit and vegetable shops in the east end. This was not as unusual as it might seem. Nearby was the Glasgow Fruit Market where masses of fruit and vegetables were brought in every day for selling on to restaurants, shops and so on throughout the west of Scotland. One of the common sources of local employment was in the Fruit Market. It didn't take long for many workers to suss out that they could make a fair profit by flogging the produce directly to the public themselves. The work had an added bonus. A few months in the market and it was easy to work out the scams on how to get the goods either at a much-reduced rate or free. Literally off the back of a lorry.

The fruit and veg folks worked in the cold, hoisting weighty bags of goods all day, and, among shopkeepers, they are the ones who are deemed to be really hard. The Welshes were the prime proof of this principle. Not a handsome family, they produced children at an amazing rate. What is more they stuck together so, at any time, there would be three generations of snarling, fighting team members, all with a natural capacity for violence. They were a formidable force in anyone's book.

The Welsh crew had been involved in crime for generations but, up until this point in time, it had only been on a petty scale. Then they took a look at their power. They were strong and united. Who better to trust than family members? And they were capable of having a go at anything, anyone. They had been carrying out debt collecting, protection rackets and reprisals for some of the heaviest players in the city for years. So, like they'd done with the fruit and veg business, why shouldn't they cut out the middlemen and do it themselves? But there was one problem – those they targeted didn't like it one bit. Who did they tackle first? The biggest and the closest, that's who – their near neighbour, Arthur Thompson.

It started in a minor way. Arthur Thompson was already seen as the big fish in that quarter of Glasgow. The place was stacked full of small-league players but he was the one with the organisation and the power. Besides, he gave a lot of the local players work. Work and wages wins loyalty. The Welsh Family didn't like that at all.

By comparison with Thompson, the Welsh Family were seen locally as scum. They dressed as if from a second-hand shop and were noted for their lack of hygiene. The area was full of folk like that. There were kids sleeping in bundles of rags on the floor, one bloke who laid turf in a bedroom for his greyhounds, mammies selling bottles of glue to the kids to sniff, folk so poor and disorganised they burned their furniture and even their floorboards. Who bothers to wash when you're burning your own floorboards? Little surprise that having a Blackhill address had the immediate impact of being discriminated against, the length and breadth of Glasgow and farther afield. But mess with these people and they fought to the death – for survival, the only thing they had left.

As they grew up, the new generation of Welshes brought added attention on the family's already bad reputation. In an area where unemployment raged at around ninety per cent, personal belongings were very valuable indeed. None more so than clothes. It was the days before automatic washing machines when mothers, invariably, took the dirty clothes in an old pram to the local steamie and then hung them out to dry in the back closes. If the precious clean clothes were stolen from the lines, it was a major disaster for the families. Locally they called such thieves snowdroppers and the most guilty of the lot were the young Welsh clan.

A lot of sentimental pap has been written about the urban poverty as experienced by the good folk of Blackhill and the like. But one general principle is true – most folk stuck together and, rather than do each other down, helped when they could. The reason wasn't altruistic but selfish. When you are that close to the edge, you too will need the help of your neighbours at times. You're only likely to get it if you willingly give your assistance when you can. The Welsh crew, on the other hand, stole from their neighbours. Not just from their washing lines but breaking into their houses, robbing their kids, mugging their old folk. It's not that they weren't liked by locals – they were hated and feared. But then they picked on Arthur Thompson.

When they turned on his pubs, demanding protection money, all hell broke loose. They were menacing the menace – what else did they expect? But Thompson himself was in for a nasty shock. After two incidents at his establishments, he gathered together a mean crew and set out for the Welsh home. The Thompson mob was armed with knives, cleavers, hatchets and pickaxe handles and they were all intent on inflicting damage.

That's how it started – as a typical Glasgow street brawl, with hand-to-hand combat the order of the day. Then, a couple of windows were thrown open in the Welsh household and shots rang out. Shotgun pellets whizzed into the air, two men fell wounded and Thompson himself felt the sting of lead on his back. If the Welsh Family had settled for the square go, even if heavily outnumbered and lost on the night as they seemed bound to, that would have been the end of the matter. Those were the expectations, the rules. But the Welsh Family didn't play by the rules. They played to win.

It was one–nil to the Welsh tribe and the whole city knew about it. Thompson didn't have any other option but to enter a war and it was a war he had to win at all costs. Overnight, the issue had moved from the Welsh Family wanting to be players rather than runners to a battle for the city. This was serious. And it was worse because the Welsh Family didn't stand alone – although they were almost large enough to do so. Patrick Welsh was the leader of that crew and his main ally was a bloke called James Goldie. These were two wizened hard men who had instigated almost every form of violence imaginable and they carried a force of weight backed up by some impressionable young men. At the drop of a hat, the Welsh tribe could turn out team-handed for any battle and often did. Worse, they seemed preoccupied with the war against Thompson and were always plotting some action. Thompson, on the other hand, had business to attend to in a number of growing concerns around the city and farther afield. He was vulnerable at home and that would never do.

In responding to the threat of the Welsh Family, Thompson imposed his will whenever necessary against whoever was troublesome. It is an old line on the street that a successful player is one part strength and nine parts reputation. If people believe they should be fearful of you, they will be fearful of you.

Confronted by a crew who always seemed to travel team-handed and armed with shotguns, he picked off lesser figures on the periphery. One time, word got to Thompson that a relative of Welsh's ally, James Goldie, was in the cemetery that ran at the side of his house. Thompson and a couple of his heavies were out there in a flash. They grabbed the young guy and beat him to a pulp. They didn't seem to care that the young bloke took no part in the war with the Welshes or that he was with his mother visiting the grave of his father who had recently died. Ignoring the mother's weeping protests, they pulled the barely conscious guy to a tree and tied him there by one hand stretched above his head so he dangled upright, battered and bloody for the world to see. It was a public shaming – an act of terror. There would be many more. This was war.

For Thompson, this was to be one of his bloodiest periods. Illegal moneylending had grown as a business concern for him. It's an arena that has always attracted those who have spare capital, enough to fund whatever market of lending they specialise in. By the early 1960s, Thompson was lending large. Many pub and club chains, now well established and straight, were kick-started by money lent to them by Arthur Thompson. Sometimes, he took a share in the business as part of his payback but, most often, he looked for massive interest rates.

Moneylenders get a bad press as being all too quick to punish late payers with extreme violence. In fact, most would do everything in their power to avoid going down that road. Hurting or killing a debtor simply reduces their capacity to raise the dosh. Moneylenders are only in the business for profit – so why debilitate the paying customers? But, with war against the Welsh Family on his doorstep, Thompson had a good reason for being vicious against all defaulters – he was trying to maintain his position as the city's top cat.

The man in Duke Street in the early 1950s was his first crucifixion. With an unpaid debt, no means to pay, a bad booze habit, a wife in failing health, whoring herself to raise their weekly cash, the man was never going to pay the debt anyway. So Thompson nailed him to the floor. And that wasn't a one-off.

Thompson was called to meet with a garage owner in the north of the city. The man had borrowed money to expand his business into second-hand car sales. Though he was a good mechanic, the borrower was a terrible salesman and quickly fell behind with his payments. Thompson had given him several extensions and, each time, the man had become more and more desperate, eventually offering The Godfather his entire fleet of unsold cars. The deal was refused on the principle of 'What do I want with your shite motors?'. If the man couldn't sell them, what worth were they to Thompson?

One week later, Thompson and a couple of minders returned. The conversation was short. One terse request for the money and, when the man started to run over his tired, old excuses, he was promptly nailed to his own garage doors.

But there was still a debt outstanding and Thompson never let anyone off with a debt. In due course, the garage was handed over to him, lock, stock, 'shite cars' and all – and he then sold the whole lot on at a handsome profit.

Thompson had developed the Midas touch with a particular modus operandi that deployed the business acumen he picked up from Mendel Morris and his expertise as a street player. He would watch local businesses like a merchant banker watches stocks and shares. If he reckoned the business was making a profit, he would move in and make the owner an offer to go into partnership. There would be some haggling over the price and the working agreement. Thompson would always say he didn't want to front the business, that he was quite happy for the current owner to continue being in charge. All he wanted was a sound investment and a bit of legitimate profit over time. No hurry. And, for all that, the bloke was being offered a handsome sum up front, a regular wage and still owned half of the business he had worked hard to build up. Moreover, with Arthur Thompson as a partner, nobody was going to mess with him, now were they? Too tempting to be true.

Sawmills, garages, pubs, corner shops, demolition businesses – by this approach Arthur Thompson ended up with a share in that lot and more. After the deal was struck, the money would be paid up promptly and all would go on as normal, as promised . . . for a while.

It might start with a lorry-load of knocked-off gear that Thompson wanted stored or some bent money he wanted put through the till. At other times, he'd borrow some of the staff to do a bit of unofficial moving work – usually hot goods that needed a lot of muscle shifting it to safety. If his business partner consented without saying a word, the demands would become more and more frequent, as would Thompson's presence at the business. If the partner objected and refused, all hell would break loose and threats would be made, leaving the poor bloke in no doubt that his life was at risk. One approach or the other always worked. That over, Thompson would just do what he wanted.

It's a mark of his power that Arthur Thompson never fell foul of the law for these capers. How do you prove a threat? How do you get the cops to catch the stolen goods without the finger of suspicion pointing at both business partners? And, as big Arthur had already warned his business partners, they were now complicit in a crime and, even if their involvement had been against their will, who would believe them? The ploy invariably worked as far as Thompson was concerned. One by one, his legitimate partners left town, doing midnight flits, scared witless and abandoning businesses they had often spent their lives creating.

Clearly, all that Arthur Thompson was after was to take over the businesses on the cheap and it worked at that. But it also augmented his reputation. Fantasies grew about why all his partners took to their heels and many simply disappeared. The reason for it had to be sinister. Well, what else could be expected of a man who crucified folk?

As well as the usual slashing faces, cracking knee bones with hammers, shooting people in the foot and then worse, that's not all he did. They had started to build the Kingston Bridge, a massive construct spanning the River Clyde at the city centre. It would take years and go on to be the busiest river crossing in Europe. The style of the bridge required enormous and deep concrete stanchions. Filling these took many thousands of tons of rubble and concrete and Thompson helped with a few bodies. The mythology would have it that he threw people in alive, then watched them sink slowly to their deaths. That is doubtful with there being too many risks of freak survival. But the reality is almost as terrifying.

9

BUILDING BRIDGES

EARLY 1960S

One man had publicly insulted a close friend of Thompson, a club owner from London. Money owed to the promoter was overdue. In his East-End club, on a night it was packed with faces, the bloke had very loudly declared that he wasn't going to pay the debt. In fact, he wasn't even going to pay for his drinks. To save his loss of face, the Londoner phoned Thompson asking for help. Anything for a pal.

Under the guise of wanting an outside, unknown face for a factory wages heist in Scotland, Thompson tempted the bloke to Glasgow. They met in the Horseshoe Bar in the city centre, an unusual venue for Thompson but it suited his plans. The Horseshoe claims to have the longest horseshoe-shaped bar in the world. While that might not be true, it is long enough and the right shape for someone to watch another without being noticed, especially on busy nights as all nights were at the Horseshoe. The Horseshoe is also situated halfway down a dark lane.

Thompson and the Londoner stood at the end of the bar farthest away from the door in the gunslinger's position from where they could see anyone coming in or at them. The pub was busy, very busy, and so loud they could have a guarded and confidential chat. In a quiet pub, the pair would have stood out because of their size, bearing, expensive suits and the Londoner's cockney accent. Everyone would have been earwigging. But, in the Horseshoe, no one paid them a second glance. The Londoner was probably impressed by Thompson's street nous.

For a couple of hours, Thompson talked quietly to the man in the guarded language the pair were so well used to. A big robbery, easy job, huge payout. A total fabrication, of course, but one Thompson didn't need much imagination to conjure up. As they talked, Thompson was the perfect host buying as many drinks as the guy could take. He took a lot.

Business finished, they worked their way through the crowds surrounding the long bar. As they reached the door, three of Thompson's men slipped in behind them. The Londoner was oblivious to this since he was a stranger in town and didn't know the local faces.

Out in the dark lane, the drunk Londoner had decided he'd found a new best friend. 'We're going to make a great team, Arthur,' he slurred, putting his arm round Thompson's shoulder.

'Aye, you're right there,' replied Thompson.

'Should've worked together long before now.'

'Right again.' Thompson was sober. All night he'd been buying his target whisky doubles, sometimes trebles while he was sticking to small beers. 'I've arranged a place for you to stay tonight.'

'What a pal. Is it the Central?' the Londoner asked, naming the only Glasgow hotel he knew – which was then the top hotel.

'It's central all right,' replied Thompson, probably with a small private smile.

'Will we get a cab?'

'No need – I've transport here.' Thompson had stopped next to an old rusty van, with a thin coat of paint hardly concealing the letters GPO of its former owners. Not exactly the kind of vehicle the Londoner expected Glasgow's top man to drive. He was right. Thompson wasn't going to be driving it.

'Right, you big English poof!' A new voice came from behind them. The Londoner turned to be face-to-face with the three heavies who'd followed them from the pub. Instinctively going for his gun, he was smashed on the head with a crowbar and knifed repeatedly in the body, arms and legs. The groaning Londoner was dumped in the back of the van and driven to a barren place down near the Clyde where the only company was derelict warehouses. All the way there, the Glaswegians had told him gleefully what they were going to do with him. When he raised enough panic to try and rise up, they'd thump and knife him again.

Depending on who the individual was, the men were ordered to kill him quick or kill him slow as the boss watched on. In the Londoner's case all he said was, 'Take your time with this cunt. He upset a good pal of mine.'

Once he was dead, they tied him in old bags weighed down with concrete blocks and wheeled him to a pit full of deep, soft concrete. They knew exactly where to take him. Thompson paid gaffers and night men on the Kingston Bridge building project regular money for just that information. For less money, he also made sure the security staff were on the other side of the river.

It was just one example but it describes how Thompson liked to deliver the concrete boots. The man who struck terror into folk by his fondness of crucifixion had added to his repertoire and his reputation.

In fact, Thompson was not the only one using this method of cadaver disposal. Many years earlier, it had been deployed by the Irish mobsters in New York and by every Hong Kong gang of note; and, most recently, the so-called New Entrepreneurs in Moscow, usually known as the Russian Mafia, have used it. Arthur Thompson was just being efficient and efficiency is frequently copied.

A recent Glasgow gangster, Stewart 'Speccy' Boyd, had bodies disposed of in the deep marshes of isolated Eaglesham

Moor and even borrowed council incinerators for the same purpose. The moor was a variation of Thompson's methods, the incinerator a sophistication. By standing on the shoulders of giants, progress is made – even in crime.

A message he had been waiting for came from London. The Kray Twins wanted to see Arthur Thompson. He needed to know more than that before he walked into the lions' den.

Thompson had rarely been in London since the time he had shown up at the Krays' club with the sawn-off shotgun. It wasn't that he was avoiding it but he had that nasty business with the Welsh tribe to deal with at home. The intermediary reassured Thompson that the twins sent their best wishes and wanted to see him about a matter of business – something that an outsider was needed for. It was a calculated risk but he took it and, yet again, traipsed off south on his own, his usual Beretta tucked neatly into its holster.

Respect is a strange commodity among gangsters. Earning it can be a complex, unexpected business and losing it simply a matter of one careless remark. When the Krays met Arthur Thompson, they made it plain he had won their respect. Free drinks, dinner, a night out at a top nightclub testified to that. Of course, this was after business had been discussed and a plan agreed.

The Krays had a bit of local trouble. It was bad enough that they and the Richardsons were at loggerheads but also there were so many individual gunslingers around London who were an increasing risk. It was a generational phenomenon and kids who had grown up copying and being taught by blokes like the Krays had now declared unilateral independence. They considered themselves hard men with guns and hired themselves out to all sorts of folk, particularly the West Indian, Turkish and Cypriot traders who were increasing in number. These people now thought they were above reproach and a few had refused to pay their dues to the Krays. Instead, they were paying the young blood and that needed sorting.

But these kids were from local families and the twins them-selves couldn't be seen to be cracking down on them. So that's where Arthur Thompson came in. A bit of muscle, violence if necessary, to get the geezers back in line. No problem to a man like Thompson.

A few months into the agreement and the Krays wanted a word. 'We're really pleased with how things are going, Art,' said Reg, annoying the hell out of Thompson by the use of the unfamiliar diminutive for his name.

'Too bloody right, son,' added Ron, nodding and smiling.

Thompson nodded with a straight face. He didn't like this.

'How do you think things are coming along?' asked Reg, adding ice to the drinks he had poured for himself and Ron. But there was no ice in Arthur Thompson's drink. He was only having a small beer. This was work.

'All right,' Thompson replied, looking back at Reg. He con-sidered Reg the more powerful of the two and Ron the more unpredictable. And, as for dangerous, well, that accolade also fell to Reg. Ron would slice you in a temper – Reg would think about it calmly and then hurt you . . . bad.

'Is there something wrong?'

Thompson couldn't stand this wavering and talking round the subject.

'Not wrong . . . exactly,' replied Reg, looking awkward.

Ron giggled to himself in the corner of the room, a grin splitting his face.

'More a matter of . . . too much.' Reg swallowed hard on his drink, loosened his necktie a little and paced from side to side.

Thompson watched him and concluded that Reg Kray didn't realise how he was behaving. More importantly, Thompson realised that Reg Kray, the more intelligent twin, was scared of him. Ron was still giggling and grinning. Thompson reckoned that he could take him out easily in a rammy – trick would be just to go for him before the crazy man even thought of violence. And that would be even before the handshakes.

'Spit it out, Reg,' Thompson said, now well pissed off with all the humming and hawing.

Reg Kray looked awkward, ill at ease, a posture that didn't befit a big man like him – a man who looked so hard.

'When you have to lean on them, Arthur . . .'

Thompson swore he noticed Reg Kray's Adam's apple bob up and down dryly in his throat.

'You're leaning a bit too hard.'

Arthur Thompson shook his head. He still didn't comprehend what the twins were trying to tell him.

'We just want them roughed up, Arthur.'

'Aye,' he agreed.

'But you leave them half-dead – sometimes actually dead.'

Thompson and the few Glasgow folk he had been using on these trips didn't like taking no for an answer. Their 'doing' is what the Krays thought of as a 'slaughter'. Big Arthur didn't see the point. You avoided going to a settler by negotiation and reason – right. But, if you had decided the rough stuff was required, what good was a slap on the wrist? But the twins were heading towards being the top team in London. They were paying him good money for these wee easy jobs. Who was he to argue with them asking him to do less?

'Right,' he said.

'Right, you'll lay off them a bit?' asked Reg, perturbed by this uncharacteristically short answer from Thompson.

'Right, I'll tell them the big, bad bogieman will get them in their beds if they don't behave. That'll be just after I wipe their arses and buy them bags of sweeties.'

Ron was looking worried, edgy. He always struggled to understand what Thompson was saying and had taken him to have a broad Irish accent at the beginning. Reg just stared at Thompson, no sign of anxiety now, just looking and trying to fathom what he really meant. Thompson broke into a large smile.

'Bastard,' said Reg, 'I thought you'd gone bad on us there for a sec.'

As Reg guffawed and Thompson smiled, in the corner, Ron Kray grinned and relaxed his grip on a long-bladed knife under his jacket. He thought no one had noticed – Arthur Thompson had.

Amongst all the big names like the Krays, the Richardsons, Joey Pyle, Frankie Fraser, 'Pretty Boy' Roy Shaw, Lenny McLean and the whole hard lot of Londoners, Arthur Thompson was the only player ever asked to be gentler. Thompson promised he would be and then did what he always did – regardless. As he always did.

The London scene was going very well for Thompson yet again. But he had tried to quash the Welsh Family overnight and he hadn't succeeded. Arthur Thompson was about to regret it big time.

10

SPORTS CARS, VANS AND GREAT BIG TRAINS

MID 1960s

There was a lot on Arthur Thompson's mind as he drove alone through the outskirts of Glasgow. It was a funny thing – the more successful he was, the more he fretted. Let's face it, he had made a killing, in every sense of the word. 'Killing! I made a fucking killing!' That type of double entendre tickled Thompson's humour button more than once.

He had more businesses than even the rumourmongers imagined. With protection rackets, he had practically a monopoly in the city. At least in those parts of Glasgow that pulled in decent cash and the borrowers paid regularly – well, most of them.

There were others in the business too, of course – like Walter Norval and that young boy, Jimmy 'Babyface' Boyle, from the Gorbals. Norval was his own man with his own plans that didn't impact on Thompson – as would be revealed when he was outed as the leader of the XYY Gang, a notorious and successful team of armed robbers. Boyle was just one of the young crew – promising, yes, but Thompson didn't reckon he'd last. In a sense, Thompson was right. A few years later, Boyle was sentenced to life for the murder of money-lender Babs Rooney and he went on to earn himself the reputation as Scotland's most violent man – in jail, that is. So Thompson was happy to leave them their punters, as long as they left him alone. They did.

As far as moneylending was concerned, he now specialised in high loans at extortionate interest rates and with short repayment periods. He mainly dealt with so-called legit enterprises who all knew whom they were doing business with. In one deal, he had made £10,000 for a twenty-four-hour loan to some guy who made an overnight profit, buying and selling some company. He couldn't complain about that. In fact he had cornered that market. Well, you would.

Down south he was still doing the odd job for this one and that. Strictly a freelance, nobody told Arthur Thompson whom to work for. In spite of the two teams being at loggerheads, he had carried out a number of jobs for the Richardsons as well as doing his work with the Krays. The Richardsons were the strongest team in London, he reckoned, and they were smart and intelligent – they would last the pace long after most of the others were in the jail or the morgue.

The Richardsons weren't as flamboyant as the Krays. Thompson liked that. They wore good suits and drove decent cars, of course, but they didn't swan their colours with B-list celebs, boxers and pop singers and get their pictures taken for the press. That just wasn't the way you handled yourself, according to Thompson. If you had it, you didn't flaunt it. All that glamour gangster stuff was just asking to be taken out. The Krays were good but they weren't infallible. Eddie and Charlie Richardson suited him better.

Frankie Fraser had become a good pal. Wee Frankie was totty – *really* small – and he reminded Thompson so much of Glasgow guys. Small men forced to be ultra vicious to make up for their lack of height and weight. Like Toe Elliot, 'The Little Emperor', a tiny wee bugger who was one of the most lethal men on Glasgow's streets and that was saying something. Toe always wore a coat that trailed on the ground making him look like some kid who had inherited his big brother's hand-me-downs. Hell mend anyone that slagged him off about it within his hearing for they soon found out why he wore such attire. A loaded shotgun down the lining at one side and a large, sharp-bladed cleaver down the other. The Little Emperor never hesitated to use the tools of his trade. That was Frankie Fraser's style too. Go in first, go in hard and go in to kill. A little big man all right and good friends with Thompson.

One regret he had was missing out on the big one. Thompson had heard from his London connections that a group of well-known faces were working on something. They weren't a group that normally associated with each other and so it had to be something different and very well rewarded. A get-out-of-the-game card – that's what Thompson had been looking for since his ill-fated robbery of the Commercial Bank at Beauly.

He had let it be known around various pubs and clubs in London that he was available for hiring and hoped that his reputation would stand him in good stead. He even spoke to his good mate Buster Edwards since he'd heard a rumour that he was involved. Edwards didn't admit or deny his involvement in something big and Thompson didn't expect him to – that would have been unprofessional. All Buster said was that, if he heard anything, he'd be sure to recommend big Arthur. That was the best Thompson could expect and he waited, hoping for the call. But the tap on the shoulder never came.

On 8 August 1963, Buster Edwards, Bruce Reynolds, Gordon Goody, Charlie Wilson, Jimmy Hussey, John Wheater, Brian Field and Ronnie Biggs committed the crime of the century that would become an icon of that period – the Great Train Robbery. When news came out that they had netted £2.3 million, Thompson was fit to spit teeth. That's what he called a jackpot. If only he'd been included, he could have left these streets forever. When things started to go badly wrong for the gang and, one by one they ended up in jail or having to flee abroad, even then Thompson didn't change his mind. He could have handled having that kind of heat. He'd been handling it for years. Exclusion from the Great Train Robbery was something he'd regret till his dying day.

Years later, Buster Edwards revealed that Arthur Thompson had been very close to being asked to join the gang from early on. The Great Train Robbers were no ordinary mob but a deliberate combination of intelligence and business acumen as well as experienced robbers. It was felt by some that Thompson fitted all the bills. Others didn't want another split in the proceeds. Indecision led to inaction and he was never approached. If he had been, the rest of this book would be very different – as would the annals of crime.

London had not forgotten about Thompson, though – quite the reverse. When Ronnie Biggs escaped from Wandsworth Prison, he had unplanned company in Robert Anderson, known as Andy Anderson. Given that Anderson had just taken a risk in tagging behind Biggs, no preparation had been made to hide him on the outside. Somehow, Anderson made it to Tottenham Court Road and the back entrance to Atlantic Machines, a company distributing gambling machines or one-armed bandits as they were known then. It wasn't an accident. Atlantic Machines was run by Eddie Richardson and Frankie Fraser and Anderson asked them for help. There was no question they wouldn't but London and the south were too hot with cops searching for Biggs and, of course, the same heat applied to Anderson. Fraser knew just the man to bail them out – Arthur Thompson.

A few hours after his phone call, Frankie Fraser arrived in Edinburgh with Anderson in tow and handed him over to the care of Arthur Thompson. For the next few months Anderson lived an almost normal life in a safe flat in Edinburgh and even went out to work every day as arranged by Thompson. It was a great example of how Thompson's power and connections extended well beyond Glasgow.

Eventually, Fraser arranged for Anderson to move to Manchester where, a short while later, the fugitive was nabbed by the cops. But Arthur Thompson had done well and, again, it was noted. It was a service given and a service to be repaid. From then on, any Scottish player needing help in hiding out in London was given the best of care by the most experienced faces. As long as Arthur Thompson asked, that is. Now that was real power.

Success was written all over Arthur Thompson as he drove alone through the familiar streets of Glasgow that day. He and Rita had a nice home at 176 Provanmill Road and now they had two children, Margaret and Arthur Junior. Life was good but, in a way, the wee ones made another niggling issue even more of a worry – the Welsh tribe. That's when he heard a thump and his car swerved, almost careering into a wall at the side.

Regaining control, Thompson looked around, searching for the cause of the grief. He was sure he'd heard a bump but he hadn't hit anything. Then a van pulled alongside him and he saw the smirking faces of Patrick Welsh and his close ally, James Goldie. 'Bastards!' Arthur Thompson was furious. He could have had Rita and the kids in the car. His weans might have been damaged by that scum. They really didn't care who they hurt or when. No code bothered them yet Thompson generally played by those rules – do not attack non-players and no violence with women and children present. The Welshes didn't play by those rules and that was just what worried Thompson. The safety of his wife and kids was at stake. Thompson lost his temper big time. He'd show them.

Arthur Thompson accelerated his car and rammed the van side on. That took the smirk off their faces. But they were hard, fearless bastards and weren't about to pull back from any fight. The van caught up and slammed into Thompson's rear bumper before pulling alongside. One of the men was looking for something behind his seat and started to pull it up. A shotgun – that's what it looked like to Arthur Thompson. Fuck that. He yanked his steering wheel hard to the side and, when the vehicles crashed together, he kept the lock on, pushing down hard on the juice, forcing the van closer and closer to the side until . . . the van smashed into a wall before running square into a lamp post.

Patrick Welsh and James Goldie were killed outright.

Arthur Thompson was unscathed but he was in big trouble – he was charged with murdering the two men. Everyone knew that Thompson and the Welsh clan were at war. This incident had happened in an unplanned way, with no cover, excuse or alibi. Arthur Thompson was facing serious jail time.

Three months later, Thompson was going about his business as usual. He was resting easier these days, reckoning that the deaths of Goldie and Patrick Welsh would have knocked the stuffing out of the rest of the family. They would probably wait and watch now and line up to give evidence at his trial for murder, determined to have him sent away for as long as possible. But he had plans for that trial and, in Joe Beltrami, he had a young lawyer who was the bee's knees. With Joe on board, Thompson didn't think the Welshes should feel so confident about him going down. So now he resumed his daily routine, driving to a few places of business. It was a good day.

Rita had asked him to give her mother, Margaret Johnstone – who was also known as Margaret Harrison – a lift. No problem. Thompson got on well with Maggie. He believed in family. That day he took his MG hardtop sports car. In his business, it was asking for trouble to drive the trendier convertible soft top. He would be stopped at some traffic lights and some idiot could just shoot him through the roof. Thompson wasn't that careless.

After helping Maggie into the passenger seat, Thompson fired up the beautiful purring engine and set off down Provanmill Road, driving past the cemetery that ran behind his home. The roads were clear, the weather good, everything was in its place. Then the car exploded.

Remarkably, Arthur Thompson survived but poor, innocent Maggie Johnstone was killed outright.

The death of a parent is a blow to anyone – a sudden death even more of a heartache. But a sudden violent death, what does anyone make of that?

There are those who say that Maggie Johnstone was aware of how her son-in-law earned a living and, therefore, she knew and accepted the risks. Yet, crime families are just families with everything that goes with them for you and me. These families have members who are not involved in breaking the law and who often disapprove of such activities yet cannot help loving even the ones who do cross the legal line – loving the person, not what the person does. By all accounts, this is how Maggie Johnstone was and she deserved the right to a long life.

How Arthur Thompson felt is another matter. Responsible? Guilty? Ashamed to be alive? If he had any of these emotions, Thompson kept them close to his chest. Yet, in spite of having a wife and kids to think of now, he didn't stop his involvement in organised crime one bit. Maybe he didn't feel that responsible. Maybe he wasn't feeling guilty at all.

So, to Glasgow High Court, the North Court thereof. This place has the same sense of history as Court One at the Old Bailey – just with different accents. Everyone and anyone in the annals of bloody crime in Glasgow has been there. Dr Pritchard was sentenced there for killing his mother before he was taken out and hanged, the last man in Scotland to be dispatched publicly by the state. John McLean, the great Marxist Red Clydesider, was tried there for sedition, in 1919, when a certain Winston Churchill had ordered troops and tanks on to the streets of Glasgow for fear of a revolution. Peter Manuel, the first identified and convicted serial killer, ably conducted his defence there though he lost and was hanged. After that, every murderer, child killer, bomber and poisoner had been hauled through that court. The place stank of fear and power. But it didn't bother Arthur Thompson one whit. He had another trial to deal with before his own.

Three of the Welsh Family stood accused of murdering Maggie Johnstone by planting a bomb underneath the car. Thompson, of course, had been called as a Crown witness. He could hardly refuse, as would be the normal expectation, given that he had been sitting next to Maggie when the car exploded. But just because they put him in the witness box, it didn't mean he would give evidence against his mother-in-law's killers. And he didn't. It wasn't that hard. He hadn't seen who had planted the bomb, after all – though he knew it was the Welsh tribe. A normal citizen, grieving the murder of a close one, might be forgiven for embellishing their evidence against the accused if they believed them to be guilty. But Thompson was expected to work on the opposite principle. Don't cooperate with the cops or the courts. He didn't. He would sort this problem out by himself – on the streets. The three men were found not guilty.

As soon as Thompson was finished with the Welsh trial, he crossed the corridor of the High Court. He had a minor matter of his own trial for killing two men to deal with.

By the start of Thompson's trial, clever work by his lawyer, Joe Beltrami, saw his charges reduced from murder to culpable homicide. Beltrami was already well known in the criminal circuit but was about to make his name big time when the jury found Thompson not guilty after less than an hour's deliberation.

According to natural justice, Thompson should have been found guilty of murder and jailed for life. But, then again, it was just a matter of chance that Welsh and Goldie ended up on a cold slab that day rather than Thompson himself. Either way, it was a tremendous victory for Joe Beltrami who would go on to represent Thompson for three decades. It was the kind of result that would create the catchphrase 'Get me Beltrami' every time some street player faced an impossible case.

These trials raised a furore of media attention. It was as if the criminals in Glasgow had gone killing mad. Commentators remarked that, if the death penalty had not been suspended the year before, they would not have been so quick to be so murderous. They missed the point.

Thompson and the Welshes were playing a deadly game day after day. Even while hanging was still a possible out-come, they had been busy, violent and lethal players for many years. Arthur Thompson was well prepared to run the risk of hanging as a price for his lifestyle. Did that make him dangerous? The cops thought so.

During these trials, one senior policeman and his family moved out of their family home in fear of attack. Immediately after the case, another cop moved abroad permanently. These were not lily-livered officers but brave men who knew the score.

All of that action and legal shenanigans resulted in three deaths and no one jailed. But, as far as the public was concerned, there was a feeling that it didn't really matter. After all, it was just criminals killing criminals, apart from Maggie Johnstone, of course. However, if anyone thought it was all over, they were jumping to the wrong conclusion.

Rita Thompson is the epitome of the gangster's wife – fully aware of what her man was up to but not involved. She held her tongue and was loyal all her life. She was a good mother and she was just as hard as her husband – only in a different way. Her business was the home and family while the streets were Arthur's concern. Except it was her mother someone had killed and someone was going to pay for it.

Rita Thompson packed two knives and set off for the Welshes' house with a handful of helpers. It was settling time. They burst in through the front door and all hell broke loose.

Rita found herself face to face with Ma Welsh, the matriarch. The two women didn't talk – they went at each other as if their lives depended on it. And they did. By the time the police arrived, there was blood and gasping prone bodies everywhere. Ma Welsh was seriously injured and rushed to hospital. Rita was fingered and was in trouble. She didn't care any more. She wanted a life for a life and she hoped the woman died. Ma Welsh survived and Rita faced trial. Found guilty, she was sent down for three years. One month later, Arthur's brother Robert was also found guilty and jailed for assaulting one of the Welsh brothers in the same battle.

Robert was used to it but it was a bad result for Rita. No matter to her. She had made her point and sent her message out loud and clear, 'Don't mess with me or mine.' Trouble was, the Welsh tribe weren't very good at listening. But, as Arthur was about to find out, certain other parties were. His life was about to go off the rails.

11

BIG TEX AND THE SPOOKS

LATE 1960s–1970s

Arthur Thompson had even more secrets than he had money. They went with the territory.

On the streets information is all. Visit any prison and the inmates heave with enough accurate information to make an average crime writer green with envy. If some titbit about a major player gets out, it gets around. So Thompson made a lifetime habit of keeping his own affairs tight-lipped and private. But those were normal business secrets. This one was special, life threatening.

Back then, Glasgow was even more divided by religious tension between Roman Catholics and Protestants than it is today. It mirrored Belfast, with certain areas identified with one particular religion and annual parades erupting in violence. Some trades were closed to a young man if he had gone to the wrong school and marriages between the religions were frowned on by most folk. But, as in business, a gangster intent on real power couldn't be seen to have one allegiance or another. He had to be acceptable to work with absolutely anyone or it would attract aggression and introduce ill feeling when there was already enough to go round. Finally, and most importantly to Thompson, it would result in him losing money. So Arthur Thompson had no religious beliefs at all – or so people thought.

In fact, he was a strong Protestant – not religious but sectarian, zealous and political. As the Troubles in Ireland brewed, Arthur decided he had a contribution to make to the Loyalist side. A regular visitor to Belfast and Dublin, he had strong contacts with the Loyalist politicians and military wings. His first contributions were made in money – cash, of course, usually hot from some robbery but legal tender all the same and in low denominations. One night, in some heavily fortified illegal drinking den in Belfast, he discussed how he could help further. Money and weapons were what they needed. Money and weapons were what Thompson would get for them.

There were Loyalist supporters all over the north of Ireland and they worked in all sorts of positions. Part of the unrest was caused by certain industries refusing to employ Catholics and just having Protestants on their payrolls. While that was well known about the shipyards, it was also true of large department stores, the post offices and the banks. The banks. Thompson's Loyalist friends revealed that they could pass any currency of any condition made by any back-street forger in any bank – no questions asked. That was handy. Before long, Thompson was shipping tens of thousands of pounds and dollars – bogus, of course – to Belfast every month. The brothers were very happy, especially when all he asked for in return was enough to cover the cost of purchase. What they didn't know was that he was making a handsome profit every time. But then they were making an even bigger skin and maybe they just didn't care.

Once every two to three months, a large cattle transporter would pull into working yards in Bridgeton or Dalmarnock in Glasgow. Those areas, the traditional homes of the old Billy Boys razor gang, were big on Orange Lodges and Loyalist supporters. It wasn't hard to find willing locals to cooperate with the venture.

In Glasgow, there were many serving officers of the Ulster Defence Association. The UDA had the networking off pat and used to hold ceremonies all over Scotland appointing people as honorary majors or brigadiers. Usually their only role would be to collect funds, though they swore to raise arms should the occasion ever arise.

Bridgeton and Dalmarnock are also heavy industrial areas – or at least they were. No one paid any attention to a large wagon reversing into a yard at night, especially one already carrying a noisy load of cattle. The proximity of the slaughter-house in Duke Street had made folk immune to this scene and the racket. And everyone knew that many of the Irish drivers diversified by carrying out a little smuggling on the side. Nobody in those areas would grass someone for trying to earn a few bucks more.

Once in the yard and with the gates closed, boxes, usually marked Corned Beef (Argentina), would be loaded into the back in sections under the floor where the cattle stood and paced anxiously. The poor beasts would be really stressed, having been picked up at so-called friendly farms in Ayrshire or Lanarkshire, particularly near Larkhall, earlier that day. There were no rules and regulations regarding feeding, watering or resting the weary beasts back then. The few rules that did exist were strictly ignored by the driver and his mate. Who cared about animals? This was a war that was being fought. It wasn't their dead and processed cousins under the beasts' stamping feet but boxes of guns and ammunition.

The guns were mainly Second World War issue or older, stolen from army dumps. There were Thomson submachine guns, 303 rifles with long barrels and ammunition beginning to turn rust red in crumbling damp boxes. But who cared? With a little attention, the majority of the guns worked and, usually, the ammo fitted. With a bit of oil, adjustment, repair and testing, they became killing machines – just what the

Loyalist soldiers needed – and they were cheap. Arthur Thompson only asked for a nominal contribution – enough to cover some of his purchase costs and a few bribes. The bribes were the biggest outlay – or so he said.

He wasn't lying. He was paying guards to be far away, checking a perimeter fence, when his lorries rolled in and helped themselves to the goods at weapons dumps in rural Wales, near Newcastle, Dumbarton and elsewhere. But he also used the Loyalist ticket when he could to convince other people that they should supply the weapons for the 'cause' – free of charge, of course. The best weapons he kept for his own people and the rest were passed on to the Loyalists, at a price. It was a very profitable piece of altruism for all concerned but especially for Arthur Thompson.

These exchanges meant Thompson was now having to visit Belfast as well as taking his frequent trips to London. No one in Glasgow thought anything of the Irish trips. Most didn't know and those who did assumed that he, along with half of the city's population, had relatives across the Irish Sea. But someone else noticed.

Due to his association with the major gangs in London, Thompson had been under the close scrutiny of MI5 for years. The security services were alarmed by the growth and strength of the London firms and the Krays' swaggering publicity seeking also troubled them. They saw Thompson as an outsider and, as such, a possible weak link.

On one of his visits to London, MI5 made an approach to Thompson around 1966. They wanted information on the London gangs and, in return, they would allow him a degree of immunity from prosecution for his own rackets. Arthur Thompson told them to sod off in no uncertain terms.

That should have been an end to it. But Thompson did something strange. He didn't tell any of his associates. It would have been expected for him to warn the London firms. At the very least, the approach to Thompson was a warning about exactly the kind of game MI5 was playing. Arthur Thompson said zilch. Why? Nothing Thompson ever did was accidental or casual.

A couple of years later, in 1968, Arthur Thompson was arrested and charged with a warehouse robbery. It wasn't a big haul but, given his past record and his reputation, the authorities had no hesitation in locking him up in jail on remand to await his trial. This was the place Thompson hated and he had done everything he could to avoid it. But now it looked like he was going down for a long stretch.

While on remand, Thompson was called into the governor's office. This was a walk that a prisoner took only when he was in big trouble and in line for internal discipline – or when his wife had died. Thompson had been a lippy but well-behaved inmate – no trouble at all to the screws. As she displayed on her regular visits to the jail, Rita was in the rudest of health. So, if anyone had really thought about Arthur being summoned to see the governor, they might have been suspicious. But he was Arthur Thompson, The Godfather, and the other prisoners just assumed he had been raising hell. A few inmates who did show curiosity about big Arthur's visit to the governor were quickly distracted by the prison officers – particularly the ones on Thompson's payroll.

The governor wasn't in his office. Two high-ranking officers from MI5 were there, one of whom was a Scot seconded from Glasgow City Police.

'I've given you my answer before,' Thompson said when the introductions were made, 'now fuck off and leave me in peace.'

'We haven't asked anything yet,' said the most senior spook.

'So this is a social call, eh?' replied Thompson. 'Where's my chocolate and tobacco then? Mean cunts.'

'It's a social call, all right. Just doing you a favour.' The MI5 officer was a handsome, big hulk of a man with a taste for expensive suits. He passed Thompson a buff-coloured folder and sat back, lighting a cigarette. There were two A4 sheets inside the file and, on the paper, points were marked out by numbers down the left margin. There were around forty lines in all, not many more than three hundred neatly typed words. Not much at all, except when Thompson read it and it spelled out, in some detail, the history and extent of his dealings with the UDA. The colour drained from Thompson's cheeks. The defiant look melted. Arthur Thompson was a dead man.

If this intelligence got to the Republicans, he would be taken out – never to be seen again. If he was prosecuted, it would mean a lifetime in jail and still he would have been at risk of a violent end from the host of IRA supporters in Scottish jails. All it would take was for the UDA to learn that this meeting had taken place and the cops had solid info on Thompson for them to consider a hit job to stop him talking. If all MI5 did was circulate the file's contents on the streets of Glasgow and London, Thompson was finished. Whatever happened, his life was never going to be the same again. He knew it and the MI5 officers knew he knew it.

And that's when they made the second offer of an arrangement. With the full dossier they had on him, they had Thompson by the balls. They still expected some hard bargaining – maybe some heroics. The man could be motivated by political principles after all. But they had got him all wrong and what they didn't reckon on was Thompson's hatred of prison. The prospect of being tried and found guilty of terrorism charges and being sent down for life was, for him, a fate worse than death. For a change, Arthur Thompson was very cooperative.

The deal was that they wouldn't interfere in his current charges. It wasn't that they couldn't have them dropped, knobble a witness or two or ensure the court dispensed as light a sentence as they could. All that was well within MI5's power but they didn't want to attract any suspicious attention to Arthur Thompson. MI5 saw him as a big fish, one of their best catches to date in gaining inside info on the UDA and the London firms at the same time. They wouldn't risk that for anything.

'Unfortunately, Arthur, that means you're going down for a while,' said the senior MI5 officer who didn't notice a small tremor run through the prisoner. Thompson truly detested jail. 'But, as soon as that is over, we'll cut you some leeway in return for regular reports.' The copper allowed the thought to sink in. 'Unless you're very greedy, you'll never go to jail again.'

The MI5 man kept talking but he needn't have bothered. The deal was already sold to Arthur Thompson. No more jail time, guaranteed – that was the get-out-of-jail card he had always been searching for . . . and with bonuses. He could keep to his way of life, pick and choose, make a good few quid and know that, if he ever got caught, he was still a free man. Perfect.

The offer wasn't unconditional. Thompson could continue with his protection rackets, moneylending and his more dubious business interests. He also had to continue his gunrunning to maintain the crucial contact with the UDA. MI5 didn't care how much he made out of that deadly business or how many weapons he shipped into the Troubles as long as he brought good information to them. The UDA was their top target but they were also interested in the London firms. So, again, he should continue as normal. They didn't care what he got up to as long as he gave them incriminating information on the big London faces.

The deal was struck and Thompson went on trial for the warehouse job. He was sentenced to four years, the expected term for such a conviction. But, in jail, he had thinking time again. Something had been intriguing him for a while. What was it that big bugger from MI5 had said? – 'And you can even do a bit of drug dealing if you want. As long as it's small scale, right?'

Thompson had never dealt in drugs. There was no big profit to be made in it, what with the kids only recently taking to cannabis in substantial numbers. So he hadn't bothered. But now heroin was appearing on the streets and that was a different proposition. At that time, the heavy smackheads needed thirty- or forty-quid's worth of the drug every day and it had been getting very popular in places like New York, Paris, Amsterdam and now London. Why should the Glasgow kids be deprived of the pleasure if that's what they wanted? But that was one for the future, Thompson decided. Definitely a nice earner – especially when you had MI5's permission to trade.

Within two years, Arthur Thompson, the perfect prisoner, was back on the street. He followed through on his new licence to deal drugs and quickly set about sussing out the trade.

It was 1970 when Thompson brought his first shipment of smack into Glasgow. Later, he would claim not to be a drug dealer. Later still, his oldest son, young Arthur, known as Fatboy, would be described as the one who dealt drugs. But Arthur Thompson Senior contributed to kick-starting the heroin epidemic that swept his home city, particularly in areas such as Possil, Springburn and Royston. He didn't deal, of course, or handle the goods but simply applied his usual style of delegation, taking minimum risks while scooping maximum rewards. He was good at it so the heroin trade in Glasgow boomed.

MI5 sorted Thompson out by allocating him handlers and giving him the code name Big Tex. Whether it reflected Thompson's love of cowboy films isn't known but it suited the man. One of his key MI5 contacts at the time said, 'I'd never had to deal with such a powerful figure as an informant before. Usually they were small bit-part players – insignificant, except they had access to the top gang-sters and the planning process. Here we had a man who was practically running crime in Scotland and a major influence in London and Ireland. The type of bloke who could have you killed within the hour simply by lifting the phone.'

But that was not how Thompson acted in his dealings with his handlers. By then, his home was nicknamed The Ponderosa after the main house in the popular TV western series *Bonanza*. Although it was originally a small rented property, he had given it many additions and extensions. In that area of low-grade council homes, the Thompson resi-dence stuck out. Although never one for ostentation, Arthur wasn't hiding his wealth – or his power.

While most of the meetings between Thompson and MI5 took place during his trips to London, one undercover agent recounts his single visit to the lion's den, The Ponderosa:

> He was the most polite and hospitable of people. The only time I went to his house I was greeted warmly, offered a drink of my choice and we sat there supping and smoking – more relaxed friends chatting than an informant meeting his handler. I've felt more threatened meeting some two-bit pimp in a public house. Arthur Thompson was the perfect gentleman.

Life wasn't all calm control for Thompson, though. The enormity of his weakness now that the security forces had him down on paper, film and audiotape was too much to miss. He was The Godfather, after all, surviving among hard men, streetwiser than the streetwise, and the rules of this game were exactly the same. That made him very worried. The MI5 officers saw it as some form of weakness:

> He was paranoid. Totally out of his box with worry that his phones were tapped or there was surveillance being kept

on him by rogue agents. Every time we met with him, we had to reassure him it simply wasn't true. We would have known if someone else was on his case.

But Thompson wasn't far from the reality. Occasional meetings were taking place between high-ranking officers of the Ulster Defence Association and Arthur Thompson who, by then, was a major provider of arms for the Loyalists. These get-togethers were handled with utmost care and total security. No one who had not been authorised by the UDA was allowed within miles of the venue. But that wasn't secure enough. An IRA undercover agent, working for the UDA – we can't name him due to current threats to his life – ran back to his mother organisation and gave them the low-down on the big Scot who was providing all the weapons to the UDA. The irony is that there were two members of the UDA present at these meetings who were double agents for MI5 and they didn't spot a thing. The IRA took prompt action.

The order went out to Cyril McFeeley, an IRA assassin. It was straightforward enough: travel to Glasgow and shoot Arthur Thompson dead. Addresses, usual pubs, businesses and so on were provided. It wasn't just MI5 who were good at surveillance.

Unusually, in this type of operation, there was a written command that read, 'Insist that Thompson desists from sup-plying arms. Only if he refuses, shoot him.' But McFeeley was an assassin not a negotiator. And why would you reason with a man with clear Loyalist sympathies and who was known to be an arms supplier to one of your enemies? You wouldn't reason with someone like that in Belfast so why should you in Glasgow?

The message was simply a ruse intended to address any breach of the IRA's communication system by the security services. If Thompson suddenly disappeared, then the IRA would know that communication channels with McFeeley had been breached. It would also have meant that Thompson was under the protection of MI5 and he was, therefore, a grass. If none of that happened and Thompson was killed and McFeeley was subsequently arrested with sound evidence against him, the hit man would argue that Thompson tried to kill him first after he had raised the issue of his gunrunning. He was only following orders. He would be a soldier of the cause with a self-defence alibi, in other words.

In fact, the IRA had problems of their own. Unknown to them or Thompson, several of their high-ranking members were spying for MI5. That's why on the day they arrested McFeeley the authorities showed no clue as to what his real mission was. To do so would be to reveal MI5's links to Thompson and the IRA double agents. Instead the spooks passed information to the cops that McFeeley had no right to be in the UK and was wanted on offences in Ireland. Little did the cops know, at that time, that they had just saved the life of The Godfather, one of MI5's most senior informants.

Arthur Thompson was proving to have a charmed life and he was now entering a new phase when all seemed peace and calm. But a friend of his was in deep trouble and it would take a murder to solve it.

12

A FIGHT FOR JUSTICE?

MID–LATE 1970s

Paddy Meehan had a turbulent time in prison. Serving eight years for the botched robbery of the Co-op in Edmonton, he argued and fought his way through his sentence and even tried, though he failed, to escape from Nottingham Prison. To rub acid in the wounds, his wife Betty had had enough of their lifestyle and started divorce proceedings.

Meehan's troubles had started with that £100 note Arthur Thompson had paid as his part of the funds for the robbery with Teddy Martin. Meehan had a reputation for being keen on the money and a bit tight-fisted so it was no surprise that he kept the note, dangerous as it certainly was. He cashed in the banknote, going to different shops and making purchases to reduce the denomination and, of course, lose the rare banknote with such an easily traceable serial number.

While going through this process, Meehan later claimed an anonymous man tried to recruit him to help to break the spy George Blake out of jail. Blake was a notorious double agent who'd been caught passing classified information to the Russians. According to Meehan, the man had admired his role in getting Teddy Martin out of Peterhead and thought this would make Meehan the ideal candidate to help free Blake. Straight out of Hollywood as this may seem, it has to be remembered that those were the days of the Cold War where espionage was rife in this country. The links between street players and states were well established. Remember Johnny Ramensky being parachuted behind enemy lines?

Meehan went to jail, of course, and was in deep trouble. But he did escape from Nottingham on 20 August 1963, using the diversion of a cricket match. He and another inmate, named Hogan, went through the perimeter fence at a certain point, to be met by an escape car – a well-orchestrated dash, in other words. During that spell of freedom, Meehan claims that, after dumping Hogan, he travelled to Dublin and then was flown to East Germany where he helped the authorities with questions they had about aiding George Blake and other spies held in the British penal system to escape.

Whatever the truth of those months of freedom, Meehan was recaptured and sent to Parkhurst, the top-security prison on the Isle of Wight. It was the least he could have expected. There, he met two people he was to become very close to. Infamous serial killer Archibald Hall – also known as Roy Fontaine or The Monster Butler for his habit of posing as one and killing his employers – made for an unlikely close companion. The other, Rochdale man James Griffiths, was more obvious. Griffiths, a robber of some repute, was also an escape artist who achieved the rare feat of escaping from the Isle of Wight prison and actually getting off the island. Griffiths and Meehan became very close and plotted joint enterprises that they would carry out when they were both free.

Released in 1968, Paddy Meehan had gone straight by 1969 – or so it seemed. He had a small business inserting spy holes into front doors. The robber had turned home security man – but not for long. Griffiths turned up on the scene in Glasgow and the pair were soon plotting jobs.

One night, they travelled down the south-west coast of Scotland to case a possible robbery on the motor taxation centre. That same night, in Ayr, a robbery was taking place in a house and it was going to end in absolute tragedy. Rachel and Abraham Ross were elderly and wealthy and, as such, prime targets for tie-up merchants who specialise in robbing such homes. The two robbers were heavy handed in the extreme. Abraham had a knife stuck in his neck and an iron bar was smashed over his head. One of the robbers knelt on frail Rachel's chest and she died a few days later. This was a murder case and the cops had Griffiths and Meehan in their sights.

The evidence against Meehan and Griffiths was understandable. The robbers had called each other Pat and Jim and two girls identified the pair as having given them a lift near Ayr on the night of the robbery. That Meehan and Griffiths, as experienced thieves, were unlikely to either kill or use their real names was not considered by cops desperate to get two killers of old folk locked up. When Meehan was pulled in, he had another problem. He did give the girls a lift that night – but how could he explain why he was there when the reason was that he was actually plotting another robbery? That information could only be revealed with James Griffiths' agreement and he was yet to be lifted.

When Griffiths heard of Meehan's arrest and that the police were searching for him, he went crazy. Griffiths really was terrified of jail and vowed never to go back. What resulted was a bloodbath.

When cops called at Griffiths' home at 14 Holyrood Crescent in Glasgow, they were met by a bizarre and deadly sight – James Griffiths, with bullet belts draped across his chest, coming out shooting. A chase ensued and it led to a siege in Springburn Road. When the siege ended, a few hours later, the tally was high – eleven civilians and five cops shot, with James Griffiths and one civilian killed.

With James Griffiths dead, Paddy Meehan had just lost his alibi. The police had no other lines of enquiry open so he went on trial for robbery, the assault on Abraham Ross and the murder of Rachel Ross. Meehan was found guilty by the slimmest of majority verdicts, eight votes to seven (Scottish courts have fifteen jurors), and was sent to jail big time. But all was not lost – it just felt that way.

Paddy Meehan's lawyer had been the bold Joe Beltrami, Arthur Thompson's famous lawyer, and his QC was a certain Nicholas Fairbairn who would go on to hold government office as a Tory MP. Beltrami was convinced of Meehan's innocence and had orchestrated a strong case at his trial by impeaching a fellow called Dick and one Ian Waddell as the guilty parties. The ploy hadn't worked but had split the jury almost down the middle. After Meehan's conviction, Beltrami wasn't about to let go of what he saw as an injustice. And neither was someone else – Meehan's old pal, Arthur Thompson.

Thompson used all his connections to draw in information from the street on who killed Rachel Ross. It was an invaluable assistance to Beltrami as he himself admitted. Then a complication emerged. A long-term client of Beltrami, a William 'Tank' McGuinness, began to pay him office visits although there were no cases to be dealt with at that time. The purpose of these appointments was for McGuinness to give clues, bit by bit, that, along with Ian Waddell, he had, indeed, been the second man in the Ross murder.

Eventually, McGuinness became extremely helpful to the Free Meehan campaign which, by this time, included TV presenter and writer Ludovic Kennedy. But there was a catch. Tank McGuinness had not given Beltrami permission to use the crucial information he had provided on the basis that it would incriminate him. So, while McGuinness was, for whatever motivation, assisting the Meehan campaign, he didn't want the man released at the cost of his own incarceration. Beltrami was bound by client confidentiality and must have gone through a long, frustrating period knowing that Meehan was innocent but being hog-tied.

Then someone started hunting Tank McGuinness down. In 1975, there were three separate attempts on his life – one of which involved men bursting into his home with shotguns. Luckily for McGuinness, he was out so only his ceilings and wardrobes suffered. McGuinness was a hard man, accustomed to a life of chaotic violence, but now someone was out to get him in an organised way.

On 13 March 1976, McGuinness was found, almost battered to death, in Janefield Street, near Celtic Park, in the city's east side. After thirteen days in a coma, he died. Now, with McGuinness's family's permission, Beltrami was free to use the key information that would free Meehan. Paddy Meehan was granted a Royal Pardon within a couple of months. Ian Waddell was charged with the murder. He was acquitted – only to be brutally murdered by a pal, Andrew Gentle, in a drunken brawl in 1982.

And 'Gypsy' John Winning was charged with the murder of his long-term friend and crime partner, Tank McGuinness. One reason given was that two members of their respective families had started a relationship which displeased the men and they went to war to resolve the matter. Winning was acquitted of the charge but confessed a short while later, when he was terminally ill.

All the while this was going on, the presence of Arthur Thompson was very much there, just slightly in the shadows. Thompson took an active role in disposing of Tank McGuinness, offering a handsome payment to whoever took him out. Good friend as he was to Meehan, whom he visited regularly while he was in prison in England, that alone seems insufficient motivation for Thompson to take a hit contract out, especially on McGuinness who had worked with Thompson many times over the years. So why?

One view is that Thompson was concerned that, if the case had gone to court, a good contact of his would be compromised. Charlie Craig was the top detective in Glasgow. Old school, he had come close to losing his post several times due to being drunk on duty, acting with violence and taking bribes. He was close to dismissal when one David McNee took over command of Glasgow City Police. McNee rescued Craig's career and gave him a final chance. Of course, he was eventually to go on to become Sir David McNee, Commissioner of the Metropolitan Police, and one of the most influential cops of his time. In that role, McNee made a defence of what he called 'moral perjury', meaning that it was OK for cops to lie if they knew the accused was guilty of something. Charlie Craig knew all about moral perjury.

Craig and Thompson had had a working relationship for years – one that served both of them well. Thompson got information and tip-offs, which meant he could avoid trouble, and, in return, Craig got money and occasionally sufficient information to allow him to arrest people, whether they were guilty or not. Craig's clear-up rate was very high but his name was all over numerous cases of wrongful conviction and some are still coming to the fore. One example is Raymond Gilmour who was convicted of raping and murdering a young woman, Pamela Hastie. Early in 2004, Gilmour was released from jail, pending appeal. Craig was in charge of the investigation.

It was only a matter of time before Craig got caught fixing investigations and that would not have suited Arthur Thompson one bit. He needed Craig in his post or the cop was useless to him. McGuinness had all sorts of information on Charlie Craig. If he had gone to court accused of a murder, he would have had nothing to lose and he was, therefore, likely to have threatened to expose the detective. Thompson couldn't allow that.

One beat cop recalls the night Tank McGuinness was murdered, saying:

My usual route was the streets around Celtic Park and it was a busy beat with arrests every night. It was a terrible night of rain and wind and I wasn't looking forward to the shift. I had started off as usual till a police car pulled up and I was given the order to leave that area and move to what was a much quieter area. I was dumbfounded. It was like inviting crime to happen but an order is an order.

A coincidence? Maybe. But listen to the cop one more time:

The beats were sacrosanct. Decisions on the routes to be covered were made at the highest level – we all knew that. The order for me to move off that beat must have come from the top. If I had been on my usual beat, I might well have saved Tank McGuinness's life.

If Tank McGuinness had lived, Charlie Craig might have led a very different life. Instead, he went on to be a high-ranking cop in all the major cases in Glasgow for several years. One case he was involved in, in 1984, was the killing of six members of the Doyle Family in a fire in their house as a result of what was dubbed the 'Ice-Cream Wars'. It was a horror of a murder, even for that bloody city, and the police had to catch the murderers. They convicted Joe Steele and Thomas 'TC' Campbell, the son of the same Bobby Campbell who had given young Arthur Thompson his early breaks and inducted him into the world of armed robbery. 'Free the Glasgow Two' turned into the longest fight against injustice in Scottish history and concluded in 2004 when both Steele and Campbell won their appeal against conviction on all counts.

The murder of the Doyles was a big case yet, in Craig's career, there have been many, many more of similar standing that have never been caught in the glare of publicity. To this day, criminal lawyers and the like still talk of 'one of Craig's lot' – that is, a cop who had been trained by Craig and reared to such practices. Some are still around.

Arthur Thompson was no fool. He knew he had made a pact with the devil, the very type of cop who could have stitched him up in a flash if it suited him. But then Craig wouldn't do that to his partner who was sitting on substantial evidence of his own corruption. They were tied together, another good reason to keep him onside.

Thompson's association with Charlie Craig was to pay dividends over the next few years, not least with a small matter of rape and murder. But there was much deeper trouble coming Thompson's way that no one had foreseen – from within his own family.

13

PALS' ACT

LATE 1970s–1980s

Arthur Thompson wasn't a great one for holidays. Yet, by the 1970s, he had houses in Spain, Port Seton and the Scottish holiday island of Bute – although, with good reason, he hardly used them.

The image of the stay-at-home Thompsons clashes with that of the perma-tanned gangster families hanging around their pool-sides in Malaga or Benidorm half the year. But that whole scene of the Costa del Crime was just in the making when Arthur's very good friend, London face Ronnie Knight, evaded trial in the UK by holding court there for years. That whole trend was started by Knight and his peers who had to get out of the UK for fear of arrest. Before that, street players rarely left home for fear of losing power in their absence.

By the mid 1970s, there were other pressures on Arthur Thompson, big-time gangster or not. He and Rita had four children. The oldest two, Margaret and Arthur Junior, were well into their teens, almost adults, while Tracey and the youngest, Billy, were still at primary school. The kids needed a break from the harsh streets and regular trips to Port Seton became a feature of the Thompsons' lives.

A quiet, picturesque spot on the east coast near Edinburgh, Port Seton was one of those traditional holiday spots for city-dwelling Scots. Having access to sea and sand was ideal for the younger Thompson kids but not for Margaret and Arthur

Junior, who were at an age when they needed more than buckets and spades to keep them amused. Just like any other family. By all accounts, Margaret was a popular, well-liked young woman with the adventurous spirit of many people her age. Arthur Junior was another story.

Always overweight, Arthur Junior was given different nicknames by other kids. Around Blackhill he was known as Arty Farty for his constant, noisy habit of passing wind, something that went hand in hand with his love of food. The name that stuck into his adult years, however, and was adopted by the media was Fatboy. As a younger child, his peers give different, apparently contradictory descriptions of Fatboy. Some say he was constantly bullied – others that he was the bully. Both are true. Fatboy was a braggart, fond of the company of younger, smaller children whom he could lead and always beat in a fight. They would often find themselves on the sharp end of his boot or fist. It seems he took great pleasure at other people's pain, an attitude he never lost. Boys his own age and older spotted him for what he was and weren't slow to put him in his place – thus, to that extent, the claims that he was bullied are true. The perpetrators would, of course, say that Fatboy was occasionally getting his just deserts.

When you are ten or eleven years old, you don't care whether someone's father is a bus driver or a plumber or, like most in the area at that time, unemployed. The kids didn't care that Fatboy's father was the most powerful gangster in Glasgow. Why should they? Arthur Thompson would encourage his oldest boy to settle his own battles. Most nights, he would come home from school with tales of how he sorted out this one and that – mostly his own fabrication. Fatboy had his father's desire for power but not an ounce of his physical strength and courage.

Even though the other kids didn't know or care about his background, Fatboy had an acute sense of who his old man was from an early age. 'Do you know who my da is?' was a refrain often dropping from his lips as some boy decided to sort him out. The boy didn't care. But Fatboy remained arrogant, full of himself, and what he couldn't win in a straight match he'd cheat on. By the time he reached his teens, he was conniving, vicious and exploitative and, as such, most people treated him with suspicion and some were afraid of him – with good reason.

Fatboy was also known to buy his power. Even at school, he'd pay a couple of heavy merchants to beat up someone who was bothering him. Most of the kids in school came from families who struggled even to feed themselves. Yet this teenager could put up a few quid just to watch someone having their head kicked. And he watched every time, grinning, squealing and tormenting the poor guy who was being pummelled on the ground.

By his mid teens, other kids had well sussed who Fatboy's father was and, by that time, it was important to them too. Soon they would be adults trying to claw an existence in Arthur Thompson's world. Many were already involved in the crime scene, shoplifting, robbing factories and stripping lead from roofs. Many had ambitions to work with a top player like Thompson. Others simply wanted to avoid his wrath. The intimation was: mess with Fatboy and you mess with The Godfather. So the young Thompson was left well alone. He was tolerated in company who despised him and had his jokes laughed at whether they were funny or not.

It sounds like a lonely existence, and it would have been for most folk, but it seems that Fatboy neither realised how others viewed him nor cared much. He'd emerged into adulthood with a sense of his own power and didn't mind what he did to get things his own way. Nobody on the streets and especially in Blackhill called Arthur Thompson The Godfather – except Fatboy.

Arthur Thompson was one of those fathers who acknowl-edged that, when he was growing up, he broke every rule in the book. He accepted that his own sons would do the same and wanted them to be open about it. So Fatboy got an early introduction to the basics of his father's occupation. Aged fourteen or so, he would accompany Thompson on certain business meetings, sitting among the powerful, hard-faced men as an equal. He wasn't, of course, but the message was clear. Fatboy was the man of the future and everyone had better get used to the idea.

Fatboy particularly enjoyed fast cars but was obsessed by the guns stored in an arsenal built into a tunnel under The Ponderosa. The teenage Fatboy would take a pistol from the store and go around the house pretending to shoot family members, insisting that young Tracey and Billy fall over when they were 'shot', all the while making realistic gun noises. He wasn't playing – he was practising.

All Arthur Thompson was doing was showing his boy, his heir, the ropes of the family business. What he didn't notice was that his oldest son had become fascinated with guns and what they could do – a fascination that was to prove disastrous in the future.

Breaks at Port Seton held other attractions apart from the pleasant environment – the nightlife in Edinburgh. While Arthur Thompson always felt free to socialise in Glasgow, he could never entirely relax. People would come up to him con-stantly with business proposals, problems they were seeking help with or just to chat so they could boast about it to their friends. In his home city, he suffered all the trappings of fame with the added danger of some crazy young gunslinger decid-ing to make a name for himself by shooting The Godfather. In Edinburgh, he felt anonymous and he certainly let his hair down in the pubs along the Royal Mile or in Rose Street.

Another attraction with Edinburgh was its young women. With two universities, masses of colleges and a tourism market to support, it seemed to be much fuller of trendy young females, dressed to the nines, than Glasgow. Arthur Thompson wasn't slow to chat up the young good-time girls, buy them drinks and go all the way if they were willing.

Fatboy was only sixteen years old when he was allowed to join his father on these nights out and the tempo increased. While a pleasant looking guy, Fatboy was certainly no Casanova. The young man copied his father's sense of style with short hair and wearing suits or sports jackets rather than the fashion of the day. Total confidence and a thick wallet of money made up for any social defects.

This is how one of their contemporaries described their behaviour:

> The Thompsons were outrageous. Edinburgh was sin city in the 1970s and those two took full advantage and then some. They would breeze up to any young women they fancied, buy them a few rounds of drinks and the young Thompson would roll a joint or two. They were flash and generous. Then they'd ask the girls outright to show them their tits or flash their knickers. If they did, then anything could have happened after that.

Edinburgh city centre attracted a large number of prosti-tutes and was well known for its high-class brothels but the Thompsons preferred to pick up girls from one of the many pubs. It seems that, while the father was as outrageous as the son, he wasn't too interested in following through if sex was on the cards, leaving that to Fatboy. Fatboy, on the other hand, once boasted, 'I've had more blow jobs up Edinburgh closes than I've had Mars bars.' It was both a boast and a joke against himself since he was well known for eating several chocolate bars at a time.

It's maybe not everyone's idea of how a father and son should behave. It was harmless enough in itself but it was to land them in deep trouble.

Seventeen-year-old Christine Eadie and Helen Scott were best friends. They had not long left home and moved to Edinburgh and they were intent on a great night out. It was October 1977, a good time to be young, and they intended to enjoy it to the max.

They could have gone to any number of pubs but for some reason they chose the World's End on the Royal Mile. The place was packed and the music was loud – jumping, just the way they liked it. It was no surprise when two men moved and sat beside the two attractive young women and began chatting them up. The two other friends Christine and Helen had arrived with decided to move on but the young women stayed on, chatting happily with the men. Late that night, they left the pub with the two blokes in tow. That was the last time they were seen alive.

The next afternoon, around 2 p.m., on the foreshore between Aberlady and Longniddry, East Lothian, a young couple found Christine Eadie. Naked, badly beaten and with her hands trussed behind her back, she had been strangled with her own tights.

Early that same evening, a gardener, walking his dog in a field near stables in Haddington, found Helen Scott's semi-naked body. She too had been badly beaten and had her hands tied behind her back.

The young women's deaths sparked one of the largest manhunts ever. Extra police were drafted in to trawl for clues, as huge floodlights lit the scenes. Most of their clothes were found but not their handbags. All surrounding roads were blocked, drivers and passengers questioned. Hundreds of cars were traced that had been spotted in key locations – with no results.

Photofit pictures of the two men were issued by the police, around Edinburgh and to the press. The media appealed for witnesses time and again. Two look-alike policewomen carried out a re-enactment in the World's End, sending shivers down the spine of any caring person. But there was still no breakthrough. The men had short hair, unusual for 1977, so the police interviewed every male soldier stationed at Redford Barracks and started to trace those now posted abroad who were in Edinburgh that night. It was one of the biggest manhunts Scotland had ever seen and it turned up nothing.

Across in Glasgow, two young women, Agnes Cooney and Hilda McAulay, had been found murdered. The similar circumstances of both their disappearance and deaths to those of Christine and Helen were chilling. Were the murders committed by the same person or people? Could there be a serial killer at loose in Scotland? The first one since the Bible John mystery of a decade before? It was a serious question and the cops had to get the answer right.

Edinburgh cops thought it possible the four murders were linked and kept officers on the cases, chasing every angle. For some strange reason, the Glasgow cops quickly concluded the cases weren't related and had little to do with the major investigation being carried out in the east into the World's End murders.

But it was a set of crimes that horrified and terrified the public. Anonymous calls and letters flooded in to the cops, many of them cruel time-wasters – as is usual in such murder hunts. Then a letter arrived that opened cops' eyes.

Anonymous but postmarked Wishaw, the letter claimed that the World's End murderers were two well-known criminals from Glasgow. It didn't name names – didn't even offer any clues as to their identities – and the cops laid it aside, thinking it would just be another dead end. Then a second letter came in naming the men. At the time, the police didn't release the details but we can reveal that they were Arthur Thompson and his son, Fatboy.

By the early 1980s, Thompson had simply grown stronger and stronger. Even the media had taken to calling him The

Godfather, the Mister Big in crime, even though he hadn't faced prosecution in years. The murder investigation team were sitting on dynamite.

The Glasgow cops again were very reluctant to act. Of course, Charlie Craig, Thompson's pal, was still in charge of the detectives and all investigations. The rationale was that the Thompsons were hard and lethal but were old-time gangsters with that value base that detested all rapists, women beaters and sex killers. It was an over-generalised viewpoint that clearly didn't hold water, as we have learned from a number of serial killer cases since.

Eventually, Arthur Thompson and Fatboy were formally interviewed about the World's End murders and they willingly cooperated with the police. They were in Edinburgh on the night Christine and Helen were killed and went drinking in several pubs. They couldn't remember which ones. Yes, they had been in the World's End, it's a popular bar, but they didn't know if they were there that night. They couldn't remember how late they were out or who they were with and, like everyone else, they'd seen the photographs of Christine and Helen in the newspapers but, no, they didn't recognise them. They would have contacted the cops straight away if they had. They hated sex killers and rapists – to them, hanging would be too good for them. The cops must know that they'd do anything they could to help track those killers down.

The Thompsons might have cooperated but they still didn't help the police one bit. If the cops had been aware of the father and son's outrageous behaviour on their nights out in Edinburgh, they might have persisted longer in their investigation. The image of a sixteen-year-old Fatboy sitting in crowded bars, with his hand up some utterly drunk or stoned young girl's skirt, might have raised the cops' concerns. Well, they should have been concerned. Instead they scrubbed the Thompsons from their inquiries.

As this is being written, the police have announced that, by using new, sophisticated DNA forensics, they can confirm that the World's End murders are linked to four others around that time in the Glasgow area. The Thompsons' names haven't been whispered by anyone in this connection. The suspect is Angus Sinclair, a convicted sex killer, though, at the time of writing, whether he is guilty or not has still to be decided by due legal process. The forensics will be accurate, of course, and let's hope the killer is caught soon. Yet, back in the 1980s, the police did Arthur Thompson and Fatboy an immense favour by keeping tight-lipped about them being interviewed in connection with the World's End murders.

There are many clichés about life in the world of organised crime and many of them are inaccurate. But it is true that any connection at all with the ill treatment, never mind the rape and murder, of women is held in utter contempt. For that very reason, the police would usually have let this information slip into the public domain.

Glasgow, in common with every other police force, has a well-tried system of leaking sensitive information into the public domain. A group of cops are on social terms with journalists. Off duty, they meet with the journos in a bar for a few drinks and slip them information on crime stories. In return, payments are made – strictly cash, of course – with the amounts being determined by the newsworthiness of the story. Some of these cops are strictly freelance but some work to an agenda of the force, passing intelligence on with some strategic purpose in mind.

In the early 1980s, Arthur Thompson was the major crime figure in Scotland and farther afield yet he hadn't been prosecuted for years. He was exactly the type of target the cops would use propaganda mechanisms against but, in this instance, they chose not to. Was this down to the intervention of his MI5 handlers? Unlikely. Thompson, being an MI5 informant, was kept top secret especially from the local police force since it leaked like a sieve – as most do. The order to keep quiet would have come from the leading officers of the force – from none other than old Charlie Craig, Thompson's mate. As much as Thompson needed him in the cops, Craig needed Thompson at the top of the crime ladder. It was a partnership made in hell that suited them both. But would it be enough to protect Thompson from his next challenge that was to emerge from his own backyard?

14

OLD FEUD, NEW FACE

EARLY–MID 1980s

'Can I speak to Mr Thompson, please?' The young, fresh-faced man stood at the door of The Ponderosa while, across the threshold, Rita Thompson eyed him warily. She recognised him fine – a local boy, a couple of years younger than Arthur Junior and no threat there.

'Big one or young one?' Rita asked. The teenager was flustered for a second at this unexpected query. There was Arthur Thompson then there was Fatboy Thompson, at least that's how he and his mates thought of them.

'The old man.'

'Arthur,' Rita shouted into the house, 'young boy here wants a word. Come in, son.' The young man followed Rita into the living room. It was the most luxurious room he had ever seen, even on the TV or in the movies, and this was real. Everything seemed to be leather or covered in dark fur. The fitted carpet was so thick it held on to his feet and each step left an indentation of his footprint. Arthur Thompson stepped into the room, jacketless, his shirtsleeves rolled up. He nodded grimly at the young man. 'What can I do for you, son?' Thompson asked. The two men stood and faced each other across the lounge of The Ponderosa.

'It's about that car crash . . .' the young bloke started, hoping that Thompson knew what he was talking about. The old gangster looked a bit quizzical. '. . . where the woman got run over and killed.'

'Aye, right, that accident.' Thompson's face never flickered for an instant. Poker straight is the cliché but it applied to him that day as most days.

'You might have heard . . .' the young bloke hesitated, 'that my sister was interviewed by the polis?'

'Aye.'

'Well, I'm here to let you know that she'll be telling them nothing. As far as my family is concerned, these matters should be sorted without the cops.'

Thompson was nodding. He knew the significance of this visit all right. A cousin of his had been pissed out of his box and driving a car round the Blackhill streets at great speed. The car had mounted the pavement and slammed right into a woman, killing her outright. The mad bastard had just kept driving on, of course, but the police had caught him and charged him. He had no licence, no insurance, was a banned driver and the motor was stolen. No hiding place for him really and all he needed was a witness to finger him as the driver and he'd be sent away for a long spell. It was a bad one, killing that poor woman just because he was drunk. Thompson didn't blame the young lassie for spilling everything to the cops. Most people would. But here was her brother reassuring him that his family were going to do the right thing and tell the cops nothing. He was a good man.

'You'll be a Ferris then?' asked Thompson.

'Aye, Paul Ferris.'

Thompson nodded approval. 'I know your old man, Willie. A good man. One of the best.'

It was Paul Ferris's turn to nod – and to blush a little. 'Cheers.'

'Here, son . . .'

Big gangster or not, Paul Ferris wished Thompson would stop calling him son. He had only one father and that was the way he liked it.

Thompson stood with a half bottle of whisky and three twenty-packets of cigarettes. '. . . for your father, with my best wishes.'

Paul Ferris left The Ponderosa a little perturbed. He had had to intervene hard with his youngest sister. The two were closest in age and were well used to arguing. He had had to be very insistent she didn't speak to the cops – no problem. But now the expectation was that Arthur Thompson would deal with the matter himself. That should include substantial compensation to the victim's family – God knows they had little enough – as well as some form of punishment for the boozed-up driver. Those were the rules, the expectations that Paul Ferris was working to. Thompson hadn't mentioned any of that so how could Paul be sure they would happen?

'Because he's Arthur Thompson, ye mug,' Paul muttered, telling himself off. 'Of course he'll do the right thing.'

Ferris was eighteen years old, a Blackhill boy through and through. In fact, he'll point out that he came from the better-off part of Blackhill at the top of the scheme and had it easy with his father being a good earner and his mother, Jenny, a good mother and housewife. A bright, fair-haired young man, he had a regular job delivering spirits to shops and pubs and seemed set to work his way out of that scheme.

Young Paul was the major income earner for his home. His oldest brother, Billy, was in jail for murder – a crime of passion in revenge against two men who had taunted him about how they'd had affairs with his wife. His father had lost a small bus company when he was jailed for tax evasion. Serving that sentence, he had planned an audacious robbery with three others. On his release, he got a job driving school buses. The four men robbed the bank and then escaped in a bus full of kids, with Willie driving along as if nothing had happened. It almost worked but one of the associates started flashing the cash. He was arrested and coughed on all the others. Willie was sent away again for a while and would now struggle to find legitimate employment for the rest of his life. So, young Paul's wages were crucial in supporting the family.

But Paul Ferris's friends were always from the heart of Blackhill, the dark centre of the scheme, and, being an accomplished joyrider and robber of warehouses, he had adapted easily to their ways. It wasn't big-time crime – just what most young men from that scheme got involved in, even the ones who went straight as Paul was going straight. Then, one night, a friend visited him and all that changed.

It was a Friday night, wages night, and Paul had just paid over most of his wad to his mother for housekeeping. Up in Paul's bedroom, the friend proudly showed him a huge roll of banknotes then gave him £500 because 'I'm flush and you're a mate'. Outside in the street, a taxicab waited for his friend, its meter running. The guy was eighteen years old and behaving like a toff. Paul was eighteen years old and hardly had enough money for one decent night out. The friend revealed he had made the cash robbing stores, mostly jewellers, and reckoned there was a fortune to be made every week. As well as the story, he had a proposal – that Paul join him in the enterprise. Young Ferris thought for no more than a minute and said, 'All right then.'

That was the very instant Paul Ferris decided on a life of crime. Few others can trace their lifestyles back to one conversation but he can. Then, it seemed like an everyday decision, no big deal when you lived in Blackhill. What he wasn't to know was that it was the start of a criminal career that would bring greater notoriety and controversy on him than anyone else had ever had in Scotland before. But, at that time, he was just a young man going out thieving.

The Welsh tribe were still around, making life very difficult for the Thompsons. While little was drawn to the attention of the cops and never reported in the media, there were gun battles, stabbings and assaults on a weekly basis.

The Welsh Family have been more or less written off as having one major contribution to modern day crime in Glasgow – their war with Arthur Thompson. But this is far from accurate with the brothers working in all sorts of robberies and scams, particularly when violence was required, and not just in their home city. One story involving one of the great characters of the streets might demonstrate this.

Willie Leitch was an old-time player – the type of guy who applied cunning and intelligence to his trade rather than plain brute force and violence. As with so many of his generation, Leitch detested prison and took every opportunity to escape. On one occasion, he was holed up in Edinburgh's Saughton Prison. Somehow, Willie had managed to get the cushy job of prison gardener. This allowed him loads of outside work, sun, fresh air and free rein of the grounds. It was the type of prison job old trusties fight over but it wasn't enough for Willie Leitch. One day, he was tending the governor's garden, a secluded wee patch away from the prying eyes of the screws. He'd heard that there was to be a big road race that same day and the runners would pass by Saughton Prison. Within minutes Leitch had hatched a plot.

As soon as he heard the first group of competitors pad past the jail walls, Willie stripped off to his regulation prison underwear, white vest and boxer-type shorts. With a pen he had for marking the little tickets identifying the names of different plants, he scrawled a number on the vest. Without further ado, he hopped through the perimeter fence at a spot he had long before worked out in case of just such a chance opportunity.

Willie Leitch hit the pavement running, something he was no slouch at, and took off in the direction of the race. In his white vest, shorts and prison issue plimsolls he looked for all the world like just another runner. Leitch had almost covered a mile from the jail when up ahead he spotted a line of panda cars blocking the road, surrounded by a posse of cops hefting rifles and sporting bullet- proof vets. What was he to think but it was roadblock set to nab him? But what was he to do? The police had seen him so there was no point in turning back. Only one thing for it – keep running, probably straight back into custody.

As Willie Leitch neared the barricade, he was amazed to see two armed cops stand aside and wave him through. Were they taking the piss? On he went and, sure enough, straight through the blue cordon. As he passed, he noticed that some coppers were training their guns on a car they had stopped while others were searching the boot. In the car sat the sullen faces of four of the Welsh Brothers. The boot of the car was full to the gunnels with rifles and handguns. The Welshes had just been nabbed attempting to make a delivery in Edinburgh – trading in guns on a large scale which was just one of the many businesses they were involved in.

Willie Leitch ran on to freedom where he stayed for some time. His audacious escape earned him the sobriquet of the Saughton Harrier, a name that has stuck with him since. But, for the Welsh Brothers, it was just another day, just another charge.

The Thompson and Welsh Families continued to live a matter of a hundred yards from each other. It was like a Mexican stand-off, one that had lasted twenty-five years – the longest street feud in UK history – and it was beginning to wear Arthur Thompson down.

And, for the Welshes, trouble was emerging from an unexpected source. Ten years earlier, one of the younger brothers had had a playground scrap and lost. He ran home to tell the older crew and they returned and beat hell out of the eight-year-old who had fought with their brother. This was nothing unusual for the Welsh Brothers but, for this victim, they made a habit of it, beating the youngster up several times a week for years. The Welshes probably saw that as good sport – a big mistake.

The target of the Welsh Brothers' bullying was Paul Ferris. Small for his age, father and brother in jail, he was alone in having to face a tribe ranging from school age to adult years. Ferris paid a huge price for the attacks with chronic psychological psoriasis plaguing his formative teenage years, not to mention the attacks that grew more brutal every time. By the time Ferris was sixteen, they were attacking him with hammers team-handed and for no reason other than that's what they did. Ferris couldn't and wouldn't run or hide. He took the beatings and devised a new approach – he laughed as they crushed his bones. The strategy spooked the Welsh Brothers who thought Ferris had gone crazy. He hadn't. He had grown smart.

One day, Ferris went to Arthur Thompson's local, the Provanmill Inn, to meet a couple of friends, Blink and Alco McDonald, with whom he had been planning a job. As usual, the pub was crowded and the air heavy with tobacco smoke. With no sign of Blink or Alco, Ferris asked around, to be told no one had seen them. As he was leaving, a voice said, 'Paul.' It was Fatboy Thompson. 'Could I have a word?' Ferris and Fatboy knew of each other, of course, being only a few years apart in age and living very close to each other. Paul wandered over to the end of the bar. This was the gunslinger's seat, Arthur's usual spot which was now kept warm by Fatboy. 'Can I buy you a drink?' This was a first and obviously meant something else was coming.

'Aye, cheers, I'll have a half pint of lager.' Ferris wasn't a big drinker and didn't even like lager but just wanted to show willing.

'Nonsense,' blurted Fatboy for all to hear, 'you'll have a pint and chaser. Vodka?'

Paul Ferris thought arguing would seem ungracious so he just nodded his head.

Fatboy moved further into the corner so that he and Ferris could talk privately. 'Wanted to say that The Godfather's really happy with what you've been up to lately,' said Fatboy once the drinks had been served.

'That's good,' replied Paul, taking a sip from his beer though wondering what sort of bloke called his old man The Godfather. 'Cheers. But I'm not sure what you mean.' Ferris had been robbing a lot of jewellery shops at night and doing a fair trade with the reset merchants out the east end. How could that please Arthur Thompson?

'With those Welsh BASTARDS,' Fatboy roared the last part of his sentence. He slapped Paul on the back, looked round the bar, grinning, and saw all the faces grinning back.

'Oh, aye, cheers.' Ferris thought of the issues between him and the Welsh Family as entirely personal, nothing to do with anyone else. He had been picking off all the Welsh men, one by one, and systematically gaining the revenge that had burned in him for years. By this time, he was as big as he was ever going to be – although that was still smaller than any of them.

One night, when a friend was being attacked by one of the most vicious, brutal players in the scheme, a man much older than Paul, he discovered a surprising gift. He had intervened to save his friend and had drawn the knife that he always carried. All Ferris's mates would also have carried knives and, like them, Paul never planned to use his. But that night, he stuck the blade into the gullet of the guy who was having a go at his friend. The man fell, gurgling, struggling for breath and almost died. Paul Ferris had felt nothing – absolutely no emotion whatsoever. On the hard streets of Glasgow, to swiftly gut someone without a pang of conscience, regret or hesitation was a gift. That's when he knew he could get back at the Welsh crew – and how he would do it.

'Yeah, well . . .' said Paul, unsure of what response to give, 'I've got some old business with them.'

'Business! Good one, man. That's doing the business all right, scalping that fucker.'

'Eh, aye, but it wasn't as bad as he deserved.' Ferris was embarrassed by this. That day, he had spotted one of the older Welshes on Royston Road. He just happened to have a new Bowie knife tucked in his belt and, crossing the road quickly, he decided to do him on the spot. Welsh saw him right at the last minute, when he was only two steps away. The man reached for his own blade but too late. Ferris had his knife in his hand, grabbed the front of his hair and sliced. And sliced. Five seconds later it was over. Paul Ferris was back on the other side of the street, knife back in its sheath, leaning into the breeze. A few hundred yards away, he stopped and, as he lit a cigarette, he turned and glanced back. Welsh was slumped on his arse on the pavement, back against the wall, his scalp flapping. There was no noise but Welsh's mouth hung open in an interminable howl. That Welsh would survive and wear a hat for the rest of his life. It was horrible but not enough for the years of torture he and his brothers had handed out to Ferris. It was personal – nothing to do with Fatboy.

'We thought it was cracker when you slit that other Welsh's throat but a scalping . . . Ha!' Fatboy continued and then he asked Paul to tell him in detail how it had happened.

The request made Ferris a little uncomfortable since the Fatboy was obviously savouring every minute – he seemed to be living through the pain inflicted on his enemies as if he had been there.

Paul had slashed a Welsh's throat in another chance meeting. Also, while on remand in Longriggend Remand Institution, Ferris had spotted an ally of the Welsh Brothers and had slashed him badly in the exercise yard. In spite of the area being full of prisoners, not one of them had seen a thing – or so they said. There had been others. It was a one-man, pay-back-time roadshow.

From the first hit, locals had declared Paul Ferris a dead man. After all, he was a small guy, without the backing of a major team, no record for street violence and yet here he was picking off one of the most dangerous gangs in Glasgow. His odds didn't look good but, a few bodies later, it was Ferris who was alive and in one piece and the Welsh Brothers who were being taken down.

'They deserved it, but,' said Paul, having relayed the details to an increasingly excited Fatboy, 'they're just animals. Worse than animals. The Brothers Grim just hurt for fun.'

'It's like this, Paul,' said Fatboy, now pulling his stool closer and talking in a hushed conspiratorial voice. 'We hate the Welshes too. Old score to settle. Maybe we can help each other out. Work together, like. What do you think?'

'Well, I do a bit of business with a few pals,' said Paul, trying to assess what sort of deal Fatboy was proposing and hoping he would expand.

'Sure, but the old man, he wants you on board – part of the team.' Ferris was being asked to work for the man in charge of Glasgow. It was a huge honour and the young man was flattered.

By the time Paul Ferris left the Provanmill Inn, he had agreed to sign up with the Thompsons. For Fatboy, it had been a good day's business. After all, he had just recruited one of the best young players in Blackhill. Little did either of them suspect that life was about to become very hot indeed.

15

BRIDGES, BRICKS AND IRN-BRU

MID 1980s

'Paul, this is Tam,' – Fatboy was making a polite introduction, as you do when two of your acquaintances meet for the first time. In this instance, he was teaming up two of the most dangerous young players in Glasgow.

Tam Bagan was small, slim and dark – a perfect bookend to Ferris's small, slim and fair. He was a good-looking young man, pleasant faced and bright eyed but his style of dress gave him away. Bagan could usually be found in dark suits, long black leather coats and gloves to match. It wasn't the fashion – except for hit men, that is.

Bagan and his siblings had been raised by a relative of Arthur Thompson. From a very young age, he had been around the Thompson Family at close quarters and had watched old Arthur very carefully. Arthur treated him warmly, much as he did his own oldest son, showing him the way to deal with adult life – the Thompson way.

By the time he reached early adulthood, Bagan had a reputation for being fascinated with guns. But he was entirely different from the childish braggart that was Fatboy. Bagan didn't like to play with guns, respecting their power too much. You didn't mess with Tam Bagan. If he thought you had crossed him, he would calmly, coldly take you out – well, that was how others saw him. By the time of his introduction to Ferris, Bagan had already clocked up two shootings in Easterhouse and many others besides. As an adopted member of the family, Tam Bagan would be the natural successor to Arthur Thompson if his own sons couldn't hack it.

Together, Ferris and Bagan made a formidable team. They were immediately set to task, collecting debts and protection money. Not that they were ever told why they had to get so much dough from some Joe Soap. They were just told by Thompson or Fatboy to go and collect it, no questions asked. Much of this was trouble free since most individuals were happy to have Arthur Thompson's patronage and protection rather than his wrath. But, from time to time, payments were short or unpaid, or the amounts were in dispute. That's when the fun started.

These were two very young men and they were being sent to some of the oldest, hardest faces in the city to collect money. It would be natural for the young team to be hesitant or fazed. Not a bit of it. If the money wasn't forthcoming, the quietly spoken Ferris would make it plain what havoc and pain would visit the debtor unless it was paid up pronto. It must have unnerved these more experienced gangsters to be calmly threatened by two fresh-faced boys. And it would have been even more terrifying for them when word got around of how these two lads had delivered on just such threats to men with well-established reputations. Arthur Thompson was a very happy man.

During the early evening at The Ponderosa, there would be a knock at the door. At this time, Rita would have been busy watching *Coronation Street*, her favourite soap. Fatboy would be upstairs watching a *Godfather* video, reading comics or playing with a gun. The daughters would be hanging around or out for the night. Usually the elder, Margaret, wasn't there. Rumour had it she was involved in drugs with some boyfriend. Everyone else would have been too busy, so Arthur Senior would have had to go to the door.

'Aye, lads,' he'd say by way of greeting, walking back into the lounge and leaving Bagan and Ferris to shut the front door. 'How did you get on?'

'No problems,' Ferris would say.

'What, no arguments?' Thompson would have walked through to a small workroom off the lounge.

'Aye, a bit of a grumble but it was settled after a wee discussion,' Ferris would have reassured him.

'It's all there,' Bagan would have said as he dropped the plastic carrier bag or cheap holdall on to a table.

'All of it?' Thompson wouldn't have been convinced.

'Aye.' Ferris would have been unable to see what the issue was.

'Fuck. Ha. Rita, shout the boy down. You got every fucking penny? You sure?'

'Aye.' Ferris would have been getting pissed off with this now.

And Bagan wouldn't have liked it either but he was well used to Arthur Thompson's ways.

Money was the Thompsons' god and seeing was counting. By the time Fatboy joined the company, his father would be counting the notes, licking his thumb and forefinger for greater speed, the tip of his tongue poking out at the edge of his mouth. Fatboy would appear, looking like he'd just wakened, a .30-calibre or a half-eaten bar of chocolate in his paw – sometimes both. He'd look at the pile of banknotes and smile.

'Any trouble, boys?' he'd ask. The son loved the dough almost as much as his father but a better pleasure for him was to be told every detail of any violence in Technicolor. So Ferris or Bagan would have to recount exactly what form of persuasion they had used – their final duty of the night.

Right there and then, Ferris and Bagan would be given their next day's task. They got no thank you, well done or bonus – just instructions for another job or two that would provide more money for Arthur Thompson.

Although Fatboy wasn't rated on the street, he was an industrious type. A bloke called Martin Ross almost had a monopoly on the drugs trade in Glasgow. Fatboy had teamed up with him for a while and then plotted a takeover.

Fatboy ran a garage in Maryhill and serviced Ross's cars for free, in that kind of barter system street players use to support each other. A few days after he'd had his car serviced there, Ross was jumped by the cops at the Duck Bay Marina on the banks of Loch Lomond. The team went straight to the steering wheel column where they found enough smack to put Ross away for a long time.

Word was passed to Ross in jail that a competitor, Walter 'Wattie' Douglas, had set him up. But it wasn't Douglas. It was Fatboy using a device he'd deploy many times in the future – planting drugs, guns and ammo in people's cars then belling the cops.

Ross hadn't swallowed the idea that it was Douglas who had set him up – instead, he'd sussed it had been Fatboy. Thus, Douglas was free to go on trading without threat. Fatboy had hoped that Ross would hire a team to wreak revenge on Douglas thereby removing another of his competitors in Glasgow's drugs trade. Instead, Wattie Douglas moved in on some of Ross's drugs patches – much to Fatboy's fury.

If Ross wouldn't sort out Douglas then Fatboy would – by paying a team to beat and knife him, of course. Ex-milkman Douglas was a thief and a dealer, not a hard man. No way was he going to stick around when The Godfather's son was out to get him. He took off to the Continent where he'd create a whole new crime experience with some other refugees from The Godfather. But more of that later.

Meantime, Fatboy wanted rid of another drug dealer, a bloke by the name of Ted Hughes. One day, Hughes set off down south to pick up a consignment of smack. For the job, he'd just bought a big black BMW off Fatboy. The car was stolen and had been 'ringed' – that is, the registration plate and other identifying features had been changed, making it ideal for such a dodgy itinerary.

Heading back up north with a boot-load of heroin, as soon as Hughes had crossed the Strathclyde Region demarcation line for local Glasgow cops, he was pulled in by a police car. Hughes was expecting a speeding ticket even though he reckoned he was well within the limits.

'Ted Hughes,' said the cop, once he had Hughes out of the car, 'we are arresting you under suspicion of . . .'

The police knew who he was without asking and they knew which car to stop. Even Ted Hughes's wife didn't know what car he was driving. Only one other person did – Fatboy Thompson. With Hughes held on remand, Fatboy promptly took over his trade, expanding on the heroin business his father had kicked off on a smaller scale years before.

Word got around that Hughes's wife might sing the whole story to the cops and land Fatboy in it big time. The very next day, live ammunition was put through her letterbox. The message was clear. She and her kids left the city soon after that and, when Hughes was eventually freed, he joined them.

Fatboy's cunning and utter disregard, booted into him during his childhood school years, were paying dividends. Or so he thought, as did his father. Fatboy Thompson did nothing without first consulting his old man. Arthur Thompson was as much involved in drug trafficking as his son was.

While Arthur benefited immeasurably from the work of Bagan and Ferris they were seen as Fatboy's men. As such, he expected the pair of them to drive him around and be at his beck and call. On one occasion, Fatboy combined his love of guns with his love of cars and Paul Ferris's indisputable skills behind the wheel.

Bagan had got hold of a small but fast hatchback and asked Paul and Fatboy to go for a spin. Out they went on to the little winding country roads close to Blackhill. Fatboy pulled a large pistol from his jacket – he always carried a gun, just like his father – and started firing at objects in passing fields. Discovering that the new motor had a sunroof, he opened it and stood up, blasting at road signs and telegraph poles as Ferris drove at speed.

By this time, Bagan and Ferris were getting weary of his childish games and pled with him to call it a night and go home. Fatboy refused, twisting this way and that, blasting away as if in a Hollywood blockbuster. Then he tired and tried to sit down. No chance – he was wedged tight.

This was the best fun Ferris and Bagan had had since the night began and they took Fatboy home the long way round. Ferris knew those roads intimately but Fatboy didn't. Half an hour longer than necessary, they eventually pulled up at The Ponderosa where Fatboy was eventually prised free. The trouble was that he really had been wedged in tight and getting him out had damaged the sunroof. When Bagan complained that his new motor had been busted, Fatboy asked how much the car had cost.

'Seven grand,' replied Bagan probably upping the sum a bit.

'You hang on there,' said Fatboy, disappearing into The Ponderosa. Five minutes later, he re-emerged and handed something to Bagan. 'It's all there,' said Fatboy. 'Get one with a bigger sunroof next time.' He'd just handed Tam Bagan £7,000. Generous? It wasn't in his nature. But Fatboy had just been the butt of a joke and, as well as his backside, his ego was bruised. The man couldn't stand that so flashing a large amount of cash restored the balance – or so he thought. Bagan and Ferris had different values.

Arthur was still playing an old game. Why stop when it paid him dividends? In the 1970s, a bloke called Peter Ferguson had built a small but thriving business, Maryhill Cash & Carry Carpets, on Maryhill Road, near a busy junction. The charismatic owner attracted custom from all over using advertising to great effect. Even if you hadn't actually bought carpets or cushion floor from his shop and didn't live in the west of Scotland, you would know about Maryhill Cash & Carry Carpets. It represented a juicy target for Arthur Thompson.

Thompson made Peter an offer he couldn't refuse. It was to be the usual arrangement – Thompson investing as a partner, saying he wanted nothing to do with the day-to-day running, leaving it a wee while and then moving in to compromise the original owner. But, in this instance, successful as the store seemed to be, Peter had run into major cash-flow problems. Without Thompson's money, he would soon be declared bankrupt. If he had known what was about to happen, he may have chosen financial ruin as the preferred option.

Thompson's first request was straightforward enough – just some boxes of goods he needed stored overnight till another warehouse unit was ready. No problem. Overnight became a week and then a week turned into a month. Peter started asking about the load that was taking up valuable space on his floor. Well, that's what he said the issue was but it was more likely that he was worried about Thompson's reputation and that the boxes might contain hot goods. Peter was a polite big man and gentle with it. No way did he want to offend The Godfather.

'Want them shifted?' Thompson asked the obvious question since that's exactly what the big fella had been requesting. 'No problem.'

Two mornings later, Peter went in to work to discover that Arthur Thompson had been true to his word. The original boxes were gone but had been replaced by an even bigger load. Enough was enough.

Peter carefully pulled back the cardboard edge of one box marked Ground Coffee and found . . . ground coffee. It looked as if they were damaged goods since some packages had burst and rough, strong-smelling granules spilled over the floor. He left it at that, feeling a bit foolish for suspecting foul play.

Yet, later in the day, he was still worried. Why would Arthur Thompson buy a job lot of expensive coffee that clearly was a mess? Peter went back to the boxes and dug in deeper. Drugs weren't his scene but he knew that big, solid mass in the middle of that box wasn't coffee. In fact, it was cannabis resin. Several kilos of it were stashed in each box with the aroma of the coffee designed to put sniffer dogs off.

Peter had no choice but to confront Arthur Thompson. We're not privy to what actually happened that night but we know that, from then on, big Peter was a broken man. He lost weight, his appearance became shabby, he had no sparkle in his eye and no sense of humour. Not like him at all. When he and Thompson appeared at public events together such as smokers with dinner on the table and boxing as the entertainment, his friends really started to worry about him. Arthur Thompson was treating him with utter contempt in front of people. Jokes would be cast at his expense and Peter would be sent off to fetch the drinks like some personal waiter.

Within a year big Peter went from a happy, successful, popular businessman to a sad statistic. One day, he killed himself, quietly and with dignity, the way he led his life. He became just another notch on Arthur Thompson's killing belt and, yet again, no murder was committed.

When Arthur Thompson had first invested in Maryhill Cash & Carry Carpets, he acquired an adjacent garage. Fatboy took this over as a going concern, a responsibility that could allow him to potter about in his second-favourite hobby, cars. Over that time, the cops found several players with heroin stuffed into the panels or steering columns of their vehicles and they all went down. The one thing those gangsters had in common was that Fatboy had given them free servicing and repairs on the vehicles. It was a barter, common among players, and they would be expected to repay in kind from whatever legitimate businesses they were involved in. Trouble was, Fatboy was planting some H and then phoning the cops so that his rivals were banged up and he was able to move in and take over their territories. Fatboy's drugs empire was growing all the time but he always had other little earners.

One day, Fatboy asked a mechanic, Willie Gibson, to drive a car to the auction yard. Of course, Gibson agreed – a wee drive was better than being stuck under a car any day. When he was booking the car in, two uniformed cops appeared and arrested him for dealing in stolen motors. It has to be asked, what had Willie Gibson expected from Fatboy Thompson?

Gibson was in big trouble – or so the police told him. They told him, and he tended to agree, that Fatboy had asked him to take that car to the auction because it was a ringer and he took the risks. Angry as hell with his erstwhile boss, Willie Gibson started to sing about all the shenanigans he had spotted going on at the garage. The cops were particularly interested in what Fatboy kept in his locker – some hard porn, a change of overalls and a collection of guns and ammunition. Fatboy was maybe in trouble but word was that Willie Gibson was a dead man.

Gibson might have been a non-player but he wasn't blind to what he had done. In double quick time he and his immediate family moved down to England, destination not advertised. As far as Arthur Thompson was concerned, his honour had been met. The Gibsons had shown fear, terror even, enough to up sticks out of Thompson's territory. Arthur didn't see why he and his family should take any other risky action as long, that is, as Willie Gibson stayed out of town.

Families are contradictory phenomena. They can be so nurturing and yet so destructive – so safe, yet so dangerous. Like all good folks, Gibson loved his family and he couldn't resist a quick visit back to see those members who were still in Glasgow. It was a couple of years after the incident with Fatboy and the Gibsons assumed all that would be forgotten. It was a lethal assumption.

One night Willie Gibson, his brother, sister-in-law and his father-in-law, John Hogg, went out for a pint. They deliberately chose the Open Arms in Riddrie. It was close to the family home in Blackhill but not so close as to attract attention. The Provanmill Inn would have been the most convenient pub but no way was Willie Gibson going into Arthur Thompson's HQ. That would have been suicidal. But what Willie Gibson didn't realise was that Fatboy had been told of his return to Glasgow immediately. Fatboy consulted his old man. The decision was brief and direct: 'Nail the bastard.'

A hit man was hired and he sussed Gibson's movements. The walk back to Blackhill from the Open Arms would be perfect. The route required that the group cross the M8 motorway by way of a narrow pedestrian bridge. There, they would be exposed, vulnerable.

After a few drinks, they started the short walk home. Willie Gibson was edgy, alert. It was one thing to come back to his hometown but now that he was there, the reality of the Thompsons' wrath became so real. The three men and the woman would have noticed many things. Courting couples, groups of bored teenagers and the occasional adult using the short cut across the motorway. The spot was infamous for gang fights between teams from opposing sides of the divide. Gibson and his relatives would have been more concerned by any large gathering of young men than the car that had followed them till they mounted the bridge, then sped off only to reappear in the sporadic flow of traffic below. The car exited and came back on the other side of the carriageway, a process it would repeat several times. It was Fatboy Thompson, determined to see the hit he had paid for. Gangster movies were OK but this was the real thing.

Nor would Willie Gibson have paid much heed to the young man walking towards them at speed. At least, he looked young – small build, casual gear – but he was wearing one of those hooded tops popular with the kids and had his face covered. No worries, he walked straight past them, head down, going a place. Then he turned and pulled his gun.

The hit man knew what his target looked like. Gibson's father-in-law, John Hogg, spotted the gun and took off as fast as he could. But he had a bad hip or whatever and he hobbled along the parapet. His brother-in-law took fright and immediately jumped over the bridge's railings, landing on the motorway hard shoulder yards from speeding traffic. He was lucky – he only broke a leg.

Gibson knew he was the target. He grabbed his sister-in-law and used her a shield between him and the pistol. No way could the hit man fire now and risk injuring the woman. The gunman and Gibson stood there yards from each other, the trembling woman stuck between. Something had to give. Suddenly Gibson shoved the woman at the hit man and ran. Within a few strides he had overtaken John Hogg and the hit man fired, then cursed. He had winged the old man.

Still the gunman ran on and kept on firing until Gibson reached the other side where he carried on sprinting. Now he had entered territory where there would be witnesses and innocent bystanders. The hit man turned and quickly ran off the bridge in the opposite direction, straight past the woman who was still terrified, trembling and screaming.

Down below, Fatboy passed by in a car once more. He was laughing and cursing at the same time. It had been a good scene with bullets flying around and people diving from bridges but Gibson had escaped. That wasn't the plan at all.

Willie Gibson hadn't changed much. He gave a full statement to the cops, claiming he had got a good look at the gunman's face and he had the nickname FERGIE tattooed on one set of knuckles. Then he fingered Paul Ferris as the gunman. Small problem. All of the others had given formal statements that they couldn't see the shooter's face. Another problem, Paul Ferris didn't have a tattoo or a nickname.

Willie Gibson hadn't spotted Fatboy's drive-by but someone had. Pulled in for questioning, he gave pat answers
that he lived in that part of city so what was the law against
driving there? There was none, of course, and no further links
could be made between Fatboy and the attempted hit. Except
the cops believed it was the Thompsons' young equaliser,
Paul Ferris, who had fired the gun.

Ferris was charged with attempted murder for the first
time but not the last. At his trial, Willie Gibson swore that
he had had a clear view of the accused man's face. It was
unlikely given the chaos and panic on that bridge. Maybe
Gibson had correctly sussed that Fatboy had been behind the
attempt to kill him. Who would Fatboy ask to carry out such
a hit? The Thompsons' main man, of course, Paul Ferris.

At that time, even the cops would agree that a lie or two
would be quite moral if you 'knew' someone was guilty but
didn't have the evidence. There were a couple of problems for
the prosecution, though. Ferris didn't have a tattoo and no
one could be found who would admit to him ever having had
a street name. Another big problem was that Gibson's father-
in-law, John Hogg, stuck rigidly to his original statement. He
had not seen the gunman's face and he couldn't identify him.

The jury at Paul Ferris's trial returned a not proven verdict,
that peculiar bastard verdict, peculiar to Scots Law, that indi-
cates neither guilt nor innocence. The media had started to
notice young Ferris as they noticed everything to do with the
Thompson clan. When asked about the verdict after the trial,
Ferris said, with a wry smile, 'They thought I was guilty but
they just couldn't prove it.'

Nobody interviewed Fatboy or the man who ordered the
hit, his old man, Arthur. That was the way they liked it – with
someone else in the firing line.

A short while after the trial, a brown envelope full of
money was stuffed through John Hogg's letter box. Whoever
had pulled that trigger felt bad that the older man had been

hit. It was the hit man who compensated John Hogg but it should have been Arthur Thompson.

By that time, Arthur Thompson had bought a second house, two doors down from his own home, at the other end of the short terrace in Provanmill Road. That was to be Fatboy's home. The two buildings were decked out with the same stone cladding and appeared like identical bookends. The two wings of The Ponderosa.

Visiting journalists who didn't know the local terrain often mistakenly believed that the whole row belonged to Arthur Thompson. The neighbours sandwiched in between didn't seem to mind much. At least they are not reported as complaining.

At one point, a cop lived in one house. Next door to him was a young mother who decided to enhance her income by using her trade as a trained hairdresser, cutting and setting hair in her front room. The cop complained to the authorities about her running a business from home and she was promptly ordered to cease. But there was no smidgeon of a mutter about the goings-on at Arthur Thompson's houses.

In fact, Arthur and Fatboy's homes were joined together at one point via a tunnel they had built underground. Whether this was designed as a security measure, we don't know, but it was where they kept guns and drugs when there was no place else for the stash to go.

Arthur and Fatboy went into conference around that time. For 'conference' read a chat over a cup of tea in The Ponderosa. They had noticed an upturn in the entertainment venues in Glasgow. Trendy clubs like Panama Jax and Henry Afrika's were sprouting up all over and there was a new breed of young, trendy people with money and a taste for drugs in the city. These were the days before Ecstasy and other recreational drugs hit the streets. What this mob wanted was cocaine and dope and Arthur reckoned they should have a slice of that action.

Fatboy set about handling the contacts himself. Although he was increasingly avoiding any direct involvement in his drugs trade, leaving it to others to take the risks, this time, he wanted to set the business flow up himself. The Thompsons were always wary of people who would steal their profits and this was a sensitive one. Once there had been a few exchanges, Fatboy would delegate the action.

On the day in question, he turned up at the meeting spot in a car park hefting a holdall heavy with coke and a slab of cannabis resin. CCTV cameras weren't ubiquitous then so car parks made ideal exchange locations. Forget the movies. When the transaction involves locals, there's no checking the package or testing the drugs. The idea is to make the exchange as quickly as possible and get the hell out of there. If anyone cheated on the deal, it was for the other side to remedy the situation and, in a city like Glasgow, there were few hiding places.

All went smoothly and Fatboy returned to his house via a circuitous route. He went directly into The Ponderosa to share the spoils with Arthur. Nothing excited Arthur Thompson more than shekels to fill his coffers. This deal was worth £200,000 – not bad for an hour's work. With a gleam in his eye, Arthur Thompson unzipped the bag to reveal a brick wrapped in newspaper and a full bottle of Irn-Bru, Scotland's favourite hangover cure. Not only was the other party ripping off the Thompsons, they were taking the piss. That bottle of Irn-Bru was clearly a dig at Fatboy's predilection for drinking gallons of sweet, gassy fluids every day. Arthur Thompson didn't get the joke – neither did Fatboy.

The money was important – as it always was to the Thompsons – but there was a bigger point to settle. This team of semi-professionals had just ripped off the Thompsons and that could not be allowed to stand. If word got around, everyone would fancy an earner at their expense. On every street, the reputation of fear Thompson had worked for so long to establish would disappear like a weak puff of smoke on a windy day. No way could he allow that to happen. Junior had been ripped off. Junior had caused the problem. Maybe it was Junior every wannabe gangster thought was the weak spot. No alternative then but Junior would have to fix it.

Fatboy wasn't capable of tracking down this team on his own. Besides, he had grown up seeing himself as The Godfather's son with certain standards and privileges – like not getting his own paws dirty. Why take risks when he could simply pay someone else to dish the blood and gore? Someone who had proven very skilled at just that – Paul Ferris.

16

VENDETTA

1984

'The bastards are at it, Paul.' Fatboy was sitting on his bed in his own house, playing with a pistol, an empty chocolate wrapper lying by his side.

'So what do you want me to do about it?' Paul Ferris was direct in his business dealings, particularly with the Thompsons. Fatboy could witter on about this and that, round a topic, for ages before finally getting to the point. Paul hoped that he'd put the pistol down and not burst into a game of gangsters, shooting imaginary cops out of his window, making mouth gunshot noises. Annoying as it was, Ferris had to admit that Fatboy made the most realistic, loudest gun noises he had ever heard.

'Well, you should . . .' Fatboy rubbed his nose. He looked worried, uncertain – not like him at all. 'Let's go speak to the old man,' he finally said, following through with a loud, wet fart.

'Aye, good idea,' muttered Paul. He'd been in that bedroom before during one of Fatboy's special gas attacks. Not a pleasant experience.

Arthur Thompson was waiting for them in the front room of The Ponderosa. As usual, he looked grave and solemn, his face showing no signs of what he was about to say. 'You go all the way on these fuckers if it's needed, Paul. They've taken right liberties.' Arthur nodded at Fatboy to speak.

'They ripped us off for fifty grand,' Fatboy lied.

It had been his father's ploy. 'Don't tell the wee man how much we were done for,' Arthur had instructed. 'It might give him ideas above his station. Just make it a large enough sum to make him understand it's important. Give him some big names he knows – that'll make it real for him.'

Arthur Thompson's general approach was to keep his business to himself. It would also do his reputation a great deal of damage to reveal that he'd been taken for a ride and £200,000. Even his own people should be kept in the dark. Just because he was hiring someone to go out and terrorise – or maybe even kill – on his behalf, didn't make them anything other than hired help.

'Bastards,' Paul muttered, nodding at Fatboy.

'Bastards, right enough,' agreed Arthur. 'We'll give you a list of names. Seems there's a big squad of them.' So ended Arthur Thompson's briefing to his equaliser, Paul Ferris.

'It's that Martin Ross fuck,' said Fatboy, referring to the bloke who used to run drugs in Glasgow till he was mysteriously picked up by the cops carrying a full load. 'He's trying to get back in and get a wee bit of revenge while he's at it.'

That name meant a lot to Ferris. Everyone knew of Martin Ross.

'Then there's The Irishman,' continued Fatboy. Catching Ferris's puzzled look, he said, 'You know, big Friel, John Friel – they call him The Irishman.'

'Is that who you want me to sort out?' asked Ferris, unimpressed by anyone's reputation.

'Naw, naw.' Fatboy grinned for the first time. 'Ross is well sorted and we've planted a wee surprise for Friel.'

The day before, the Thompsons had a machine gun, ammo and a bundle of explosives planted in the boot of Friel's car. Then the cops were phoned, of course. A sticky predicament for anyone, especially an Irishman, during those troubled days in his native homeland.

'It's the rest of them we want you to sort. There's five guys,' explained Fatboy, handing Ferris a crumpled piece of paper with the names scribbled in pencil. 'Seems they're into the club scene.'

Apart from adding names to the hit list every now and then, the Thompsons would tell Ferris nothing else. That was how Paul Ferris went on a mission. He became a one-man posse, scouring the streets of Glasgow for names he had no faces to but soon would.

Folk like the Thompsons and Paul Ferris had no truck with the trendy club scene at that time. Their world of socialising was all about working-men's pubs with dominoes, card schools and the occasional rough-and-ready singer the closest they ever got to entertainment. The young teams might occasionally hit the discos but it was places like The White Elephant or *The Tuxedo Princess*, specialising in underage drinking and as pulling places for teenage boys and girls alike. As soon as that was out of their system, it was the old-fashioned pubs for them.

But the new clubs were easy to find. Ferris calculated that, if these guys were regulars, they would continue to be regulars. They had brazenly ripped off Glasgow's top gangster so why should they hide now? Besides, these folks didn't know they were being hunted, never mind the ID of their hunter. And they weren't going to the clubs to sup orange juice and stay alert. They were going to be drunk, stoned, exhausted and vulnerable.

If Paul Ferris had been told that it was a coke deal they had reneged on, he'd be even more confident of his plan. A snout full of charlie might make you feel confident but it didn't increase your strength or make you more prepared. It just made you think you were. Besides, they were smoking dope and drinking booze as well as hoovering up the white snow – not a great combination when you are about to have a knife held at your throat.

Ferris picked the team off one by one. Ambushing them outside clubs in the early hours, paying them a home visit just as dawn broke, tapping them on the shoulder as they left their offices. His request was clear: tell him what they knew about the unpaid dough and they'd be fine. There was small print, of course – if they struggled, lied or held back, then they got hurt. To start with, they took one look at small, fair-haired, fresh-faced Paul Ferris and told him to fuck off. Big mistake.

The list of wounded kept rising every week. This team might have thought themselves smart because they had money and flash cars but they were ignorant in the ways and the faces of the street. If one of them had an iota of knowledge, they would have known what Ferris looked like – and they'd have known to be scared, very scared. Instead, they were hurt, badly hurt.

Ferris reported back to the Thompsons every time he had tracked one of the team down. On one occasion, he had his eyes opened.

'So he's strolling out of the club, his arm round some hairy with a skirt barely covering her arse, thinking he's got nothing to look forward to but a good shag.'

Arthur Thompson, the old man, was asking Paul Ferris to recount every detail of the violence. Now he understood where Fatboy got his fascination with violence.

'I slipped out of my motor and ran straight over. I'm on him before he knows it.' Paul had no option but to play along. This was the boss after all.

'Fucking great!' laughed Fatboy. 'Out of the dark and then right there in his face.'

'Then what?' asked Arthur.

'I asked to talk to him,' replied Paul. Arthur and his son's faces fell, disappointed.

'Talk to him?' blurted Fatboy.

'Aye – his girlfriend was there,' replied Ferris thinking that was adequate explanation of the old rule – no violence in the presence of women or kids.

'Ach,' Arthur Thompson was disappointed.

Fatboy glowered at their equaliser.

'But he was terrified,' continued Ferris, 'and gave me a couple of names. I'm going to check those out the day and, if he's lying, well . . . I know where to get him.'

Arthur Thompson and his son, Fatboy, nodded. This was a result and a rare occasion when their man didn't have a lot of bloody action to report.

They were becoming increasingly impressed by Ferris's approach. The man was totally dedicated. They'd never seen him drink anything stronger than a half pint of beer, hardly smoked these days and didn't touch any of that filth all of the young ones were into. If catching someone meant hanging around in some street for hours late at night, that's what Paul Ferris did. Usually, he gave them a wee reminder that it wasn't the done thing to cross the Thompsons. All told, they could live with Ferris's old-fashioned moral code.

But Arthur Thompson and his son hadn't sat on their backsides while all this was going on. Believing that some of the team were the money behind the clubs, they made an arrangement or two – usually with good-looking young women. Dressed to the nines, the women would go for a night out at a certain club, courtesy of the Thompsons. At that time, the bouncers would always allow unescorted, good-looking, trendy young women in without question or search and always before any men in the queue at the door. Available female talent drew in the bears to spend large. That was the theory and it worked. It also meant the dames could carry in anything they wanted and they often did.

Usually, it was a bit of speed or coke for consumption later in cahoots with boyfriends who would arrive separately.

Sometimes, they worked for the male dealers. The Thompsons had more sinister plans. One girl would plant a pistol, often behind the cistern in the gents – these were not shy, retiring ladies. Another would drop some live ammunition for that very gun. The task completed, a call would be made to Fatboy who then gave a tip-off to the cops. Variations of the same game were made with cocaine, heroin and, on one occasion, two particularly strong-stomached women dropped dead rats near the kitchen.

As much as Arthur Thompson had good fun at this harassment game, the real task was in tracking down the bodies.

'We've got a new name for you, Paul,' said Fatboy. 'Raymond Bonnar. He's the guy behind all this. No doubt. Got it from a good source.'

Ferris didn't know Bonnar from Adam but, a few days later, he'd succeeded in obtaining the make and registration of his car, his home address, the pubs and clubs he hung out at and a resume of his personal habits from women friends regarding the style of clothes he wore. Not long afterwards, he was driving through the east of the city centre, close to the Cathedral and the Royal Infirmary, when who did he spot in the car in front of him but the bold Raymond Bonnar? Waiting till they had both been stopped by traffic lights, Ferris jumped out of his car and knocked on Bonnar's window. The unsuspecting man rolled his window down.

'Are you Raymond Bonnar?' Ferris asked.

'What's it to you?' asked Bonnar, aggressively.

'I'm Paul Ferris,' replied Ferris, with a smile, 'and you're in trouble.' Ferris pulled a knife and, through the open car window, started to repeatedly stab Bonnar down the nearest arm and in the chest.

Fatboy had said that Bonnar was the team leader and Paul Ferris believed him. Why shouldn't he believe him? They were both on the same side. For weeks he had been trying to track down the bloke behind this team, hurting and terrorising as he went. Now Ferris had him and wasn't going to let go. Suddenly, Ferris's arm was being torn by sharp teeth. Bonnar's Alsatian dog was in the back seat and took exception to his master being attacked. The dog gripped Ferris's arm in his jaw and wouldn't let go as Bonnar tried to get his car into gear and take off. No choice but to stab the loyal dog, something Ferris regretted more than the numerous puncture wounds Bonnar had suffered.

Eventually Bonnar managed to fire his motor into first and sped off with Ferris back in his car and in hot pursuit. A harum-scarum race through the busy city-centre streets came to a halt on Bell Street when, to Ferris's amazement, Bonnar actually stopped at red traffic lights. What was it with him? Was he more concerned about getting a traffic ticket than a blade in the throat?

The junction was busy with cars and the pavements were mobbed with lunchtime pedestrians taking breaks from their office jobs – too dodgy for Ferris to get out with a bloody knife in his mitt. So he rammed into the back of Bonnar's car hard and repeatedly. Every time the metal crunched Bonnar's vehicle edged farther out into a main road which was nose to tail with fast-moving cars. Another couple of rams and he would be side-swiped big time. Then the lights changed and Bonnar was off again at speed.

Ferris tailed him all the way till he pulled in at a cop shop and half-ran, half-staggered through the front door. Safe inside, he collapsed in a bloody heap. Outside Paul Ferris drove past the police station and turned away. Time to report back to the Thompsons.

At The Ponderosa, Arthur and Fatboy listened to the story with raw glee, interrupting only to ask for more lurid details or to act out poor Raymond Bonnar being struck with a blade. They were in their element, almost watering at the mouth. In Paul Ferris, they really did have the most dangerous man in Glasgow working for them.

After the car chase and ramming exercise, it was agreed that Paul Ferris's car was now a liability for him. Never mind the passers-by who had stood ogling as Ferris bashed repeatedly into the other car, in the hectic chase Bonnar himself had had plenty of time to catch the number plate. Worse, the car was a big Renault, innocuous enough in itself, but had a neat registration plate with the numbers 666, the sign of Satan. It gave Paul and the Thompsons a wee laugh at the time but now it was like a noose around his neck. The motor had to go. It was parked at the rear of The Ponderosa and he was given the keys to the only spare car at the house, a Volkswagen Beetle. Not his style but it would do.

As Ferris drove away from The Ponderosa, he noticed two cop cars speeding in the opposite direction. Two minutes later, a squad of cops broke into the back of the Thompsons' house with a warrant for Paul Ferris. The cops tore the place apart and paid special attention to Ferris's car.

The following day, Paul went round to The Ponderosa for his next assignment. The laughing, good-humoured atmosphere had disappeared to be replaced by big Arthur Thompson in a very sullen and serious mood. Fatboy fidgeted nervously and ate chocolate at a greater rate than usual.

'We've had word the polis are after you, son,' said Arthur to Paul Ferris.

'Big time,' said the anxious-mugged Fatboy. It was an unusual look for a young man who thought he was untouchable.

'They've a warrant out for your arrest for that Bonnar thing,' added Arthur. 'Attempt murder.' He allowed the words to sink in. This was serious. 'You're going to have to shoot.' Arthur Thompson didn't mean grab a gun and start blasting his way out of some police ambush – he was suggesting Ferris should get out of the city and fast.

Within ten minutes, Paul had been given the keys to the Thompsons' flat in Rothesay on the holiday island of Bute, far down the Firth of Clyde. Next, he needed transport and he was amazed when Arthur Thompson threw him the keys to his very own Daimler, his pride and joy. Now that was something special.

As Ferris drove away from The Ponderosa, the two Thompsons started laughing.

'Ach, it's a waste, you know,' said Arthur.

'Aye, you're right,' smiled Fatboy. 'So you're not making that phone call?' A smirk stretching his face.

'Eh-let-me-think-about-it-I've-thought-about-it-and-right-I've-decided-I'll-make-the-fucking-call,' rattled Arthur at top speed, laughing aloud. Then he scooped the phone from its cradle and dialled a familiar number.

Paul Ferris went directly home to see his girlfriend, Anne Marie McCafferty, then heavily pregnant for the first time. He didn't know how long he'd be away for and couldn't leave Anne Marie alone with the baby's arrival so close. So they agreed that she would come along but would travel by a separate car later that day. Though it wasn't necessary, Anne Marie was told not to tell anyone, even close family where they were off to. Just pack and leave.

That night Paul and Anne Marie were well ensconced in the Thompsons' Rothesay flat. It was an OK tenement flat on the seafront, looking out over the broad, picturesque expanse of the Clyde. Next to an ancient ornate church and a jeweller's shop that rarely saw a customer, the place felt soporific and quiet after the anarchy of Glasgow's streets. When the Thompson clan spent time there, the locals didn't know who they were – well, most of them didn't. Quite a number of legitimate businessmen also kept houses down there and knew Arthur Thompson by sight – some had even borrowed money from him. They now laugh at recalling the fierce gangster in his suit, probably carrying his Beretta, walking his wife Rita's tiny pooch along the seafront every morning. They laughed but didn't say anything. Rothesay was the kind of place they left you alone. Usually.

Anne Marie was making dinner in the kitchen while Paul lounged in the living room watching some European football match on TV. He was in trouble, that was for sure, but he was being taken care of by Arthur Thompson so why should he worry? Rothesay might be just the place for a wee break anyway. The enforced absence would give him and Anne Marie some time together in this peace and quiet. That was when three armed cops smashed through the door.

Before he knew it, Paul Ferris was down on his back, this huge cop with a ruddy complexion and pure white hair waving a gun at his head. Then the cops discovered that Anne Marie was there and panicked. No woman cop present. Had to get a female polis in attendance, double-quick time.

They manhandled Ferris like a rag doll, handcuffed his hands behind his back and searched the flat. Helpless, he sat there and watched, just as the cops intended. One came in and took Ferris to another room, asking him to count some money he had found on the mantelpiece so that there was no dispute later. That done, the florid-faced cop grabbed Ferris by the cuffs and pulled him bodily through to another room, the small man trailing on the ground in the wake of this giant.

Dumped on the bed, Paul Ferris heard a thump and looked down to see that the cop's gun had fallen to the floor. Ferris kicked the gun sending it skidding across the floor just to annoy the cop.

Ferris watched the cop rifling through his discarded clothes. The cop pulled out a plastic bank bag, the type they use for coins of small denominations, from one of Ferris's tracksuit pockets and held it up to his prisoner and asked, 'Whose is the brown powder, son?'

'Fuck knows,' answered Ferris.

'In that case, it must be yours, eh?' answered the big cop with a smile.

At that time, Paul Ferris didn't use any kind of drugs and nor did he deal. He was the equaliser for Arthur Thompson and that meant steering clear of lager shandies, never mind smack. Instantly, he knew it was a set-up and lost the place, promising the big cop that, if anything went down like a stray bullet or one hair on Anne Marie's head was hurt, he would track him down and kill him.

The cop looked back with an arrogant but wistful look. It said, 'Come ahead. Please just try.' And he held the gun out, pointed at the smaller man.

Paul Ferris and Anne Marie were taken to the local cop shop that night. He was booked in and charged with the attempted murder of Raymond Bonnar and was warned he was being investigated for thirteen similar offences in total. He was twenty-one years old and in serious trouble. Then, of course, there was the small matter of the 'brown powder' to be considered after it had been forensically tested.

Anne Marie was grilled for hours before being given a cup of tea and allowed to sleep in a dank cell in the police station. Down the corridor, Paul Ferris hoped and prayed she would be OK . . . that the trauma and questioning hadn't upset her health . . . that their unborn baby would be fine. He had too much on his mind that night to think of other things like how the cops knew where he was. That would come later.

Back in Glasgow, life was going on as normal. Fatboy was watching *The Godfather* for the umpteenth time, blurting out the dialogue in time with Marlon Brando and the other cast members. Arthur had watched *Coronation Street* with Rita before going out to have a few drinks in the Provanmill Inn. He had a few whiskies and small beer chasers – not enough to get drunk but enough to add cheer. Life was good and had just got better. A dangerous man who might have taken over had just been dealt with.

Little did he know that his own older son's sloppiness would take the smile off his face. Big time.

17

EVIL STENCH

1984

'That'll be him then,' said Fatboy to his old man, Arthur.

'Aye, well done,' Arthur replied, not looking up from his copy of the *Glasgow Herald*. He was reading the obituary page, hoping for some clues on some rich guy or dame, preferably a widower or widow, who had died leaving some vast country mansion full of antiques as empty of life as the grave they were heading to. It was an old line of business but a lucrative one. Why should he drop it especially now he delegated the hard work to others and still made maximum profit?

It was the day of Paul Ferris's trial. The bold Raymond Bonnar had withdrawn all charges and none of the others would stand the scrutiny of the court. (Years later, Ferris would discover that Bonnar had nothing to do with conning the Thompsons out of fifty grand and would apologise for the mistake and the hurt caused. Remarkably, Bonnar accepted his words, shook hands and had a few drinks with him.) So now Ferris stood charged with dealing in Class A drugs and a few other allegations. No way was he going to win through. The cops had seen to that.

'What about that other business?' asked Fatboy with no further explanation because none was needed with his father.

'Ach,' muttered Arthur, throwing the *Glasgow Herald* on to the floor in disappointment and sweeping up a handful of tabloid newspapers. He was going to read the football pages for the second time that day for want of anything better to do. 'We'll use Tam.'

Tam Bagan was not to be underestimated. While Ferris was catching the limelight and getting the major jobs from Arthur Thompson, Bagan was active and feared all over. As a double act, Ferris and Bagan were awesome – maybe too much and too good even for Thompson. As individuals, they could usually do the jobs. It was a simple business decision by Arthur Thompson to maximise resources by splitting their partnership. They had sent Bagan on a contract to London with a team of others. Nothing fancy for the boys – just an old van as their transport and accommodation. After a couple of nights, life was so miserable they booked themselves into a cheap hotel, only to find later that Arthur docked their wages. But Arthur was smiling. The job got done.

'Divide and rule,' Arthur had laughed and said to Fatboy.

'Aye, Dad, sure,' said Fatboy, not quite understanding but thinking he had heard that phrase in some movie. Or was it 'all for one'? 'But what about the wee man? He's a bit . . .'

'His goose is well roasted.'

'Deep fried,' laughed Fatboy.

'Ha. Aye, like a fucking black pudding,' roared Arthur Thompson, praying that he was right.

In court, Paul's solicitor, Peter Forbes, and his QC, the bold and idiosyncratic Donald Findlay, were in top form. Peter, very careful with every detail, had had a problem with Paul's version of events. Ferris told him that all three cops had had guns yet the official report stated that only two firearms warrants were issued that night.

Ferris had scratched his nut over that one. Maybe, just maybe, the high drama of the situation had made him recall things wrongly. But he had this memory that haunted even his dreams of that door going in, him jumping to his feet and three cops, each brandishing a gun, bearing down on him.

The big ruddy-faced polis who had roughed him up and 'found' that brown powder wasn't officially issued with a pistol that night. Ferris admitted he was angry with him all right, so maybe he was putting a gun in his hand that really wasn't there. Then he remembered the bloke had dragged him into the bedroom, yanking him along the floor by the handcuffs, his arms behind his back, when a heavy, shiny, silver metal pistol had dropped with a thump from the cop's jacket. Ferris had kicked it along the ground just to irritate him.

'Cunt,' Ferris had said. 'You're nothing but a cop prick and you'd better not try anything nasty tonight. Or I'll get you.' It had been a mistake, a grave mistake to make any such threats. Paul Ferris knew that threat had been an error and it might come to haunt him. Yet, if that was real, surely the gun was real.

After Peter Forbes interviewed Ferris's girlfriend, Anne Marie, he didn't need any further convincing. Ferris had made a point of keeping his work separate from his personal life. Anne Marie knew very little about what her man got up to work-wise. Forbes knew that and knew she had no experience of cop raids or investigations. When he asked her to tell him what happened, she gave him the full, lengthy details down to what the cops were wearing and that they all had guns. Three guns. Now he was convinced.

So, what was it? A mistake by the cops they were covering up? Scarlet-jowls's own shooter? Or a wee rogue number they were intent on shooting into the ceiling above their heads a few times, after they had killed Ferris in 'self-defence'? An unregistered gun to be placed in the dead man's fist? A tactic the security forces were using in Belfast against the Republicans all the time. Was he saved because Anne Marie was there? A heavily pregnant woman that even they couldn't kill? How could they explain that away? Say that she looked as if she was carrying a gun instead of a wean? Aye, right.

Hit man, equaliser, heavy for The Godfather, whatever else he was, Paul Ferris was putting more of his conscience into remembering the incident accurately than the cops. They stepped into the witness box and, working to a script which they thought was watertight, told their story.

Ferris was allowed to make a Judicial Statement, a peculiar Scottish phenomenon that is a right of freedom for any accused. With his scribbled notes running on for pages on the cheap jail-issue paper, he stood up, cleared his voice and made the longest such statement in the history of Scottish criminal law. He didn't know it at the time, nor would he have cared. All he knew was that he had a few things to say. It was impressive but the cops' story was not – they had knocked on the door and shouted before kicking it in; the accused had been read his rights; notes had been found referring to drug deals; there were only two guns issued; two officers were present during the search of the accused man's clothing where the heroin was found. It was going to be a case and a half.

Paul Ferris didn't worry about the Thompson father and son not being present at the court. That didn't happen. It would attract too much attention and allow the media, under their limited privileges reporting on court proceedings, to go to town about Arthur Thompson and, by so doing, condemn Paul Ferris. Normally, they would have had a spy in the public benches to report back every night but, in this case, they didn't. Ferris had too much on his mind to worry over that detail.

During his spell in jail on remand awaiting trial, Ferris had been starting to worry over the details of that day in Rothesay. Fatboy Thompson visited him but didn't mention what he had done to take care of Anne Marie for a very good reason – the Thompsons hadn't helped her at all. Instead, he spoke about some gangster movies he had been watching, acting out different scenes, before telling Ferris that he was in good company. Some guy called Mark Watt was also on remand there and was involved with the team who had ripped them off for £50,000.

'Ideal opportunity, Paul,' said Fatboy, getting up to leave. 'Give him a right doing.'

It was as ideal an opportunity as the condemned man carrying out a hit job on the screw escorting him to the gallows. Either way, he was in big trouble. Prisons are full of street players, many of whom have scores to settle. But they are staffed with officers whose main duties are to keep the peace. Screws then didn't care if you were happy, unhappy, innocent or guilty. They were paid to keep you locked up, alive and out of trouble for the duration. To relieve the boredom, they like nothing better than getting a couple of cons in hot water for slicing lumps out of each other but, after it's finished, that's when they would start in with a good kicking as well as putting the cons on formal report. With his difficult trial ahead, Paul Ferris needed this like a slug in the head.

But his word was his word. Tracking down Mark Watt was easy. All he had to do was look for where the light was blocked out. The bloke was massive, huge, with great clumps of fists. Nothing to do but to do. Ferris collared Watt, challenged him and then hightailed it back to his cell to prepare. Trouble was, Watt came calling early.

Watt thumped and squeezed the life out of the wee man in the confined space of his cell. He would have killed him for sure had the alarm not gone up that there was trouble on the wing. The flap-thud-flap-thud of the screws' boots running got louder and louder, nearer and nearer. Watt took off, thinking he'd won the joust and wanting to avoid further days in jail. Ferris, bleeding from his face and skull, ripped a metal slat off his bed base and took off after him.

Halfway down the landing, Ferris took a high dive, grabbed Watt round the neck with one arm, clenched his legs round the big man's waist and battered him senseless with the improvised weapon that he held in his other hand. In the melee, the metal slat was sent sailing into the air, over the railing and landed on the safety net one floor below. With no weapon and, of course, no witnesses, it was lucky but it saved Ferris a further conviction and extra months in jail.

The whole episode had been high risk but then he didn't think so. After all it was for Arthur Thompson, The Godfather, and he was looking after him. Except he wasn't. Thompson was giving him more dangerous work in a place he was almost bound to get caught. And he was lying. Mark Watt had nothing to do with that bad deal either.

That was in the past now as Ferris's trial at Dumbarton for possession of Class A proceeded. The rogue gun was a case of his word against theirs. It didn't look good. If in doubt, judges and juries believe the cops. But the 'little brown powder' was a different matter.

It was quickly proven that Ferris's fingerprints were not on other incriminating items taken from the flat like telephone directories and a note that read:

Sulph 10
Black 50
Coke 4
£50,000
£75,000

It was a drug dealer's list and was not in Ferris's handwriting. In fact, it would prove to be Fatboy's writing – a sloppy act that his father would roast him for and one that was to bring great trouble to his door.

Tackling that bag of 'brown powder', Donald Findlay and Peter Forbes hired an independent forensic expert to analyse the plastic cash holder and tracksuit bottoms. Throughout the trial, Findlay forcibly presented the view that the drugs had been planted which, of course, the cops and their expert witnesses strenuously denied. Then the defence's forensic witness was called.

The foremost forensic expert in his field demonstrated that the heroin couldn't have been in the tracksuit pocket. The design of the plastic holder and the fine grade of the brown powder meant that there would have been spillage. Yet absolutely no trace was found on the material of the pocket. It was impressive evidence but it was technical and in the realm of magic as far as the average court was concerned. But the forensic expert wasn't finished.

'You'll note the plastic of this holder is green in colour,' he said in response to a question by Donald Findlay. 'This has been tested under laboratory conditions. If it contains white powder the contents appear green. If it contains black powder the contents appear green. And if it contains brown powder the contents appear green.'

The implication was obvious. The cop had already sworn that he pulled the bag out of Ferris's tracksuit and asked, 'Whose is the brown powder?' Well, how could he have known the powder was brown if brown contents looked green in that plastic bag? An example was shown to the court. Seeing is believing. The judge gave a summing up to the jury that spelled it out clearly. Believe the cops, convict Ferris. Believe Ferris, find him not guilty. The jury retired to consider and debate.

Back in Glasgow, Arthur Thompson was on a mission. He wanted to access more weapons and Tam Bagan had set up a visit to a dealer, driving The Godfather to the venue. All the way, the old man was on good form, cracking jokes and teasing Bagan. When they got there, Bagan and Thompson went into the house. Suddenly they were confronted by rows and rows of guns of every type. The dealer was chatting away, explaining what he had that was a bit special and Bagan was trying out a few that caught his eye when he looked up and saw that Thompson was chalk white and shaking.

'Is there something the matter?' asked Bagan.

'Fucking hell . . .' stammered Thompson, 'there's enough here to start a war.' Thompson then staggered to the door and left, followed by Bagan still apologising to the gun dealer.

On the way back home, Arthur Thompson was quiet, saying nothing. There was a terrible stink in the air and Bagan just assumed it was dung or agricultural fertiliser that had been spread in some fields they had passed but to break the tension of the utter silence he said, 'Evil stench in this motor.'

Big Arthur's cheeks reddened slightly and he replied, 'Sorry, Tam, that was me. I farted and followed through.'

Arthur Thompson had been terrified at the sight of such major weaponry. So much so that he had literally shit himself. Could this be the same Arthur Thompson who sent folk off on hit jobs and nailed men to garage walls? Bagan wondered what the hell was going on. Was the reputation of Arthur Thompson more smoke and mirrors than anyone suspected? Or was the old gangster losing it?

Back in the court, the jury declared after only one hour. Paul Ferris was found not guilty of the serious charges of drug dealing. They had believed him and not the cops.

What the verdict really meant was that those fifteen good folk and true believed Scotland's finest detectives had planted heroin on Paul Ferris. The judge had explained to them that was what a not guilty verdict would mean. No police officer was charged with having that extra gun but the jury seemed to believe Paul Ferris on all counts. If the accused was telling the truth about the drugs, why should he have lied about the gun? If the cops had lied about the drugs, why should they be believed about the gun?

Two members of the police disciplinary staff sat in the court throughout the proceedings but whatever action they took, if any, was kept strictly confidential. There's no doubt what would have happened to those cops if the members of the public sitting on the jury had been allowed to decide.

Paul Ferris wasn't off the hook entirely. Many months before the Rothesay incident he had been tooled up for a spat with the Welshes after they had fired shotguns at his car with him and Fatboy in it. As it happened, Arthur Thompson had ordered that no retaliation was to take place yet the cops had stopped Ferris and searched his car, finding a pickaxe handle and assorted weapons. Those charges had been added to this trial and he was found guilty of them. Normally, they would carry a six-month jail penalty but this time Ferris got eighteen months.

Ferris would be away for a while – some thinking time. A time that would change his life and, as it happened, that of Arthur Thompson.

18

WALLS HAVE EARS
1985

'Good to see you again, Arthur.' The MI5 agent shook Thompson's hand warmly.

They were sitting in an office in Charing Cross Road, Soho, sleazy premises wedged between a private gay club and a strip joint. After the downfall of the Krays, law and order agencies had grouped together to smash organised crime in London and set up their secret HQ here. Now that the emphasis had turned to Ireland, the office was still used as an occasional meeting point with informants, especially well-known ones like Arthur Thompson.

'I wish I could say the same.' What on paper looks like a negative retort was, in the context of this now longstanding relationship, a friendly tease. It was a very Glaswegian habit of Thompson's to make negative, critical comments as a way of being close to someone.

The MI5 man was well used to his informant's ways. 'What brings you down this time?'

The two men chatted for a while about how all the old London firms were either on their last legs or being pushed out by the younger, hungrier teams. Crews like the Adamses, the Arifs and even the younger Brindles were showing a disregard for the old ways and a mean touch with shooters. The MI5 man and gangster agreed that the drugs market had changed the way crime was organised. Now it was a hard-headed business with fortunes at stake so no one was allowed to step in the way. Then you had money men with a nasty streak like Kenny Noye, an outsider but more active in London than some of the most notorious East-End faces of twenty years before. Cop and con agreed that things had changed for the worse and would never be the same again.

'We hear you've been doing a bit of trafficking yourself, Arthur,' said MI5, finally getting to his main point.

'Aye, as you know, not much. Just enough to keep my hand in,' replied Arthur Thompson wondering where the hell this was leading. They had given him a licence to deal in drugs without prosecution. They had actually given him the idea to get into that business in the first place – so what were they doing now? Changing their minds?

'We got word that you've been meeting with some of the local Turks?' The MI5 man's eyebrows raised in an arch, encouraging The Godfather to tell him all about it but reminding him that he'd been seen.

'Aye, a couple of meetings to explore some trade. You have to talk to them these days if you want to shift drugs. It's either that or the Scousers and you know what they're like.' Thompson drew a one-fingered crazy sign at his temple.

'They're radio rental right enough, chum,' MI5 smiled warmly. 'Don't blame you for giving them a body swerve.'

'Like the ugly lassie at the dance, I'm never in that corner,' smiled Arthur.

'And the Turks, how much are you up to with them?'

Thompson knew he would return to that question and was ready. 'A few kilos of dope every month. Just the usual but a new supplier. Better quality, cheaper product.' Both of these statements were true but only half the story. If you have to lie, do so by telling some of the truth was Arthur Thompson's approach. He was happy to play along with this guy – after all, an MI5 licence to commit certain crimes wasn't easy to come by.

'Good, good. And what about that boy Ferris? Is he coming back to you?' Paul Ferris was in prison, serving time for possession of a pickaxe handle and other weapons. But MI5 knew that Arthur Thompson had set him up in Rothesay and that that had failed.

'Well, aye. It's what'll have to happen,' Thompson spread his hands asking that the security agent understand his position and how things had to work on the street. How he had to behave as expected or folk might begin to suspect his role. His cover as an informant might get blown.

'Sure, I understand. Tell me, do you know a man called Benjamin Al Agha?'

Thompson thought for a brief minute and answered, 'No' unless he serves me a curry now and then.' Like a lot of Glaswegians, Thompson was a big curry fan. Indeed, the city claimed to be the UK's curry capital.

The MI5 man smiled. 'Well, he won't have been doing that for a while. He's been away and Ferris has been visiting him.'

MI5 gave Thompson a potted history of the man known on the street simply as Ben. The grandson of the Shah of Iran, he was brought up in palaces. He trained as a lawyer and worked for the Iranian secret police as a torturer. That was before the Shah was deposed by Ayatollah Khomeini. That was when Ben moved to London. Shortly thereafter, he was caught in a massive scam selling non-existent missiles to the Iranians – a ploy that had involved taking bank managers and diplomats hostage. On his team was a member of the Arifs, an up-and-coming London family. Ben was also found guilty of raping his secretary.

Now he was about to be freed. Ferris had met him through his brother Billy who was in the same jail as Ben. The Shah's grandson had recognised young Ferris's talents and MI5 said they feared the combination of the former's money and international contacts with the latter's intelligence, guile and street nous.

'Sounds like a fucking James Bond movie,' blurted Arthur Thompson, who knew nothing about Ben. Thompson wasn't the only one who could keep things to himself.

'Yeah,' MI5 smiled and agreed, 'except this is real, Arthur. And we need to stop things, eh, developing.'

Thompson nodded.

They were returning to an old point of discussion. Certain players' development had already been abruptly ended with Thompson's help. This time, it was one of his guys. Very close to home. Thompson already feared Ferris anyway. The man was too smart, too young and had a growing following on the street. So far, Ferris didn't realise this but, when he did, what was to stop him taking over? Arthur Thompson, that's who.

The MI5 man had rattled on about how dangerous Ben might be if he hooked up with Ferris. What he didn't reveal was that Ben had registered as one of their informants while he was in jail and had already helped imprison some drug dealers and expose an IRA cell. MI5 weren't worried about Ben – they had the same arrangement with him as with Thompson. What they wanted was for Thompson to sort out Ferris – he was a real threat as far as they were concerned.

'I'll see what I can do,' answered Thompson, knowing from experience that MI5 wouldn't want the gory details. But, if he failed, they would want to know why. Sometimes Thompson wanted to tell them to stick the agreement. He hated being held on a leash by anyone, even when they had a shared goal.

'Good, I know you will,' smiled MI5. 'How's the oldest boy?' he asked as if had suddenly changed from business to personal chat. He hadn't.

'Fine. Absolutely fine.'

'Still working hard in the family business, eh?'

'Aye.' What was this?

'Behaving?'

'Of course.'

'Not freelancing or anything?'

'No, no. Arthur's a good lad,' reassured Thompson.

'See it stays that way, Arthur,' said MI5, standing up and signalling that the meeting had come to an end.

Thompson stood up too but he wasn't finished. 'About my phones. Have you checked those again? I keep hearing a clicking noise on the line and . . .'

'How many times, Arthur? Your phones are absolutely clear of bugs, taps and even crossed lines. You must have the most secure phones in Glasgow.' MI5 was walking Arthur Thompson to the door as he spoke. He didn't want to waste any more time on this subject yet again. But, of course, Thompson's phone line at home was tapped. What did he take them for, MI5 or MFI?

Travelling home from London, Arthur Thompson mused over the discussion. Did the spooks really know what he was up to? He was buying a few kilos of heroin off the Turks every few weeks and, through some people he had in Blackpool, he was also doing some drugs business with the Scousers – not to mention a fair amount of trade in cocaine and the usual racket of cannabis. He'd been conning MI5 for years now and pretty soon he'd be conning them even more.

Fatboy had already upped the operation and no wonder. The demand had increased. He was a businessman so what was he meant to do? Ignore the customers? The drugs trade was worth too much money to back out of now. It was a big risk if MI5 found out but what the hell? He had managed to get off with it so far. He'd do it for another while. Anyway, they would struggle to link that business back to his family – even to Arthur Junior. Or so Thompson reckoned.

Fatboy had been getting paranoid lately – so much so that his old man was beginning to wonder if he was sampling his own produce. Fatboy had gone to the family lawyer, Joe Beltrami, and got him to write to Strathclyde Police on his behalf. The letter claimed his client had strong evidence that the cops were planning to set him up as being in possession of heroin. Beltrami warned that, if any such action took place, he had been instructed to take the strongest possible legal action on his client's behalf. Arthur Thompson had to worry about that boy sometimes – he really did.

A few weeks later, Fatboy was driving home late one night. He had just dropped Tam Bagan off when he suddenly spotted an unmarked cop car come flying up behind him with two more on its tail. He took off, flying homewards the long way, determined to reach The Ponderosa and call for legal help before the cops nabbed him. He never made it.

Right there and then, they charged Fatboy Thompson with dealing in Class A. They would go on to say that, during the car chase, he was witnessed throwing £10 wraps of smack on to the street and they produced some as evidence. The arresting officers were not the usual faces. Nothing could be done to divert the Fatboy from jail.

Arthur Thompson cursed, remembering what the MI5 had asked of Fatboy, 'Behaving?' It had been a serious warning he hadn't recognised. Now Fatboy was heading for big trouble. But Arthur Thompson wasn't finished. Others were going to be punished for this grief. You wait and see.

19

DIRTY PICTURES
1985

Arthur Thompson was livid. Someone had set up his boy with heroin and no doubt. Arthur knew his elder son's weaknesses better than anyone but now he regretted thinking he was paranoid. Fatboy had been absolutely right to suspect the cops were setting him up. Him being cooped up inside that jail was proof enough.

Even those who hated Fatboy Thompson sniffed a rat. The man was well known for never getting his mitts dirty, particularly with drugs. He behaved like some white settler in the days of the British Empire, swanning around, giving orders and never touching a grain himself. There was no way he would have a stack of tenner wraps in his car – especially when he already suspected the cops were on to him and planned to set him up. His father knew that more than anyone and he was going to have revenge.

Fatboy was charged along with Tam Bagan and a recent recruit called 'Blind' Jonah McKenzie. Jonah had lost an eye in one of many brawls as a young man and henceforth was called Blind Jonah. He had been the leader of one of the east-end teenage gangs for years and, even before he was old enough to leave school, had a formidable reputation as a street fighter. Small and slim, he didn't look the part. But he was courageous and fearless and fast with a blade.

Blind Jonah had gone to work for another east-end player, Thomas 'The Licensee' McGraw. McGraw was called The Licensee because he was well known as a police informant, trading information and often innocent bodies in return for immunity from prosecution.

McGraw was never rated on the street but he had developed a fair reputation as a wire man, specialising in dismantling alarm systems. For a few years he had been part of the BarL Team, Scotland's most successful and professional armed robbers of the 1970s and early 1980s. That crew planned their operations with military precision and discipline and never got caught as a group.

One of that gang, Vinnie Dickson, was caught in a farm, near Coatbridge, with a safe stolen from a pub in Clydebank. The safe still had around £30,000 locked in it and Dickson was for the high jump. Another member, TC Campbell, the youngest son of Bobby Campbell who had given Thompson his start in armed robbery, had been found guilty of killing the Doyle Family in a fire at their house in what was known as the Ice-Cream Wars. Everyone on the street knew that TC and Joe were innocent and the police should have been investigating The Licensee. Now that left a bad taste in most people's mouths, including that of Blind Jonah who promptly left the gang and moved over to the employ of Arthur Thompson's son Fatboy.

Fatboy instantly decided that Jonah's flat would be used to cut and wrap all their smack. It was a big risk but one that Jonah took with a shrug of his shoulders. Earlier on the night of his arrest, Fatboy had been there with Bagan and Jonah, talking business and checking the quality of the latest deliveries. For months before, the cops had had a stake-out in a flat across the way and were listening to and filming every movement. True to form, Fatboy had been sloppy and talked openly about this arrangement on The Ponderosa's phone. The very phone his father was so convinced was tapped and had warned his oldest son about frequently.

'The old man is fucking havering,' Fatboy had said to Paul Ferris one night. 'The stupid bastard thinks our phone's bugged. Tell ye, he's getting demented.' Paul Ferris had nodded and smiled and decided that it was the Fatboy who had lost the plot, not his father. Then again maybe he had never found it. When Arthur Thompson heard the case against his son he would have agreed with Ferris, though he'd never have admitted it to his young equaliser's face.

On the night of Fatboy's arrest, the police had been watching him in Blind Jonah's flat as per usual. They waited till he had driven away with Bagan and tailed him. As that was going on, other cops hit Blind Jonah's place team-handed. The small tenement flat was floating in heroin dust and there were bags of the stuff all over. Not so much caught red-handed as smack-pawed.

Jonah was going down – there was no doubt about that. But it seems he wasn't quite as content with the arrangement for his place to be the junk factory as he had made out. Soon he was griping that they should leave him and go after 'those cunts with the big motors'. He didn't name names, of course, but he needn't have bothered even complaining because the cops were on the case anyway.

Blind Jonah didn't know it but he was an essential part of the police's plan. They searched his place through and through and carted away bag-loads of evidence. As this was going on, the cops had deliberately allowed Bagan to get out of Fatboy's car before giving chase and arresting the young Thompson. Later that night, they arrested Tam Bagan but, more importantly, they also raided The Ponderosa.

Cops were such regular visitors to the Thompsons' house that Arthur was on first name terms with some of them. Rita wasn't quite so affable and who could blame her? The boys in blue aren't renowned for being careful with suspects' worldly goods – or tidying up after themselves. Rita Thompson was very house-proud. To her, a warrant to search was a warrant to disrupt.

They didn't disappoint her on this occasion either and searched the place thoroughly. Many, many hours of cops' time must have been wasted searching The Ponderosa since they rarely found anything they were looking for. But this time they did – in a linen basket of all places.

The basket was empty of dirty washing – hardly surprising given Rita's daily housework routine. Lying at the bottom was a girlie magazine. Not really porn, just your standard top-shelf material. No big deal except that the corner of one page had been ripped off – or so the cops said. That missing corner was then reported as having been found in Blind Jonah's flat, wrapped round a tenner deal of heroin.

'SET UP!' screamed Fatboy. 'I've been fucking set up.' He moaned openly to anyone within earshot – a bad call since he was in Barlinnie on remand at the time and the wing he was in was full of lowlife hoods claiming just that. The difference is, in his case, there was some merit to his claim.

The Thompsons had an extremely liberal approach to their kids' upbringing. Fatboy had been quite openly masturbating to dirty magazines from an early age and now here he was a fully grown man. What need did he have to hide a mild blue magazine in a linen basket? Why would he dump it in a place his mother visited every day to collect the dirty washing?

'It was mine,' Blind Jonah had confessed to Paul Ferris when they met in Barlinnie where Ferris was serving time for the pickaxe handle. 'The dirty magazine was mine, Paul. It was in my flat the night the cops raided.'

Arthur Thompson knew the score and he had other questions. Why did the cops not raid Jonah's flat when he, Fatboy and Bagan were all present? Catching all three red-handed would have made prosecution so much easier. Why did they let Fatboy drop off Tam Bagan before they arrested him? If they suspected there was smack in Fatboy's car again, it would have been more damning to catch the pair of them sitting in it.

Arthur Thompson had loads of questions no one else was going to answer. Never mind – he had reached his own conclusions.

There was no heroin in Fatboy's car. The boy was stupid over some things but was too high and mighty to take that responsibility as well as the risk.

Thompson's conclusion: the cops planted the heroin.

The dirty magazine wasn't Fatboy's. The filthy bugger had graduated to hard porn a long time before. What would he want with pictures of women with false tits and airbrushed good looks?

Thompson's conclusion: the cops took the magazine from Blind Jonah's – or Blind Jonah gave it to them.

Tam Bagan was looking cleanest of them all. Yet he was meant to get between his son and the cops. Why did they let him out of a car apparently loaded with heroin?

Thompson's conclusion: maybe Bagan was involved in setting Fatboy up.

Who was responsible for all of this when he had an arrangement with the cops to deal in drugs?

Thompson's conclusion: the cop in charge of the case must be an ambitious nutcase not willing to play the game.

Plan: Arthur Thompson was going to make people suffer for this. The cop, Bagan and Blind Jonah.

Arthur Thompson's views were cemented when, at the end of the trial, Fatboy was sentenced to eleven years, Blind Jonah to seven and all drugs charges dropped against Bagan though he was charged with some related firearms offences. Arthur Thompson was going to make someone pay big time.

When Paul Ferris was released from jail, Arthur Thompson asked to see him.

'I've a wee job for you, son,' Arthur said in his usual solemn mood. 'Pal of mine's having a wee spot of bother. One of his boys is thinking of jumping ship – changing sides, like. Needs it sorted.'

Thompson was referring to the boxing world, an interest he maintained all his life. Like many of his generation, he was a great fan of boxing and, as with many who could handle a fight, often thought he might have made a decent champ if he'd tried. Instead, he stuck to being in the audience and was a regular at exhibitions and championship bouts in Glasgow, Edinburgh, London and almost anywhere else in Britain. As a result, he had many close friends in that world like promoter, Alex Morrison. But he also knew guys in the background – guys who'd invest in fighters and expect to see a return for their cash.

As ever, Paul Ferris went along to see the man as Arthur Thompson requested. Part of Ferris's reputation was built on him never refusing a task and always succeeding regardless of the odds. He had served his full eighteen months in jail because he wouldn't lie down to the system, fighting it every inch of the way. But now it was business as usual.

The businessman was expecting him.

'You Arthur's boy, then?' he asked, more of a statement of fact than a question. Instantly, Ferris didn't like the man. He might accord Arthur Thompson respect and loyalty but that didn't mean such applied openly to all or any of Arthur's mates. Who did this guy think he was?

'Arthur asked me to visit. Said you had a bit of a problem you needed help with.'

The man explained that a top boxer, a young man called Gary Jacobs, was planning to leave for a London-based promoter. 'After all I've done for him, son. Everything I've invested in him.' The bloke was moaning as if it was his lover leaving him or someone had just emptied his entire piggy bank – a mixture of both, really. All that Ferris could see was that an ambitious young sportsman, one of the hopes for a crack at a world title, had made a business decision to try to make the most out of what was inevitably a short career span. But, for whatever reason, this guy was taking it personally. 'It wouldn't take much, son. Just a wee scar to his cheek. A wee slice.'

Ferris walked away. He hadn't liked the man. It wasn't just his sleazy attitude and the fact he was willing to ruin some guy's career but he kept calling him son. He couldn't stand that. Who the fuck did he think he was?

Gary Jacobs did move on and went on to win titles at European and Commonwealth levels as well as competing for the World Crown. Years later, after he had retired from the ring, Jacobs would admit that he knew a contract had been taken out on him. He also knew that, if Ferris had decided to slash him, there would have been little he could have done to prevent it. But, for Ferris, it wasn't just a question of right and wrong – it was also the first time he had refused to carry out an order for Arthur Thompson. Big changes were on the way.

During his jail time, Paul Ferris had given careful consideration to a host of issues that had been bothering him. The Rothesay incident stank. So he had proven that the cops had planted heroin on him. Big deal. Everyone on the street knew that was a common practice. But there had been an extra, unregistered gun that night. Did the police mean to shoot him? Was it that serious?

Why was the place littered with Fatboy's notes on drug deals? OK, he had been able to prove that the notes weren't his but what sort of a message did that send to the jury? The Thompsons were usually ultra careful and now the very place they had given him as a safe hideaway from the cops had all that incriminating stuff lying around.

Ferris had kept the note detailing drugs and amounts of money and confronted the author, Fatboy, when they had crossed paths in prison.

'For fuck sakes, don't tell the old man,' Fatboy blurted, 'he'll go fucking mental.'

So was it the Fatboy being sloppy again? It could have been worse for Ferris, as he well knew. Fatboy had discovered a new hobby – making guns and ammunition. At that time, it was possible to buy the individual components for guns – casings, powder, heads, pins – from different hardware shops around the city. Fatboy would do his shopping then disappear to the flat in Rothesay for a week building pistols and rifles and getting the right ammo. The weapons weren't flash or of a modern design. One favourite was the Webley 443, known as the Zulu Stopper, that had been around since the days of the Boer War. It was a huge revolver with an extremely long barrel and, therefore, extremely powerful. If the bullets didn't hit their mark, the weighty gun could be used to batter the target to death.

Some of Fatboy's regular productions would be sold on to other players while others fed the continuing arrangement his father had with the UDA – a family secret he, but no one else, had been let into. Arthur Thompson was still making regular deliveries of weapons to the Loyalists at night-time trysts in yards in Bridgeton. Fatboy's hobby made his father a good few quid, kept the Loyalists happy and maintained the relationship his MI5 contact demanded.

Paul Ferris knew that Fatboy made guns down in Rothesay but he was not aware of the Thompsons' links with the UDA. If he had been, he would have walked away from them pronto. Had he been lucky? If Fatboy had been really careless, the cops might have found gunpowder and bits and bobs of weapons. But there was no sign of that kind of gear – just notes and information relating to drugs transactions. So had that been a choice by Fatboy? One the cops already knew about? After all, if they had shot Ferris dead, he wouldn't have been around to point out that the notes weren't in his handwriting.

A youngish Arthur Thompson. Here, Arthur almost has the look of a matinee idol about him. There is nothing in this rather benevolent-looking face to suggest he was capable of administering the kind of violence he was to deal out with alarming regularity, during his later years.

1960s' glamorati, including the Kray Twins and, in the centre, *Carry On* star Barbara Windsor, in party mood. This was the kind of company Arthur Thompson kept while he was forging his reputation as top dog in Glasgow's underworld.

Joe Beltrami, Arthur Thompson's legal eagle for over thirty years. Known as 'The Great Defender', the first time Joe represented Thompson was when Arthur was on trial for murdering two men. Beltrami's clever work saw the charge reduced from murder to culpable homicide, before he secured a not guilty verdict. After that, the cry of 'Get me Beltrami!' was often to be heard.

Arthur Thompson's MG hard-top sports car. A planted bomb exploded, killing the front-seat passenger, his mother-in-law, Margaret Johnstone. Remarkably Arthur survived. Three of the Welsh Family were charged with her murder but found not guilty, partly because Thompson refused to incriminate them, preferring his own brand of street justice.

Peter Ferguson, owner of Maryhill Cash & Carry Carpets. Until Arthur Thompson muscled in on Ferguson's business in the 1970s, Peter had been a happy and well-liked man. Thompson wrecked his business and ruined his life. A broken man, Ferguson committed suicide just one year after becoming involved with Thompson.

The Cottage Bar, on the corner of Darleith Street. It was here that the car, with the bodies of Bobby Glover and Joe 'Bananas' Hanlon dumped in it, was found on the night before Fatboy Thompson's funeral. It was certainly no coincidence that the car was left at this spot – not only did Bobby own the pub, Fatboy's funeral cortege was due to pass along Darleith Street just a few hours later.

Fatboy Thompson's coffin being taken from The Ponderosa to a waiting hearse. Along with other members of the Thompson clan, he was buried right next door to The Ponderosa in Riddrie Park Cemetery. In more ways than one, the Thompsons spent their lives close to death.

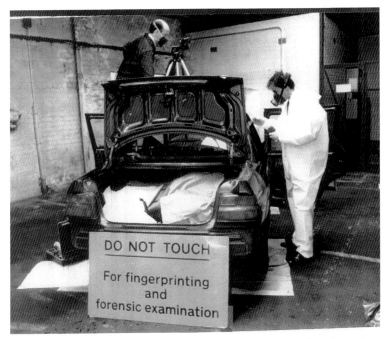

DO NOT TOUCH

For fingerprinting
and
forensic examination

Bobby Glover's Ford Orion car. Here, forensics try to obtain vital clues from the car that contained Bobby and Joe's murdered bodies. Their murders were seen as retribution for the hit on Arthur Thompson's son, Fatboy, and these three deaths led to fears that gangland warfare had erupted on the streets of Glasgow.

The Ponderosa, Arthur Thompson's home. Named after the ranch in the popular TV western series, *Bonanza*, Arthur's house is the one on the far right. Arthur's son, Fatboy, and his partner, Catherine, occupied the house at the far left of the row.

Arthur Thompson, with his wife, Rita, in the back of the car, on their way to attend their son's funeral. Fatboy was gunned down in the street by a hit man, as he walked the thirty yards from his father's house to his own front door.

Early morning outside Glasgow's High Court in July 1992. Here, Paul Ferris was on trial for the murder of Arthur Thompson's son, Fatboy, and the high-profile police presence is an indication of the trial's significance. Lasting fifty-four days and with almost three hundred witnesses cited to appear, it is the longest criminal trial Scotland has seen to date.

Photograph courtesy of Mirropix

Donald Findlay QC, Paul Ferris's defence lawyer. With his distinctive Sherlock Holmes pipe and his magnificent Edwardian-style whiskers, Findlay is immediately recognisable. His record of getting juries to return not guilty or not proven verdicts is unsurpassed.

Paul Ferris leaving the High Court, having been acquitted of the murder of Fatboy Thompson. From the look on his face, he is clearly stunned by the numbers of press and public who have come to see him walk free. Ferris's trial generated unprecedented levels of front-page news across the UK.

Great Train Robber Buster Edwards enjoying his new career working on his flower stall outside Waterloo Station. Before he committed suicide in the 1990s, Edwards admitted that the gang that pulled off the Great Train Robbery had been very close to asking Arthur Thompson to join them in their brazen crime of the century.

Arthur Thompson's funeral cortege inches its way past The Ponderosa towards Riddrie Park Cemetery. Hundreds turned up say their final farewells to The Godfather who died in Glasgow Royal Infirmary on 13 March 1993. Many others, some breathing sighs of relief, merely wanted to watch as Arthur was buried just the other side of the boundary wall that separated his home from the cemetery.

Then how did they know he was there? Ferris had adopted the habit of keeping all his paperwork and evidence from trials. It was a habit that would be lifelong and one that was to prove extremely useful in future challenges with the cops. Not only did he keep the papers, he read them – every single word – over and over. If he didn't understand any aspect, he would ask his lawyers. In the bundle from the Rothesay trial was the warrant for his arrest. It was dated the day of the cops' raid and timed at 1 p.m. That was only a short time after he himself knew he was heading to Rothesay. His girlfriend, Anne Marie, hadn't been told till 2 p.m. so that ruled out the possibility that the police had tailed her to that flat. Only two other people knew of his destination at 1 p.m. that day – Arthur Thompson and Fatboy.

There were other memories that irked Ferris's view of the Thompsons. Like the time John Redmond and his old partners in crime asked him to pass a load of stolen jewellery to Thompson to sell on. They trusted Ferris and Thompson was bound to have the right contacts. The men cancelled the deal when they were told they had been offered £20,000. The haul was worth ten times that. When the load was eventually returned, the men checked it off against an inventory they had taken and discovered twenty of the best pieces missing.

Then there was that young boy who Thompson had got to participate in his first armed bank robbery. He had been teamed up with one of the guys who robbed Govan Shipbuilders and escaped up the Clyde in a dinghy – dramatic and effective. The older bloke turned out to be useless, turning up at the robbery without his mask. In spite of all that, they had nabbed the money and escaped. The boy was expecting £80,000 but then, at pay-out time, Thompson had read out a list of deductions and cuts that went on and on. Eventually, the boy had been made to feel very lucky that he was getting £15,000. Ferris had felt very sorry for the young guy and knew Thompson had ripped him off big time.

Ever since Paul Ferris had signed up with Thompson, his father, Willie, and his Uncle Bertie had warned him off. 'What you doing working with him for?' they'd asked exasperated and worried. 'Thompson's nothing but a fucking grass,' was their assessment of the man. These were the two men Paul Ferris trusted and respected most in the world. They had guided him on the ways of life and to survival and success on the street. But he couldn't accept their strong views on Arthur Thompson. That couldn't be right. Thompson was the top man in Glasgow. An old-fashioned player whom everybody respected, even his enemies and the cops. He couldn't be a grass, could he?

The arrogance of youth, thinking he knew it all, aligned with the great compliment of an unknown young man being employed by the top man in Glasgow, had carried Ferris away. He had ignored his father's and his uncle's advice but their words never left him: 'What you doing working with him for? Thompson's nothing but a fucking grass.'

Now Paul Ferris was wondering if they had been right all along.

'You know they bastards set up my boy?' Arthur Thompson was meeting with Paul Ferris again. The matter of the boxer was never mentioned. Thompson had been surprised that Ferris hadn't followed through and had fully intended to call the cops after it was over. Being done for slashing one of the UK's top young sports hopefuls would have lost Ferris allies and he would have been hammered by the courts. Though it didn't seem much, it would be just the thing to get the wee bastard off the streets again – exactly what he and the cops wanted. But this was better and it was personal.

'Aye,' agreed Ferris because, whatever the Thompsons were up to, Fatboy still had the heroin planted on him. 'The whole case stinks.'

'It seems the cop in charge is a bit of a fucking zealot,' said Thompson. 'He's determined to destroy my family and other folks' – whatever it takes.' Arthur Thompson wasn't in the habit of using words like 'zealot'. This he had borrowed from the description given to the lead officer in Fatboy's case by one of his own police contacts. His cops didn't like colleagues on a mission. They upset normal business.

'Seems like it,' responded Ferris, agreeing but not commenting further. What could you do about a cop bending the laws to suit himself?

'Thing is he's no' finished there. He'll keep going at it with his dirty tricks. None of us is safe.'

'Aye,' agreed Ferris, 'but what can we do?'

'Teach him a lesson,' replied Arthur Thompson getting to the point. 'A lesson he'll never recover from and no other bent polis can ignore.'

Paul Ferris was beginning not to like the sound of this. 'How?'

'We're going to bomb him in his motor.'

20

THE REVOLT OF THE MICE
1985–86

'He's got to be fucking joking,' Ferris thought but he kept schtum. Arthur Thompson didn't joke about such lethal matters as bombing a cop unless the joke was on the victim.

'If we don't fix him, there'll be a lot more folk in trouble,' muttered Thompson. 'It has to be something obvious – that sends a message to others like him.'

'But how would we get access to his car?' asked Ferris, touching on just one of many issues that troubled him. Thompson had first mentioned the proposed hit on the detective who booked Fatboy for heroin dealing just a couple of days before. Yet, of all the issues Paul Ferris had been asked to deal with, this one bothered him most.

'Not *his* car,' answered Thompson, 'but *a* car. One he can't resist.'

Ferris wondered what the hell he meant. A top of the range Mercedes, a BMW convertible? What?

'This guy is determined to make a rep for himself catching big names. Apparently, anything to do with drugs and he's on its tail, fast as you like. Wants to be seen to be doing better than his mates. He doesn't trust cops even.' Thompson rattled out the words without a glimmer of humour or irony. His contacts in the police had told him that they really despised this particular cop and that nobody would mourn too hard if some dreadful, unfortunate accident befell him.

Arthur Thompson intended to oblige but it wouldn't be any accident.

'So we're talking about a set-up,' said Ferris. 'Get a motor, plant it some place and then somehow get a message to him that it's got a big consignment of drugs stashed in the boot.'

'That's the idea,' agreed Thompson, almost smiling for the first time that day.

'And you reckon a bomb?' Ferris had to get Thompson to spell out what he meant. No room for even slight confusion in this one. There was little history of the street players in Glasgow using bombs. The attempt on Thompson that killed his mother-in-law was one of the few examples.

'Aye,' replied the old man, 'that way no one needs to be in the vicinity.'

'Sure, but what about the bomb itself?'

'Eh?'

'Materials, making it, being sure it will work?'

'Don't worry about that,' said Thompson, dismissively. 'I've got enough Semtex to blow away Pitt Street cop shop, never mind one wee motor. And a pal of mine is a bit experienced with the explosives.' Though Thompson never said, it's likely that that 'pal' would have been one of the Loyalists he had been trading guns with. That was a connection Arthur Thompson could never admit to anyone other than his immediate family.

If Paul Ferris had sussed it, he would have walked away from the old gangster without hesitation.

'You'll need to drive the motor there and make the phone call.'

Ferris was well aware by now that he was being told he would be the bomber.

'And hang around to be sure the job's done, of course.'

Ferris was to be the bomber all right but his question was did he want to be?

The plan was amended over the next couple of days. Arthur Thompson wanted the car left in a lane in the city centre for maximum impact media wise. If it happened out in the sticks, the cops might well write it off as minor or at least cover up some of the details. If there was an explosion in Glasgow's busy city centre, there would be an outcry, an inquiry, for sure, and it would be plastered over the newspapers for weeks.

Paul Ferris had only ever refused one job from Arthur Thompson before – the slashing of that boxer. Now he really needed to consider this one carefully. Killing a cop was serious, the most serious. It wasn't that he disagreed with Arthur Thompson about Fatboy being fitted up by the cops. He really believed that was the case. It was what he was being asked to do now that bothered him. The question dogging his mind was whether or not that was the right thing to do.

To start with, he really didn't like the idea of a city-centre bomb. No matter how professionally it was made or how quiet the lane in which the car was dumped, the risks of the public being accidentally injured or killed ran high. There was the added risk that the bait might not attract the right target. Thompson seemed so confident that a phone call could be made directly to the cop in question but what if he was wrong? What if he was also mistaken about that cop keeping the job to himself? They would send at least two polis to look at the car and it wasn't every one of them that had asked for this fate. Some cops just did their jobs as best as they could, worked within the law and treated their prisoners with some degree of respect. What if it was a couple of the good guys who got it in the neck?

All that was bad enough but there was a final deciding factor for Paul Ferris. If he blew a cop to smithereens now, everything would change. As many people had predicted, Glasgow would become another Belfast. Not with the political and religious divides to the fore, but with the cops' and security forces' approach to law and order. There would be guns on the street with uniforms shooting first and asking questions later. It was a scenario no street player wanted and certainly not something Paul Ferris was keen on.

There was one final consideration for the young man – one that had been bothering him a while. If he carried out that hit for Thompson, how safe would he be? The year before, he would have been convinced that Glasgow's top player would make sure he was taken care of, whatever that took. But he knew that either Fatboy or Arthur had set him up in Rothesay. He'd been thrown to the wolves deliberately. At first, he had suspected Fatboy but now he wasn't so sure. What if Arthur Thompson was asking him to do this to get rid of one troublesome cop and Ferris himself at the same time?

It was time to move on. Without fuss, ceremony or bold statement, Paul Ferris slipped away from Arthur Thompson. All it took was for him not to look in every day for work and not to run to Thompson's beck and call. That was the easy part but now Ferris had to establish himself in his own right, to move east.

Out by Barlanark, there was a collection of players all very busy in their own right. One of the busiest was Thomas 'The Licensee' McGraw who was keen to tie in young Ferris. McGraw had run with the BarL Team, expert and professional armed robbers. Now the gang had disbanded but McGraw knew a winning formula when he saw one. Instead of participating in the heists, McGraw set them up using younger players who took all of the risks. All he took was a slice of the proceeds.

McGraw was also into legitimate enterprises such as ice-cream vans and pubs. One pub, called the Caravel, was registered under his wife Margaret's name. According to many, Margaret, nicknamed The Jeweller because of her fondness for gold chains and rings, was the brains behind McGraw. He also had another strength – backing from the cops. And Thomas McGraw was known as The Licensee not because of the Caravel but due to him having a police permit to commit crimes with immunity. In return, he gave them information and set up bodies to take the rap for offences, often ones they hadn't committed. There was no way Paul Ferris wanted to be associated with The Licensee.

So Ferris soon linked up with an older bloke called Bobby Glover. Glover and his wife Eileen were a well-respected couple in the east end of Glasgow and they ran a small, traditional pub, the Cottage Bar. The Glovers were an attractive pair. Bobby was swarthy, dark haired and confident. Moreover, he was bright and ambitious. A perfect match for the young Ferris.

Tam Bagan was unhappy. Fatboy was raving that, if he went down for the drugs, then so should have Bagan. It left a nasty taste in the mouth. The cops had decided to let Bagan out of Fatboy's car – that was their decision. But, facing eleven years in jail, Fatboy was hitting out at everyone, especially those closest to him – for the past few years, that had been Tam Bagan.

Arthur Thompson wasn't much better. He reckoned that either Blind Jonah or Bagan or both had colluded with the cops in getting Fatboy set up. Bagan had worked hard for the Thompsons, never refusing a job. He had gone south on dangerous trips and been paid a pittance. He had even put up with Arthur Thompson thinking that an old van was adequate transport for days when he was risking life and limb. All this had added to Thompson's legendary meanness but, for him to start casting doubts on Bagan's integrity, that was going a step too far.

Tam Bagan walked away from the Thompsons never to return.

Ferris and Bagan were now independent practitioners who worked in alliance from time to time. But, as former tight-knit partners, they argued frequently. During one such dispute,

The Licensee asked to meet with Paul Ferris. They met in the back rooms of The Licensee's pub, the Caravel. The only other person present was young Joe Hanlon, nicknamed 'Bananas', one of The Licensee's men who carried out some heavy work for him in dealing with other teams.

'I hear you're having a problem with Tam Bagan,' said The Licensee.

'Yeah, a bit,' laughed Paul. Bagan wasn't the easiest person to deal with when there was a disagreement.

'I could have Bagan put out of the road for you,' offered The Licensee.

'The trouble I have with Bagan won't need to go as far as killing him,' blustered Paul. 'It's nothing that can't be sorted between us.'

The Licensee sussed how Paul Ferris had interpreted his offer and was quick to explain. 'Naw, naw, I didn't mean that. No' that. I'll have him sent to prison. Just a call to some of my contacts in the force. They'd stop him in his motor, find a load of smack and he's offski. Get him out of your hair for a while.' The Licensee let his offer hang in the air for a while, unable to interpret Ferris's expression. 'What do you say, Paul?'

Ferris couldn't believe what he was hearing. McGraw deserved his nickname The Licensee and no doubt. 'I don't know about you,' replied Ferris, 'but I don't work that way. If I have a problem I fix it.'

The young man wanted to smack McGraw in the face and put him in his place. How easy was it for him to get people sent away for crimes they had not committed? How often had he used this arrangement already? And how many innocent blokes had he done this to? Ferris was leaving and pronto. As he got up to go, he turned to fresh-faced Joe Hanlon who had been watching and listening to the proceedings silently. 'If I were you, Joe,' said Ferris, 'I'd be fussier about who I worked for.'

Joe Hanlon was a street fighter extraordinaire. He came from that kind of stock. His old man had been nicknamed Shooders Hanlon – as in 'shoulders' – due to his exceptional body strength. Shooders was also one of the most feared street fighters in Glasgow till he met an early and horrible end. Someone, probably a group of heavies, shoved his own fish supper, wrappings and all, down his throat, choking him to death – a horrible, grisly end that, curiously, took place in a tenement close on Maryhill Road, next to Maryhill Cash & Carry Carpets and the garage run by Fatboy. Joe was a chip off the old block and wasn't about to let anybody else touch his fish supper.

Joe looked handy but what he achieved on his own was a different league. One time, The Licensee's son, William, known as Winky, fell for a young woman at the same time as James 'Jasper' McCann, the son of a major player from Easterhouse, did. The young guys fell out and Winky ended up being slashed. Not on, according to his father. The Licensee dispatched Joe Hanlon to the huge scheme to settle the issue. As soon as Joe parked up near some shops, word spread that he was there, as he knew it would. He just waited and, sure enough, the team appeared and set to on Joe immediately. Single-handedly he beat the lot and left the leader so badly hurt he was disabled and had to move south and retire. These were no soft touches but some of the hardest men in Glasgow and young Joe had sent them packing.

Joe Hanlon was keen and enthusiastic but he'd been having lingering doubts about The Licensee for a while. One of the jobs he did for McGraw was to man the door of the Caravel. When someone lobbed in a live a grenade one day, he had asked himself why anyone would hate his boss so much. After listening to The Licensee offer to have Tam Bagan set up with drugs, Joe was beginning to get the picture.

That same night he got a phone call from Paul Ferris. Ferris liked Joe and no doubt. He was so open and brave, who couldn't help but like him? So he wanted to be sure he was OK. Once again, Ferris counselled young Joe that McGraw wasn't a man to be trusted if he worked with bent cops setting people up. By now Joe was convinced.

Soon afterwards, Joe Hanlon teamed up with Paul Ferris and Bobby Glover. They didn't just work together – they played together. As well as associates, they were friends who trusted each other totally. They were the Three Amigos and they were being watched.

'How's the boy, Arthur?' asked the MI5 man as he faced Thompson across the scruffy room of their office in Charing Cross Road, the noise of the London traffic a faint rumble outside.

'Shorter than me, a bit heavier and a full head of hair,' replied Thompson, no humour showing on his face.

'Come on, you know what I mean.'

'And you know what I fucking mean,' growled Thompson, his jaw jutting out further.

'Is he coping OK in prison?' the MI5 man persisted.

'What do you care? Did you think of that when you set him up?'

MI5 shook his head and sighed. They had been over this before, numerous times, since Fatboy had been arrested. He had explained to Thompson that it wasn't their doing but a local matter, a cop on a campaign. 'You know we didn't . . .'

'Maybe no' but you did fuck all to get him out. You could've got him out.'

'It's difficult once someone's in the system,' replied MI5. 'Then we need good reasons.'

'So the arrangement with me suddenly isn't good enough, eh?'

'We couldn't expose you, Arthur. It would be too risky.'

'What? You can't trust a judge?'

'Well, no . . .'

'What the fuck's the world coming to?'

'It's not the judge, Tex, it's the pen pushers we'd have to involve. They're renowned for being . . . eh . . . loose tongued.'

Thompson shook his head and said nothing. He hated it when the MI5 man used his code name. It was a laugh to start with but now it sounded patronising. Worse, it served to remind him who had more power in that room and it wasn't Arthur Thompson.

'Besides,' continued MI5, 'he was asking for trouble, your boy.'

'Fuck do you mean?'

'The drugs, Arthur.'

Thompson shrugged and looked quizzical. They had agreed that the Thompsons could deal.

'He was getting a bit carried away.'

'That's just what the cops made out. Nothing to do with reality.'

'I want you to see something, Arthur.' The MI5 man opened a folder by his side and flipped out a few photographs, arranging them neatly on the table in front of them both. Fatboy was in every one. At Blind Jonah's flat . . . sitting in a car as two men carried bags into the close . . . at that warehouse in Blackpool, coming out through a doorway at the side . . . in the car park at Hogganfield Loch, less than a half mile from The Ponderosa . . . wearing dark glasses and sitting in the driving seat of his regular motor while a man with a hefty holdall walked away. There were others, all similar scenes.

'Stupid wee cunt,' spat Thompson. 'Stupid wee cunt.'

Little did Arthur Thompson know that the security services had been paying particular attention to Fatboy and another associate, Grant McIntosh. A gifted footballer, McIntosh had chosen street life and had just won a fierce, bloody battle for control of his patch – the large industrial town of Paisley that runs on to Glasgow's south-west border. Fatboy and McIntosh had joined forces with the intention of taking over the whole of Scotland and farther afield. With

McIntosh's crew of battle-hardened heavies, his own street nous and Fatboy having the backing of The Godfather, it was a sound plan. So sound, the security services started to pay them attention. Considering code names for the pair, they didn't have to scratch their nappers for too long. They just used the terms Hollywood-smitten Fatboy used – Mr Glasgow and Mr Paisley. Tarantino might have been impressed. Street players weren't.

Thompson Senior knew about the pair getting together. In fact, he had used Grant McIntosh on quite a few bits of business himself and liked the young man. Thompson knew all about his older son's deficiencies and hoped that the partnership with the harder, steadier, brighter McIntosh might just be what he needed to see him take over The Godfather mantle in the future. But then the stupid wee shite had to go and spoil it all by being careless.

'We've been watching you, Arthur, and we know what you've been up to.'

Thompson's face reddened slightly but he stared defiantly back at MI5 man.

'We estimate the scale of your drug dealing as maybe four or five times what you've told us about. That's four or fives greater than our agreement.'

No answer from Thompson.

'You've been conning us for years, Arthur. Or at least you think you have.'

'Stupid wee wannabe fucking gangster.' Thompson was looking down at the photographs of his son, still seething with anger.

'You broke our deal long before the boy got involved. We know. But, since then, he's just gone right over the top.'

'Stupid, stupid, stu . . .'

'He was careless all right. But you knew about how much he was doing.'

'I didn't . . .'

The MI5 man held up the palm of one large hand, signalling to Thompson that denial was futile. 'We know, Arthur. We've always known what you've been up to.'

The two men broke an awkward silence by going on to talk about Thompson's Irish connection. As usual, the Glasgow gangster passed on a few names of active Loyalists – some well-known, some brand new, some powerful, some bit-part players.

'My boy helped me with that, you know,' Thompson interjected. 'I couldn't have done it without him.'

'I know. And I know it has to be hard to watch your son go to jail.' The MI5 man had grown fond of Thompson over the years. But now he had outgrown his usefulness. Also, he had failed in one of their requests – to take care of Paul Ferris.

'I was that close to nailing Ferris,' Thompson explained, when asked. 'I asked him to do one job in particular. If he'd done it, you would've nabbed him at the scene with enough reasons to shoot him down or lock him away for several life sentences.'

'And?' asked the MI5 man.

'And the wee bastard didn't fall for it. He just fucking walked away. Left me and that job undone.'

'We heard that he's teamed up with Glover and Hanlon now.'

Thompson nodded a curt yes.

'A very interesting group.'

No comment from Thompson.

'And Bagan has left you too, I hear.'

'Aye, well rid.' Thompson was confirming MI5's conclusions that he had lost his key men overnight. He wouldn't see many more years at the top. The spooks had already decided that they would meet a few times more but it was a winding-down process. They wouldn't tell Thompson the deal was off. No one was ever finished with MI5 completely.

'Ferris and Bagan. That's some loss, Arthur.'

Thompson looked back at him with a contemptuous sneer. 'It's nothing – just the Revolt of the Mice.' Big grin from Arthur Thompson. 'What have I got to worry about?'

Back in Glasgow, someone was planning to pay Arthur Thompson a visit. And it wasn't social.

21

TRUE LOVE
1986

This was personal.

We'll call her Diane. She had been the most beautiful woman in the scheme as far as he was concerned. Blonde hair, blue eyes with a smile that melted ice. She wasn't tall but she was voluptuous and straight backed with peachy skin that made her gleam and other girls seem dull. He had wanted her through those school years from a distance. Being Jack the Lad, showing off in front of his mates, carrying out wee jobs that everyone else bottled from, gang fights – no problem – but don't ask him to speak to Diane without becoming a stuttering, nervous wreck.

Diane had had boyfriends and they were always older than him. Guys with a bit of money to splash on the clothes and nights on the town. He was still shoplifting to earn a few quid and he wasn't very good at it. Those guys were grown-ups and he felt like some daft wee boy. Then she smiled at him. That was the day his real life began.

They were fifteen going on sixteen and inseparable. That's the way he wanted it to stay. He was earning good wages at the Fruit Market and selling some produce on the side but they wanted to get a house together and needed more money. They both agreed their kids weren't going to get raised wanting for anything and were going to get every chance in life. That took money so he took to the robberies. It was only local factories and small-time stuff at night. Sometimes he raised a good few quid but at other times nothing. She used to tell him to stop. That he would get caught and end up in jail. But he was the boy and he knew better, making fun of her, calling her his Auntie Betty. Then he got caught.

By the time he got out of jail, he knew that she had changed. A deadness about her eyes, a stoop to her shoulders. It was as if somebody had stolen her light. It was heroin.

Some bastard had talked her into chasing the dragon at some party. A friend, of course – some friend. A junkie friend, of course. Why was it that so many smackheads wanted everybody else to join them in that gutter? Why was that? They had told her that you couldn't get addicted if you smoked the shit. Right. By the time he got out, she was mainlining and needing £40 every day to feed the habit.

They had tried to fight it together, him and his Diane. They got a council flat together in Sighthill and he went back to work in the Fruit Market. She got a job in some bar in the city centre but chucked it in after they realised their different shifts meant they hardly saw each other. Money was tight, always tight, and worse when she was on the smack.

She got clean at times and then fell off the wagon. She'd disappear for a couple of days and nights and then come back, filthy, unwashed, smelling of some dirty flat and crying. Always sorry that she had let him down. Let him down? No way. He just couldn't live without her. Whatever she needed to get by he'd get – simple as that. So he started thieving again to pay for her drugs. She didn't like it one bit but then she needed heroin. What were they do?

By the time he got caught, she was down to a tenner bag a day. She was getting there and at least now she had a life. That old Diane was with him more often than not. But he was sent away and she didn't cope well on her own. How many years had they lived like that? Him in and out of jail, her on and off the stuff?

They had a wee girl, Angela, her mammy's image, and her mammy got clean for her. That was OK by him. He understood because there was nothing he wouldn't do for his daughter either. Fuck, they were happy. Just the three of them. It was the life they had always planned. Then those old warrants came to haunt him.

'This is the last time,' he'd said to Diane and he meant every word. Why should he steal when all he was stealing for was to feed her habit, a habit she'd broken? 'One more spell away and we're thegether for the rest of our lives,' he'd promised her in bed the night before court. And she'd believed him. And he meant it. Fuck, how he hated not being with her and the wee one.

She stopped visiting him seven months into his sentence. For weeks, no one knew what was going on with her or maybe they just weren't telling. He almost lost it big time in that jail. His Diane was in trouble and he was totally helpless. One night, he lashed out at some guy who was showing off about drug deals he had pulled. The bloke was a lowlife arsehole telling stories. He knew that but he lashed out anyway. Lowlife arsehole or no, the guy had mates and one of them slashed his face from forehead to chin the next day. In a strange way, the pain helped. It was the only thing that stopped him worrying but it never lasted that long.

By the time he was released, Diane had given up the flat and had disappeared with Angela. He searched the city but with no luck. Then, one day, a guy with long hair and trendy casual gear turned up at his mother's house where he was staying. A social worker to tell him that Angela had been taken into care. Diane had given them his mother's address before she disappeared. They hadn't seen her in over a month.

He'd cried right there in his mother's living room in front of that social worker. Wept like he hadn't done since he was in short trousers and still afraid of the dark. He'd begged the bloke to tell him where he thought Diane might be. Quietly, calmly the social worker had said, 'I heard she turns up on the Green some nights.'

'The Green? Glasgow Green?'

'Yeah, after dark.' He couldn't understand. What the hell would his Diane be doing in that dangerous place at night? It was full of muggers, wild dogs, tramps and . . . prostitutes. 'She's a working girl,' the man had said, 'and she's not very well.'

AIDS. He thought that was a gay plague. Why did his Diane have AIDS? Diane told him herself after he had gone down to the Green every night for a week and eventually found her there, standing in the half light by the kerb waiting to be picked up by passing motorists.

Murderous and heartbroken – he had been both at the same time. Those filthy, fat-cat bastards in the cars stopping to look her up and down – he would have killed them all had he got close enough. But his poor wee Diane. She was skinny, her short hair greasy and straggly, her eyes dead. It broke his heart.

It took months of cups of tea and talk, talk, talk but she told him all about it. Who else would she tell but him? How she had gone to pieces after he had been jailed and had had a few hits. Desperate for money she had gone to the DHSS, the welfare and every friend she could think of. No one would help or help enough. So she went to him. She'd heard that Arthur Thompson had helped a few young women with cash. A hard man, aye, but one who loved kids and helped out if he could. All she needed was maybe £50 to pay some rent and buy food for Angela until the next giro came in.

Thompson gave her the £50 all right and said there was no hurry for its repayment. He could wait for such a good-looking young lassie. He had asked her if £50 would be enough and she had to admit that it was wee bit tight. He had offered £75 and she had thanked him very much. There was a way she could show her appreciation, he'd said, as he smiled and undid his zip.

She got down on her knees at his feet and did as Thompson wanted. She was desperate – what else could she do? He had to understand. That was her first time selling sex for money. She felt so disgusted with herself, she bought some smack and that was that. A couple of weeks later, she was back at Thompson's house. Same deal, same payment. She learned later that all those young women he had helped had the same arrangement. Feeding their kids by sucking his dick.

After that, it was easy to go down to Blythswood Square. Well, no, not easy, but it hadn't seemed such a terrible thing to do. She needed the money badly. How else was she going to take care of Angela and feed her habit? Now she had lost him, her baby and her health. All she had left was her habit.

'You haven't lost me,' he told her. 'You'll never lose me.' And he hugged her and kissed her and gave her all the money he had so she wouldn't have to go down to the Green that night. She should go home, have something to eat and he'd meet her there later. First he had a wee bit of business to see to. Something to sort out.

This was personal.

Arthur Thompson was messing about at the back of his house. He liked to keep the space well organised and clear for the various cars he brought in. Fast cars still gave him a buzz and these days he sometimes picked one up on the spur of the moment. Sometimes, they were given to him towards some debt. At other times, he'd see one he fancied and make the owner an offer he couldn't refuse right there on the spot. It was good fun and useful. If the cops and other players weren't sure what he would be driving, he was harder to keep track of. That's what he liked.

Thompson was thinking of going back into the house when he noticed a hubcap lying on the ground. It had come off a car he had just got rid of. Now that was annoying. What was he going to do? Chase up the bloke he sold it to and pass the hubcap on? Fat chance. He would pick it up and chuck it in the bin.

As he was bending over, he heard a pop just as something tugged at his trouser leg. Strange. He stood up and looked at where the noise came from. There he was, walking towards him, some old revolver, held in both hands, stretched out in front of him, pointing at him.

'See you, you bastard,' said the gunman, 'I'm going to kill you.'

Thompson straightened up and looked at the guy. He seemed familiar.

'This bullet's too good for you. I should do you slow. You deserve to roast for what you did to her.'

Her? What was he raving about? 'I think you've got the wrong man, son,' said Thompson.

'You calling her a liar, you prick?' The young man was furious, chalk white and nervous as hell. Bit by bit, he edged closer, the gun barrel pointing out at Thompson.

'I don't know what the fuck you're talking about,' Thompson said, standing stock-still, wary of making any sudden movements that might alarm the edgy young guy.

'Not what. WHO.' He was a few yards away now and Thompson could see his eyes full of tears, the gun waving from side to side. 'Diane. My Diane. What you did to her . . .'

As he had learned to do in street fights from an early age, Arthur Thompson chose his moment well. One hand reached up from the side and grabbed the gun, yanking it up as his knee slammed into the gunman's groin. A second shot popped into the air as the bloke doubled up, fell and dropped the gun. Thompson kicked the revolver away and then kicked his would-be assailant, stamping on his head again and again, all the while cursing him.

A few minutes later, Arthur Thompson had made a call to one of his people to come and 'give someone a lift'. The young man was kicked and stamped a few times more, bundled into the back of a transit van and driven away.

Thompson didn't care what happened to him after that. Either he would be dumped in some isolated scrubland outside the city boundaries or shot in the head and disposed of in a refuse dump, some deep river or maybe one of the many building sites his folk had access to. He just didn't care. When asked who the hit man was and why, he'd said, 'Fucked if I know. Just some fucking junkie that got the wrong end of the stick. I bloody hate junkies.'

The wound to Thompson's leg was superficial and he treated it himself at home with some Dettol and a large Band-Aid like he had done so many times before. Later, he had a look at the revolver – an old rusty pre-war job that hadn't been serviced or oiled in decades. No wonder it had popped rather than banged. The boy was just an amateur after all. But the incident didn't trouble Arthur Thompson for long. He had more important things to worry about.

Margaret was his elder daughter and, some say, his favourite though he loved all of his kids. People who knew her said that she had more of her father's strength of character in her than either of her brothers or her sister. If she had been a man, Margaret would undoubtedly have followed in her father's trade and been an ideal successor. But she was a good-looking young woman and was barred from taking a lead role. Did that save her? Not from heroin addiction.

Arthur and Rita Thompson had been fretting about their daughter for a few years. She kept bad company according to them and seemed to have settled with a regular boyfriend Gerry Carbin, known as 'Cyclops' since one of his eyes was badly disfigured. The Carbins were a well-known Glasgow crime family with strong links to Liverpool. Some of his family had moved out to Spain and were setting themselves up nicely trafficking drugs from North Africa. But Cyclops stayed in Glasgow for the best of reasons – he was in love with Margaret Thompson.

Under normal circumstances, it would have been a good match, acceptable to both families, but for one issue – Cyclops was a junkie. No way would Arthur Thompson have his daughter run around with a smackhead. He tried everything – bribery, threats, pleading – and nothing worked. Margaret and Cyclops were an item and that was that.

Eventually, Arthur Thompson cut her off and banned the rest of the family from seeing her. He had made several public statements saying that he hated drugs and he would have nothing to with the evil trade. Yet, there was his own lassie living with a junkie. Arthur Thompson couldn't have that. Besides, though happy to rake in the substantial profits, he did hate drugs. Heroin was for idiots, not his kith and kin.

If he had been true and open and asked then what was his biggest worry, Arthur Thompson would have replied that it was the well-being of his oldest daughter, Margaret. And he was right to worry about the young woman. But then he didn't see what was awaiting him around the corner. Thompson's worst times were just beginning.

22

DAMP POWDER,
DAMP GRASS

LATE 1980s

It was ideal.

He was a professional hit man with good reasons for hating the Thompsons. He was that kind of guy. Moral, some would say. Old-fashioned was his term. But there was a settlement due and he was happy to see to getting Arthur Thompson off the face of this earth just because he thought it the right thing to do.

We'll call him The Apprentice. It's not a name you'll hear on the street except from a select few who have decided that will be their name for the man – a man who has done much and has many secrets. They chose the name, The Apprentice, because he was so good so young – like all the best street players.

Starting with the usual teenage acts of stealing cars, joyriding, robbing shops and taking part in gang fights, he soon graduated to more serious hit jobs. At first, it was just settling old scores with a razor to the face. Then, with a gun in his fist, he found his vocation. Street fighters need to be able to deal with their pain as well as dish it out. Shooters need a calm head and detachment no matter how personal their deed. That's why he was so good.

Arthur Thompson had fallen into the habit of going to one of his sawmills every morning. It was sloppy and dangerous to let the world know where you are going to be. A time and place are the essential ingredients of any hit. That's why so many gangsters survived to die in their beds. Not that they didn't have enemies – it was just that their foes could never tie them down to a time and a place. Thompson wasn't stupid, far from it. But he seemed to think he was untouchable and had grown careless. It was a lethal mistake.

The Apprentice knew where Thompson would be and when. Witnesses were also scarce. The couple of guys working in the yard weren't happy with Arthur who had cut their wages and upped their workloads. If they had spotted the hit man, it was likely they wouldn't say a thing. Most of the time, they were lost among the piles of wood, operating one of the industrial saws that howled at its work. Perfect cover for the noise. A time and a place were no problem in this particular job.

The only worry The Apprentice had was with the gun. His usual arrangements had fallen through so he used a fall-back position. This meant he wouldn't have the opportunity to test the weapon or the ammunition. Not good. But his supplier was reliable and he assured him the piece would be in good order. It was an uncharacteristic risk but The Apprentice decided to take it. If he had cancelled, maybe the time and place would have disappeared. A free pop at the so-called Godfather was too good an opportunity to pass over.

Arthur Thompson was sitting behind his desk, rifling through some papers. He had recently started a contract with a Bridgeton family heavily involved in the demolition of old tenements. The government was paying out more grants to knock buildings down than to build new ones. Seemed stupid to him, but who was he to pass over a chance to make a few quid?

The old buildings were full of good gear, especially the wood. Hard, high-class timber that would last several lifetimes more. It was the type of material that now cost a fortune and it was in short supply. All the demolition company had to do was to stack the wood separately and then deliver it to base. He'd extended their role recently by demanding they also remove the old nails. That was time-consuming and painstaking and had been costing him good money in labour costs. Not now. The demolition company weren't happy but what did he care?

Arthur Thompson reached past the ashtray on his desk for the phone. That's when he spotted the young man standing in the doorway. The shot rang out, smothered by the howl of a saw in the yard. For a second, Thompson thought he was a dead man. But the bullet had missed, falling short into the desk.

The Apprentice cursed the gun. Something was badly wrong. Probably damp ammo. But he had a job to do. Taking two steps closer he fired again as Thompson got to his feet. The second bullet was aimed at the target's chest but fell short and into his groin. A nasty one but not enough to put him down.

Thompson was fumbling at his jacket which hung over the back of his chair. The Apprentice knew the old man's Beretta would be there and that it would be in perfect working order. If that desk hadn't been in the way and if Thompson had been at least stunned he would have pulled the knife from his waistband and finished him off up close. No time for that.

The Apprentice turned and ran out of the office, down into the yard and out on to the street. The job had failed. He had intended to leave Arthur Thompson dead on the floor and he had blown it. But calm-head time. There would be other opportunities, that's for sure, and, the next time, he'd test his weapon and make no mistake.

Arthur Thompson was bleeding badly from the wound that was just inches away from his penis and testicles. It was a bad one but it could have been worse, much worse. This time he'd need a doctor and fast. He picked up the phone, called his family and calmly told them where to find him. No details, just the location of where he would be.

Thompson struggled painfully into his suit jacket. By rights he should have dumped his pistol but he reckoned the gunman might still be out there waiting for another crack. He'd take it with him and store it before it got dodgy.

Inch by inch, he walked across the floor, hanging on to whatever furniture was at hand. By the time he had reached the yard, he was sweating and dragging the leg on the wounded side and blood was oozing down his trousers. At last, he made it to his car and, with one last effort, sat down and manually lifted his legs into the driver's seat. Now came the really hard bit.

Somehow he had to manoeuvre the pedals with one use-less leg. Thompson made a mental note to consider getting automatics in future, jarred the car into gear and headed unsteadily out on to the street. From across the yard one of his employees had watched the scene from beginning to end. He was a kind-hearted man normally but there was no way he was going to help Thompson. Why should he help someone who had cut his wages and increased his workload?

Arthur Thompson dumped his Beretta in the car's glove compartment outside the private Nuffield Clinic. Booking himself in, the old gangster claimed he had had an accident at home with an electric drill. It was nasty wound but one he would recover from quickly. The police were called, of course, and, as usual, Thompson told them nothing. It's a shame his older boy didn't keep just as quiet.

Fatboy was still griping about being set up. It got to a stage that few still under his employ, even from the jail, would listen to him – them and his young brother, Billy.

Billy Thompson was no chip off the old block. Even as a young child, the differences in how he looked from the rest of the family set tongues wagging that he wasn't Arthur's son. Gossipmongers claimed that Arthur's brother Robert was the real father but it had been typical of The

Godfather to agree to bring the boy up as his own. Whatever the truth, Thompson was to find that there wasn't so much a cuckoo in the nest as a runt in the litter.

While Fatboy at least had his father's natural cunning, Billy had very few of old Arthur's characteristics. As a young man he still looked like a lanky, awkward teenager and had the same unthinking delinquent turn as somebody ten years his junior. What he did have was that sense of arrogance that he was a Thompson, The Godfather's son, and he could get off with murder.

For a few years, Billy had been listening to his father complain that Fatboy had been set up for the drugs dealing. On prison visits, Fatboy would regale him with his latest theory and his amended hit list. Now there was a new theory and, as with all the earlier ones, Fatboy was adamant that this time he was right.

'It was that cunt McGraw,' Fatboy said in the visiting room at Peterhead Prison. 'We all know he's called The Licensee because he's hand-in-hand with the polis. Now he's taken over my trade. What better way to get that business than to grass me to the cops?' Billy listened and believed. And, by the time he had returned to Glasgow, he had decided to act.

The Licensee's symbolic HQ was the Caravel. If you couldn't get at the man, get at his headquarters. One night, Billy Thompson clambered up on to the roof of the Caravel and set it alight. He had already painted the words GRASS all over the road. That would show The Licensee.

It took McGraw two days to find out who the culprit was and he was far from happy. The pub survived, but only just, and the whole affair had punched him where it hurt – his wallet. Worse were the words GRASS painted on the roads. If he knew that Billy Thompson had been the culprit, then so would half of the east end. Having Arthur Thompson declare you were an informant would be bad for his reputation and, more importantly, bad for business.

Arthur Thompson agreed to meet The Licensee in the back room of the Caravel. Privately, Thompson was furious with Billy – not for what he had done but for acting on his own initiative. It was the sort of childish act that would cause problems he didn't need and now he had to clean up after him.

'I'm no' a grass, Arthur,' McGraw had pled.

'No?' Thompson might have privately accepted that Billy was in the wrong but he wasn't about to concede that easily face-to-face with the complainant. Besides, he suspected McGraw might have had a hand in setting up Fatboy.

'No,' insisted McGraw, 'I had nothing to do with your oldest boy going down.'

'I heard differently.' Thompson was standing, staring right back at McGraw, daring him to deny it.

'You heard wrong. You should look at that bastard Blind Jonah if you want a grass,' McGraw said, knowing that Thompson was bound to suspect Blind Jonah too.

'He'll be seen to,' insisted Thompson curtly with no explanation offered or expected.

'Aye, but this is no' right,' McGraw said as he waved his arm up at the roof. 'Amends should be made, eh?'

Two of the stingiest street players stood in the back room of the Caravel and haggled over money. It was an argument close to both men's hearts but, eventually, Arthur Thompson agreed to pay a sum of compensation. How much it was is irrelevant. Even before the pair left the bar, their eyes blinking in the sun, Thompson had decided not to honour the agreement. It was what he always did.

As Arthur Thompson and Thomas McGraw stood near their cars on wasteland next to the bar, another motor arrived at speed. It was Tam Bagan, his brother and a couple of his team and they weren't happy. Bagan was out of the car in a flash and running towards Thompson. But he was too angry and too slow. Thompson yanked his pistol from its holster and smashed Bagan across the jaw, sending him reeling.

Thompson stood over the prone Bagan pointing his gun directly at him. There was a sudden movement to the side and Thompson turned to see Bagan's brother make a move towards him. Without hesitating, Thompson spun round, pointing his gun at the brother. Big Mistake. Tam Bagan was on his feet and wrestled the gun from Thompson. The old gangster then suffered the indignity of being pistol whipped with his own gun. Bloody and battered, Thompson hit the deck. Bagan straddled him with his knees on his shoulders, the loaded gun now inches from the old man's face. Tam Bagan was going to shoot Arthur Thompson dead right there and then.

Then there was a shrill voice. 'Fuck's sake don't shoot him.' It was Thomas McGraw, The Licensee. Then, he corrected himself, saying what he really meant, 'Don't shoot him here. The fucking polis will be crawling over me and my pub.'

As The Licensee continued to whine in panic, Bagan stayed where he was, the gun still stuck into Thompson's gob. Long minutes passed and then Bagan smashed Thompson across the face with the gun. He stood up and then kicked him in the head before smashing the lights and windows of his car. His final acts might seem petty but, added to the beating, they gave a message of utter humiliation for Arthur Thompson – a message that every street player in Glasgow would understand. The Godfather was vulnerable – just look at what Tam Bagan did to him.

As Bagan and his team sped off, McGraw leaned over and tried to help Thompson to his feet.

'Take your fucking paws off me, you fucking grass,' growled Thompson. It was typical of Arthur Thompson, in one fell swoop, to show so little gratitude and to scrub the agreement that had been made between them just five minutes before.

Arthur Thompson could count himself lucky he did not die that day. In a sense, he owed his life to Thomas McGraw pleading his case. But Thompson didn't see it that way. He was alive and owed nothing to anybody. That was his way. But the word was out – Arthur Thompson was vulnerable. And in a lot of ways that people didn't know about.

23

I SCREAM

1984–89

The streets of Glasgow groaned with a sense of outrage. Does that take much in a city whose reputation is as hard as nails? No, because the people are as warm as they're tough. As keen on social justice as they are dismissive of social class. When two of their innocents had gone down for the most terrible murder in the city's history, even the dogs on the street howled injustice.

It hadn't started that way.

On the night of 16 February 1984, someone had torched the door of a flat at 29 Bankend Street, Ruchazie in Glasgow and wiped out six members of the Doyle Family, including a wee baby. It was a horrible death for them all as they struggled to protect the young and the frail and battled through the smoke to get free. Next day, the newspapers carried a picture of the burned-out shell of a house and worse.

In the back of an ambulance slumped Andrew Doyle and his brother Daniel, the skin peeling off their flesh, pain and grief scarring their faces. Next to them, a shell-shocked fireman held a wee bundle. It was the baby, Mark. A few agonising days later, Andrew and Mark died.

Theirs was not an easy death. Their burns were so severe that the level of morphine administered to cope with the pain meant their lungs couldn't work properly. Slowly, fluid filled their lungs and they drowned in their hospital beds.

The citizens of Glasgow were outraged. The pressure on the cops to find the killers was immense. Media coverage was intense.

The word was that the murders had been over some dispute about ice-cream van territories. Ice-Cream Wars. Andrew Doyle drove such a van on one of the more lucrative runs. Someone wanted him out. Well, he was out now.

It's not just decent citizens, honest cops and hard-working journalists who are interested in such atrocities. Street players were keen to suss out who was behind the killings as well and they have access to dark corners where others aren't allowed.

Even by the time of the trial, anybody who was anybody on Glasgow's streets knew they had the wrong men in the dock. None more so than Arthur Thompson. The high-profile murders had meant that the city was crawling with cops and that wasn't good for business. Besides, Thompson had inside information on the case from his old pal, top Glasgow detective, Charlie Craig.

Craig was in overall charge of the case but the main man on the ground was one of his troops – Norrie Walker, nicknamed Goldilocks by street players. So, while Walker's name was all over the case, Craig was directing proceedings from his desk. From day one, he was out to get one man – TC Campbell.

In the years preceding the Doyle murders, TC Campbell had been accused of three serious offences and had walked free every time. Charlie Craig didn't like that at all. Now he had TC in his sights on the slimmest of connections. His wife and sister ran ice-cream vans and Ruchazie was a slice of his part of the city. Slim, but enough for Charlie Craig.

Thompson knew all about this even as the investigation was going on and would have been well aware of who TC was. He knew all about TC's late father, Bobby, who had been one of the most respected robbers Glasgow had ever produced – and that was saying something.

By the time of the trial, he would have sussed who the other guy in the hot seat was. Joe Steele's father, Andy, was a well-known player as were his two older brothers, Jim and John.

When TC Campbell and Joe Steele were found guilty of the murders, Arthur Thompson was well aware of why two innocent men had just gone down. So was the investigating cop, Norrie Walker, who'd go on to commit suicide. Question is should Thompson have done anything about it?

There were plenty of players in Glasgow at the time who had inside info on the Doyle murders. But the relationship between the cops and someone with a track record isn't a comfortable one, with the law-and-order mob likely to be suspicious of any approach that didn't fit their chosen suspects. But Thompson was different. He had the ear of the top man. After all, hadn't he helped his old pal Paddy Meehan win a Royal Pardon for the murder of Rachel Ross? And Arthur Thompson knew more about what happened that night in Bankend Street than many of the cops on the enquiry.

A well-known street player was in Bankend Street that night, accompanied by two of his usual minders. His group had asked a pair of junkies to torch someone's door for them, for a payment. The junkies agreed then disappeared. Even they wanted nothing to do with that.

The man and his minders then went to a local petrol station and bought a gallon can of fuel. They were identified and the matter reported to the cops, some of whom went back to the witness and tried to persuade her it was TC Campbell who had bought the petrol. She knew TC Campbell by sight from around her neighbourhood. She knew it wasn't him and stuck to her story.

The same well-known street player owned a large number of ice-cream vans. A couple of days before, his brother-in-law had had a run-in with Andrew Doyle as they drove their vans and had come off second best.

Just after the Doyles' door was torched, a man was involved in a minor bump with another car on Bankend Street. The men in the other car took off fast. Why would they do that over such a little scrape? The ID the man gave of one of the group fits the well-known street player.

Even by the time of the trial, Arthur Thompson knew all about this. He knew too that TC Campbell and Joe Steele weren't the killers. And he also knew who that well-known street player was – Thomas McGraw, The Licensee.

Some might think that Thompson had just been handed a gift. He hated McGraw and suspected he might have some-how been involved in setting up Fatboy for the drugs. Getting him locked up for life for the murder of the Doyles would cer-tainly get him out of his hair. By the late 1980s, a campaign to prove Campbell and Steele's innocence was beginning to be accepted by the public. That would have been the time to use the information but still Thompson did nothing.

Some would say that he was working to the street rules. You don't put anyone into the cops – you settle matters yourself, on the street. But Thompson had abandoned any adherence to the code long ago. That wasn't the reason he did nothing.

Through Charlie Craig, he knew that McGraw provided a great deal of information to the cops. Because of that, he was more useful to them out of jail than in. And, if he tried to use what he knew in any way, he'd find himself losing old friends and allies, like Charlie Craig. Now that would be bad for business.

What of Campbell and Steele, by then fighting to prove their innocence? Thompson saw that as their problem. Nothing to do with him. He'd a business to run after all.

Cold and uncaring? Sure but the episode told Arthur Thompson something else. He wasn't as strong as he thought he was. When it came to power with the cops, even the corrupt cops, McGraw was beginning to be a major influence.

The Godfather had lost his stranglehold and he didn't like it. People might notice and try to take advantage.

There were folk who intended to do just that. But, first, life was to send him a blow that some thought he'd never recover from.

24

WOUNDED

1989

Margaret Thompson and her father Arthur had a special relationship. It was a modern-day tragedy that she took to company and substances he couldn't stand and he banished her from his sight. An everyday contemporary tragedy that is enacted in every street. The only difference this time was that this tragedy involved the top hoodlum in Glasgow.

Margaret Thompson was stubborn, a characteristic she inherited from her father. When she was banished she didn't stray far and she made a point of being around so her family, especially her father, noticed her. But, in 1989, in a move so audacious it beggared belief, she took her defiance of her all-powerful father a step further.

After floating around from flat to flat, Margaret and her boyfriend, Gerry 'Cyclops' Carbin, decided to try to get a council house. The perfect option came up when they were offered a ground-floor flat on the corner of Moodiesburn Street and Provanmill Road, about thirty yards from The Ponderosa. It was directly across the street in a position that Arthur couldn't avoid. There was going to be trouble or a reconciliation. Local people were betting on trouble.

Margaret was well liked by most people she met. Her new neighbours were delighted she was moving in, regardless of how they felt about her old man. But Margaret and Cyclops were still on the smack and Arthur wouldn't accept her back into the fold as long as that was the case.

The new flat had lain empty and boarded up for a long time. The young couple moved in, put a mattress on the floor and planned to clean the place up as they went. They had hardly crossed the threshold when disaster struck.

One morning, Cyclops woke to find Margaret Thompson dead beside him. Once he had pulled himself together, Cyclops ran to the neighbours for help. They agreed that poor Margaret was dead and went to fetch her family from across the way and called an ambulance and the cops. Arthur and Rita were heartbroken. It was one of the very rare occasions that anyone reported having seen Arthur Thompson with tears in his eyes – and the other occasions were due to mirth not sadness.

Margaret lay there, in that squalid flat, her heroin works plain to see by her side. Arthur knew what had killed her but he instructed the family, 'She choked, right? Choked on her own vomit in her sleep. Too much to drink. Got it?' Perishing from too much booze was socially acceptable in Glasgow and it still is.

Margaret Thompson had indeed vomited as well as urinated and defecated. But it was a heroin overdose that had killed her.

At that time, much of the smack in the city was being brought in by McGraw, The Licensee. He was using people with little experience of the drug and they had taken a consignment of exceptional purity. Margaret Thompson wasn't the only experienced junkie to die from too pure heroin that year.

By the time the paramedics were taking Margaret's lifeless body out of the flat, Cyclops was on the hard shoulder of the M8 hitching a lift south. No way did he want to face Arthur Thompson's wrath.

Parents should never have to bury a child. Some do, of course, but they are left feeling that the act is unnatural and unjust. This was no different for Arthur Thompson as his daughter, Margaret, was quietly interred in the family plot at Riddrie Park Cemetery, right at the back of The Ponderosa. As she had moved in across the road in defiance of her father in life, so she would be only a few yards from him in death. Gangster family or no, it was a tragedy.

Little did Arthur Thompson know that, out of that very tragedy and other acts of his kin, a new order was taking shape elsewhere. His influence was reaching across the seas.

25

THE TARTAN MAFIA
1989–1990s

Ever since there have been Scots, many have always gone abroad to work, till the soil, explore, run companies and almost anything else you can think of. Mostly, though, they've gone abroad to fight as mercenaries. Then you get two Glasgow guys of the 1980s and 1990s. On the run from Arthur Thompson, they went abroad to get rich – whatever it took.

Wattie Douglas was the first to flee the country with the Thompsons on his tail just because he had had the nerve to deal drugs in territories Fatboy Thompson wanted. Ex-milkman Douglas wasn't a fighter but he wasn't stupid either. Moving to London wasn't far enough to be safe from The Godfather. The Netherlands – that was better.

Tourists all think of Amsterdam's coffee shops and their liberal approach to cannabis. But importing the stuff is still illegal, especially on a large scale, and that's what Douglas did. Travelling around from country to country, he wasn't sightseeing but setting up his contacts. Douglas had spent some time in Spain in what would soon become known as the Scottish Costa del Crime, Fuengirola. The place was a holiday resort for many but that's the base from where he forged links with Moroccans who'd ship large quantities of hashish wherever he said.

With so many London faces like Ronnie Knight and Great Train Robber Charlie Wilson settling in Spain as well as a whole range of lesser-known players, there was enough people arranging cannabis export to British cities. Wily Douglas didn't want to attract their wrath so he exported to the Netherlands.

By 1989, there were already other Glaswegians gathered in Fuengirola. The Carbin family had come off second best in a gangland feud for control of the vast Castlemilk scheme and fled to Spain. All, that is, apart from Gerry Cyclops Carbin who stayed on with his lover, Margaret Thompson. When Margaret died beside him and he fled Glasgow to escape The Godfather's hurt fury, he kept going south to join his family. Now things were going to get hot in Spain.

Cyclops wasted no time in getting involved in the lucrative cannabis smuggling route from North Africa via Spain into Britain. But now he would work with other expatriate Scots such as Wattie Douglas. But there were others.

Richard 'Ricky' Hayes, from Glasgow's Easterhouse scheme, ran many legitimate businesses and ran them well but cops suspected he was a big mover in the dope trafficking.

James 'Scud' Rae, a former mercenary, had fled Yoker in Glasgow to escape car-theft and weapons charges. It was the best move of his life as he used a business importing and exporting luxury cars to ship cocaine into almost every European country and as far north as Norway and Sweden.

Pat McCadden was a young, flash tycoon running a shoe business but he left Glasgow for Spain when the business went bust. He soon found another high-profit commodity – heroin – and created effective links between teams in Marbella and Glasgow.

Tony McVey had grown up in the tough Calton neighbourhood in Glasgow. He and his younger brother Paul were known for always wearing the best suits, always looking smart even when they were dishing out the grief. In Spain, Tony McVey bobbed and weaved like an expert, constantly changing houses and cars. Paul got caught up in a few bits of action, surviving a shooting in 1990, and then he was accused of threatening to shoot seven cops after a drugs raid in Glasgow. Paul McVey was too smart for the cops. In 1994, they named him as the mastermind behind a £14 million heroin heist some of which had been left in a locker in Glasgow's Queen Street Station. McVey wasn't convicted. Not even the guy the cops claimed to have caught red-handed, Ian Allen, went down for it. The only effect the whole expensive police operation had was that McVey now spent most of his time in his luxury home near Palma Nova on the island of Majorca.

Then the Thompsons chased Wattie Douglas and Cyclops Carbin out of town and in Spain the action livened up.

First Carbin was arrested under suspicion of having murdered Norwegian nightclub owner Torborn Heia. That he and his brothers were found living in Heia's house, driving his car, wearing his clothes was a bit of a clue.

When in jail on remand, Cyclops' Spanish cellmate somehow got through a tiny window and fell to his death from five floors up. Cyclops was accused of pushing him through the window and murdering him. While he was waiting trial, Glasgow cops served extradition papers on him in connection with the death of Margaret Thompson, The Godfather's daughter. Now he was in trouble.

Back in Scotland, Cyclops was cleared of any responsibility for Margaret's death. So who had given her the too-pure smack? He was also cleared of drug dealing in that connection. So who had dealt her the drugs? Street players point to The Licensee's team but no one else was brought to book.

In Spain Cyclops was cleared of his cellmate's murder – difficult to prove with no witnesses. But Cyclops wasn't free – far from it.

In 1994, the Spanish cops finally nailed him and he got six years for cannabis trafficking. Within a few weeks of his sentence beginning, fifty bags of smack were found in his cell. He openly blamed another prisoner, an Italian bank robber, of grassing on him. Two months after the smack was discovered, the Italian was found murdered in his cell.

The Spanish cops scratched their heads. They had criminals of their own who were wild. They feared all the well-known London faces who had moved in. But these Glaswegians were pure bloody crazy.

Wattie Douglas, that other Thompson refugee, hadn't been lazy either. Russia, Canada, USA, Finland, Netherlands, Morocco, Spain, Portugal, Germany, Ireland – name a country and he had been up to devilment there. But, for years, Fuengirola in Spain was the place he returned to.

Maybe Douglas liked the climate. But for a man who had a dozen passports in different names, suffered facelifts numerous times to keep his ID different and was so good at covering his tracks that Interpol called him the Tartan Pimpernel, it was a weak spot.

With numerous European police forces believing Douglas to be behind international syndicates smuggling drugs and weapons, pressure was put on the Spaniards to act. Well, they tried.

Time after time they pulled him in and grilled him after Great Train Robber Charles Wilson was gunned down and killed beside his swimming pool. They were convinced that Douglas was the hit man but they could make nothing stick.

Then they took him the whole legal road on laundering £150 million of drugs money. The cops lost.

Douglas infuriated the Spaniards even more by teaming up with Brian Doran, a former foreign languages teacher from Glasgow who, along with his Scottish partner Ken Togher, had become the top cocaine traffickers in the world. Doran and Togher also lived in Spain. While they set another squad on the tails of Doran and Togher, the Spaniards put even more resources chasing Douglas. Then they hit it lucky.

An anonymous informant started phoning them. The only thing Spaniards knew about this man was that he was either

German or Scottish because of his accent. All the grass wanted to talk about was Wattie Douglas and he went on to prove he knew the man's activities by listing scams the Spanish cops were convinced he had been behind but couldn't catch him on. Then came a live one, 'There's a boat called *Great Alexander* setting off for Africa in two days. Watch it.'

Click. The line went dead. It wasn't much of a clue but the Spaniards were desperate. Within a few hours, they had arranged satellite tracking of the *Great Alexander*.

The crew took the ship in and out of four African states, picking up legitimate goods as well as their crooked cargo of 250,000 kilos of hashish. It was meant to be Douglas's usual careful planning to avoid suspicion. Thorough as he was, he didn't study his international politics closely enough and the poor crew sailed into two countries in the middle of civil war.

In one case, at night, with the lights off, sailing into port, they heard a THUMP THUMP THUMP against the boat. Eventually they could stand it no more and threw on a light. The water around them was full of dead bodies. Unfortunately the light didn't just show corpses but gave their presence away to the rebels on the bank.

Two weeks in a rotten jail later and having paid a huge ransom to buy their freedom, they headed for the open seas, only to be arrested within hours with their full cargo of drugs still on board. But, if the authorities thought they had finally nabbed Wattie Douglas, they were badly mistaken.

Soon it was apparent that Douglas wasn't to be seen in any of the cities he was known to visit. For a man who changed his name and appearance frequently this was no great surprise. Then a registered police informant in Amsterdam asked to meet his cop handler. He knew where Wattie Douglas was. In the bottom of a canal, dumped there by a drug-dealing associate he'd had a dispute with.

The cops just didn't take the informant's word for it. They

hunted the alleged killer, someone they already knew well, and pulled in other informants. Of course, no one would admit to the murder but the cops were convinced enough to spend days dragging sections of the maze of canals that zig-zag Amsterdam. They never found a body but knew that it didn't mean that Douglas wasn't there, stuck in the mud at the bottom.

A few months later, it was clear the cops wouldn't have been able to tie Douglas into the drugs haul on the *Great Alexander* anyway. Some forces closed their files on the man who had given them such a runaround. Others turned more of their attention on other members of the Tartan Mafia who were still active. Then Lazarus appeared – a new Lazarus. Wattie Douglas chose Russia to rise from the grave to announce that rumours of his death had been greatly exaggerated. Rumours he had arranged himself. Game on again.

It was no accident that Douglas had chosen Russia. The fall of the Berlin Wall in 1989 and the ending of the old Soviet central control meant that Russia was a particularly lawless country run by gangsters in real terms. Douglas had made a close association with top Russian players who had access to a great deal of high-quality Afghan heroin. Useful as that was in business terms, it was also very easy to disappear in that vast state when protected by people who controlled the streets.

It was a cat-and-mouse game that would go on through the 1990s but there, back in the early part of the decade, it was true to say that Douglas and Gerry Cyclops Carbin were lead-ing forces, giving an identity to a group of Scottish players abroad. In a sense they created the Tartan Mafia. Carbin even had a shop in Fuengirola that was known by locals as the Tartan Mafia.

Without Douglas and Carbin, it is unlikely that the Tartan Mafia would ever have been conceived of. Just ask the Spanish cops and the police forces of a raft of other European countries. Yet Douglas and Carbin only ever went abroad to escape the wrath of Arthur Thompson, The Godfather. European police forces might take some consolation that it was Thompson refugees and not Thompson himself who ended up on their doorsteps.

Back in Glasgow, Arthur Thompson had his hands full. There was the small matter of revenge to dole out.

26

JINXED
1989–1990s

Arthur Thompson was worried for his kids and quite right too. Tracey was the only one who was steady, bright and capable. Fatboy was still locked away and making new threats against serious people every day. Billy, the youngest, was a worry every time he left the house. God knows what he would get up to. Other people were watching Billy very closely. In typical style, Thompson soon had the chance to take it out on someone else.

Blind Jonah was delighted to be released from prison. No one likes prison apart from ancient worn-out lags who have grown so used to it they are scared to live anywhere else. Jonah was young, full of energy and he had plans.

Everyone in the Scottish jails knew he had been working with Fatboy. That hadn't bothered him to start with. In fact, he thought that his links with the Thompsons would guarantee him a safe passage and that he'd be taken care of with their pet screws delivering wee extras like tobacco or a bit of dope. They'd also take care of his family while he was away and that was a reassurance. Except they didn't help him or his at all. Old Arthur would have his reasons, Blind Jonah reckoned, and he got by as best he could.

Then Fatboy started boasting about who he was going to have killed – a whole list of folk on the outside who Fatboy claimed had had him set up. There were cop names and Willie

Gibson, Martin Ross and the Irishman, John Friel, of course. Then there was Wattie Douglas who had hightailed it out of Glasgow to Spain then the Netherlands. As soon as they set up on their own, the names of Paul Ferris and Tam Bagan were added to the top of the list. Within a couple of years, Thomas McGraw, The Licensee, was also added. Now there was a turn-up.

When Fatboy was jailed, there were business matters to take care of. Someone had to fill the gap in the drugs market and a few other scams. If he had just done nothing some stranger would have taken over and that would be that. Instead, Fatboy struck a deal with McGraw, The Licensee. It was agreed that The Licensee would take over Fatboy's dealers and his suppliers for the duration of his spell inside. Not for nothing, of course. Fatboy was to get an agreed and generous cut – an OK agreement for someone doing nothing because they were stuck in jail.

Blind Jonah had worked for The Licensee years before and didn't trust him. On two occasions, Jonah had jumped in when the man was being attacked and saved him from sure-fire doings. Those in the know would say that Blind Jonah had saved McGraw's life and lost an eye in the process. How had he been rewarded? He wasn't – simple as that.

Jonah had stayed close enough to McGraw for years to know how he traded information with the cops and often set people up for offences they hadn't committed. As long as he made money and avoided jail, he didn't care. McGraw would have shopped his granny for a couple of quid. So Jonah wasn't surprised when Fatboy started bleating that the payments from McGraw had dried up. That was McGraw's name on the list.

Now Jonah was free and, in spite of Fatboy's hysterics in prison, he went directly back to Arthur Thompson to work for him. Old Arthur was a different type all together, Jonah reckoned. Somebody you could trust. That's when Arthur Thompson crucified Blind Jonah.

He was no pushover, unlike some of the others Thompson had nailed through the flesh. It took four heavies and a bloody beating with boots, bats and a metal bar before Jonah slid to the ground. Even then, he'd protested his innocence of setting Fatboy up. Arthur Thompson didn't listen.

It was an old wound that would never heal. Never mind that the security forces had shown surveillance photographs of Fatboy at the bad business. Thompson couldn't hurt MI5 and he needed to hurt someone. Those who knew Fatboy also knew he wouldn't handle the drugs himself but let others take the risk. The way he was caught throwing tenner bags out of his car window as the cops chased him suggested someone had set him up. Thompson couldn't exactly let it be known that MI5 were involved, could he? Jonah would have to do.

Besides, Arthur Thompson did suspect that Blind Jonah was involved in some way in setting up Fatboy with the drugs that led to his eleven years in jail. Whatever Jonah said would make no difference. Well, a confession that he had done it would have made a difference – it would have result-ed in his death. All the man could do was to keep repeating and swearing he had nothing to do with it. He tried to tell Thompson about the girlie magazine the cops had lifted from his room to plant in Fatboy's linen basket. He hadn't seen them take it but they took so much that night. He used differ-ent paper to wrap the heroin in but never the corner of a page from that magazine. Why would he do that?

Jonah had wanted to tell Arthur that all along, thinking that the old gangster would visit him in jail but he never came. Now it sounded like he was making excuses, filling in the gaps when it was too late. Well, it sounded like that to Arthur Thompson. To Blind Jonah it sounded like the truth.

Still they nailed him to the floor and beat him again. It was in a deserted council flat in Blackhill – just one of many with the windows boarded up. Then they left him there, skewered to the floorboards. Next morning, one of the men visited to check if he was alive. Blind Jonah took more killing than that. So, he was prised free and left to find his own way to safety. He did – but not for long.

As soon as The Licensee heard that Blind Jonah wasn't with Arthur Thompson any more, he decided that he had a few scores to settle. When Jonah had split from him, he spoke openly about The Licensee trading in flesh – how he was a grass and a paid police informant. Those were the kinds of words McGaw couldn't allow to circulate on the street.

A group of McGraw's men huckled Jonah into the back of a van one night. Much of the fight had gone out of the young man since his time in jail and his beating from Thompson. His heroin consumption had been well established for years but now it was close to getting out of control. Once wiry, strong and a born fighter, he was now weaker, unfit and always look-ing for his next hit. The old Jonah would have given that team a good fight. The new Jonah just gave in.

They dragged him into a disused warehouse and tied him to a chair. The Licensee had brought some new young blood in for the job. It was to be one of their tests to see if they could make it into the senior team. To pass, they would have to prove they were cold and efficiently vicious.

Billy McPhee was a big bloke who liked to call himself The Iceman. However, that name belonged to another street player with an even fiercer reputation. McPhee had been a Rangers football casual who specialised in slashing fallen opponents as they lay on the ground. A Stanley knife was his blade of choice.

Then there was Gordon Ross, a big handsome bloke from the east end. Ross had the golden touch with women and could have made a living as a gigolo if he hadn't chosen crime. But he had a collection of weaknesses – money, violence and sex in descending order. And sex he could get anywhere, anytime. Teaming up with The Licensee would give Ross unlimited opportunities for violence and he reckoned he was smart enough to earn a fortune even given The Licensee's legendary mean streak.

Both of these men had been individual practitioners who had worked with a variety of players. Paul Ferris noticed they were occasionally linking up with McGraw and had given them the same warning that he had given Joe Hanlon – to watch their backs and get the hell away from him. Both had said they had listened and agreed but continued to do what paid best. That night was to be their big test and they knew it. Neither would fail.

They tortured Blind Jonah for hours, partly for revenge and partly for information. The Licensee wanted to be sure he had all of Fatboy's contacts for the buying and selling of drugs. One of his strengths was that he trusted no one. That very strength was also a weakness as he slunk home before dark every evening and sat sleepless in a house surrounded by the most sophisticated security systems in Scotland.

Hours later, Jonah was slumped in the chair, his body and face broken and slashed. Soon he would pass out again and become oblivious to the pain. Billy McPhee wasn't satisfied. He had something to do while Jonah was still awake, still feeling. Something the young man wouldn't forget.

McPhee slammed the blade into Jonah's good eye and twisted. A low yelp was all the poor guy could muster.

'Blind Jonah, eh?' screamed McPhee. 'Well, you're really fucking blind now.' McPhee and Ross carried Blind Jonah's limp body out of the warehouse and dumped him in the street.

A couple of weeks later, a friend of Jonah visited him in the Royal Infirmary. The patient was delighted to have the visitor's company but he was worried sick, nervous. 'I can't see,' he said. 'Fucking anybody could walk in here and I wouldn't know. A sitting duck, that's what I am.'

The friend stayed for an hour and suggested that they go outside for a smoke. Jonah asked for his arm and he led the way. Instead of walking down the corridor, the pal headed towards a wall and then let go of Jonah's arm, reassuring him it was clear ahead. Four steps later, Jonah bashed his wounded face into a wall and fell back howling in agony. He was blind all right. That's what McGraw had paid his pal to go and check.

Jonah McKenzie's friend walked out into the daylight and phoned McGraw. 'He's blind in both eyes all right.'

'Are you sure?' McGraw showed his usual paranoia and lack of trust.

'Of course I'm fucking sure.' He hated McGraw, he really did. He felt cheap, treacherous, a Judas for what he had done to his friend.

'How do you know?'

'I just know! Right, you prick?' After that, he hung up and punched at the nearest wall, wishing it was McGraw's head at the end of his fist. There was no good punching bricks and mortar – no good at all. He shoved his hands deep in his pockets and headed off down the road, tears streaming down his face for what was to become of his friend.

For most people, their stories would have ended there but not Blind Jonah. More than anyone else, he was shocked when Arthur Thompson took him back into the fold. What good was he to himself, never mind a gangster? But he accepted and did what he was asked to do, which didn't seem much compared to the old days. Asked why he had taken Blind Jonah back, Arthur Thompson had replied, 'The blind bastard knows too much about me and my family. Better he's under my feet so I can keep an eye on him. An eye! Hee, hee. Get it? Keeping an eye on Blind Jonah.'

Some say Jonah was a jinx. Some say Arthur Thompson was cursed. Others thought there was a reckoning due for his years of cruelty. Whatever the reason, Arthur Thompson's worst years had arrived.

27

CLOSE CALLS
1990

Arthur Thompson had a debt and this time somebody was insisting it was paid. Thompson hadn't paid one bean of the money he had promised Thomas McGraw, The Licensee, for the damage caused to his pub's roof when his son, Billy, had set it on fire. McGraw had asked for the money but was treated with contempt by Thompson. He would have to be persuaded to cough up.

McGraw had just the man for the task in hand – Gordon Ross. Ross was one of the men who had tortured Blind Jonah and he was now fully ensconced in The Licensee's camp. They had a simple plan – kidnap Billy Thompson and hold him to ransom.

Billy drank regularly in the Open Arms pub in Riddrie. It was near to his home and it was also in the shadows of Barlinnie Prison, making it popular with off-duty prison staff. A quiet pub, in other words, where Billy felt safe. Bad call.

Billy was having a drink inside the pub.

'Billy Thompson?' asked one of two large men in suits.

'Aye, what's it to you?'

'Police,' said one the men, flashing some ID. 'Will you come with us, please?'

'Naw,' Billy's voice was getting louder. 'No way, man.' The men took a firm grip on Billy's arms and started moving to the door. He dug his heels in and hollered, 'No fucking way are you bizzies, man. No fucking way.' His calls were attracting attention from other drinkers and the men had to work fast. One pulled a set of handcuffs from his pocket and, after a struggle, they had Billy Thompson's wrists secure. Still, the skinny young Thompson wasn't going to leave easily so the two bogus cops were forced to move him physically, one yanking him by the cuffs, the other pushing from behind. It was clearly not a professional arrest and it was beginning to attract a lot of attention from other drinkers. This was starting to get embarrassing.

Out in the car park, Billy continued to holler for help and lean back with all his weight. A few yards ahead, a man sat in a large white van, gently revving the engine ready to take off. In the back was a sizeable carpet into which they intended to roll Billy Thompson. This would keep him secure on the journey and help to sneak him past nosy neighbours into the safe house they had ready. Once secured there, they would tie Billy Thompson up and threaten to inject him with a syringe full of red tinted fluid and tell him it was an HIV-infected heroin overdose. They knew Billy Thompson – he would freak and go to pieces.

After that, he would do as they told him to do, including putting exactly the right sense of urgency into his voice when they set up that call to his old man, Arthur. In fact, the syringe held a harmless concoction but it looked the part. The team were confident their plan would work but, first, they had to get Billy Thompson into the back of the van.

Out in the car park, things were looking bad. Big Gordon Ross was thinking of hoisting skinny Billy up and throwing him over his shoulder. Trouble was that a crowd had followed them from the pub – all heavily built men, off-duty screws from BarL.

Billy Thompson was still pulling and appealing to the crowd that these weren't real cops. A couple of the onlookers were convinced and grabbed Billy, yanking him the other way. Then, the handcuffs snapped. That had torn it. The two bogus policemen took to their heels, clambered into the van and drove off at speed, chased by the mob.

It was a close call and even Billy Thompson knew it. When he told Arthur, the old gangster took stock. This was a bad time and he was going to have to make sure his folk got through it. But he'd been there before with the Welsh Brothers and now look at them. Most of them were dead and those who'd survived were all walking wounded, capable of nothing more serious than running brothels and selling porn magazines.

There had been that time, just a few years before, with Bobby Dempster, a well-known face from the Possil end of town some people called 'The Devil'. Dempster was vicious and ambitious and didn't care who he tackled. At one point, it looked as if he'd try to take over Thompson's ground and, in truth, he frightened Arthur. He was the only man in Glasgow who did. One time, Thompson had offered Tam Bagan a lot of money to shoot Dempster but Bagan had refused. That wasn't like Bagan but, privately, Thompson didn't blame the young shootist.

Worst of all was Paul Ferris. That elder son of Thompson had set up that daft deal with three boys, Danny Lorimer, Kenny Kelly and Martin Hamilton. He'd got them to agree to kidnap Ferris and shoot him up with a heroin overdose. Daft bugger. When the boys went to Arthur to collect the promised money, he'd told him to forget about that nonsense. He had a more straightforward plan.

Arthur had given them £20,000, two good guns and ammo and had told them just to shoot the wee bastard. They agreed and went off on the hunt. Except they didn't. The buggers had just taken the money and vamoosed. They were probably frightened of Ferris and with good cause. He was the kind of wee guy that you could beat in a square go but you had to be sure to finish him off. If you didn't, he'd come back at you one night, out of the shadows, and call your number. Ferris was a dangerous one, all right.

Arthur Thompson knew he was paying a price for being top man. The money and the power were good but he had to keep alert, looking around him all the time. There would always be someone wanting to topple him and now there seemed to be a queue. For a while, he and his family would have to be careful – stay close to home, be constantly armed, trust nobody. And that's exactly what he was doing one night when it all went wrong.

Since the kidnap attempt on Billy, Arthur had made a habit of going to the Provanmill Inn for a few hours at night. As usual, he didn't have a lot to drink that night but maybe he'd had more than he realised. He was in a good mood, wandering back up Provanmill Road, only a few hundred yards from his home, The Ponderosa.

Purely by accident, two young players with grudges against Thompson were driving down Provanmill Road at the same time. They couldn't believe their good luck. There was The Godfather, on his feet and on his own. No sooner seen than decision made.

The pedestrian spotted them at the last second and his hand moved towards his gun. Too late. The driver bumped the car on to the pavement and straight over Thompson. Fifty yards on, the car pulled to a halt. Thompson lay sprawled on the ground. The two young players were hooting with laughter.

'What you up to?' the guy in the driving seat asked.

'Making sure,' answered the driver. 'Might as well.' He shoved the car into reverse and sped up the road, mounted the pavement again and over Thompson's legs. The two men sat in the car, staring down at Thompson prone on the ground. They couldn't believe their luck and were laughing, joking. 'Fuck it,' said the driver and moved the car forward again at speed and once more over the body on the ground.

'Pull in now!' ordered the passenger as the car drew to a halt.

'Why?' asked the driver who just wanted to get out of there before someone called the cops.

'Alibi time,' said the passenger without further explanation. He was the brains, renowned as a thinker. The car was reversed beyond where Thompson lay to the spot close to where they had first seen him. Stepping out of the car and pulling on gloves, the passenger stooped over Thompson's body. From the shoulder holster he pulled the loaded pistol he knew would be there. Ordering his friend from the car, he proceeded to shoot a bullet through the windscreen.

'My fucking car, you bastard, you,' screamed the driver. He loved that car. Then the passenger dropped the gun by Thompson's outstretched hand, scanned the area to be sure no one had seen and the two men were in the car and off at speed.

It had taken three minutes to kill Thompson, so they thought. It was that easy. In spite of all the warning signals he'd received lately, the old man was getting too complacent. The two young players didn't care. They were jubilant, happy. In their opinion, Thompson was long overdue and they were happy to deliver.

The business with shooting the bullet from Thompson's gun through their windscreen was straightforward. They had mowed Thompson down in a built-up area and it was likely that the noise of the car and the shooting had caused a few curtains to twitch. If they had been grassed to the cops and were lifted in the next short while, they would argue that Thompson fired on them first and they had acted in self-defence. It was an alibi they hoped they wouldn't need but, if they did, it could mean the difference between a few years in jail or spending the rest of their lives there.

The men drove across the city, heading for some isolated waste ground where they could check the car. They were buzzing with adrenalin, pumped up with the excitement of it all. The passenger was already having thoughts about how things would change now that Thompson was dead. They had driven over Thompson three times. He had to be dead.

Or was he?

28

THE LAST CURRY
1990−91

Arthur Thompson stirred on the road. He was stunned, in agony and one of his legs had been badly crushed where the car had reversed over him. But he was alive and he would live – and he had a bit of tidying up to do.

Thompson stretched one hand out, inch by inch, any movement jarring his broken bones. Finally, he found it. His gun. He had played dead while the gun had been taken from his jacket and a bullet blasted through the car windscreen. To an old player like him, even stunned, his assailants' plans were clear. If the cops got involved, they were going to claim he fired on them first and they acted in self-defence. Not while he was still breathing they weren't.

The still-warm barrel of the gun met the palm of his hand. Twirling it round, Thompson grasped the handle, rolled himself on to one elbow and threw the gun as far as he could in the direction of the long grass of the scrubland. Then he passed out.

The next thing Thompson knew he was coming to, still on the road, and leaning over him was a familiar face wearing his usual dark glasses.

'Jonah, son, I've had an accident,' Thompson wheezed as if even a blind man couldn't work that out. 'Give us a hand, son. I'm going to need a doctor.'

Arthur Thompson had survived yet another hit. Of all the attempts to kill him, this was the one that should have succeeded. The driver was good and knew what he was doing. But on that first blow, Thompson had somehow fallen underneath a fence that the car had also brought down. So, when the vehicle was then reversed over him, the fence helped spread the weight and reduce the damage to his body. It's the kind of trick strong men use in circuses when buses are driven over their bodies on the ground. But, with Thompson, it wasn't a trick – it was sheer luck.

Thompson not only survived – he changed. Those who knew him well say that the process started from the time he was shot in the groin and it then progressed after his near-death brush with the car. He became more open to the media, giving several polite interviews in which he tried to play down his current involvement in crime. He'd say that the east end of Glasgow was a hard place when he was growing up and he had earned his reputation at that time. But, then, he'd always remind the journos that he hadn't been found guilty of any offence in over twenty years. All true, of course, but no one entirely believed him.

It was as if, with Margaret's death and his own close calls, Thompson had suddenly become aware of his mortality – an aspect he had disregarded for most of his life. The bullet to the groin and his leg being crushed under that car also left him with permanent physical ailments that his tough constitution had previously avoided sustaining through his violent career.

Thompson even claimed Disability Benefit. Not that he was a stranger to signing on as unemployed and had done that most of his life. So why Disability? Because it paid a few pounds more per week? It was unlikely those few quid would be an attraction even to someone so fond of money as Thompson. It was probably an acknowledgement that he was no longer as strong as he once was and now, of course, he was sixty-one years old and getting on. Worse still, his old detective pal Charlie Craig wasn't around and he'd clearly been given the shoulder by MI5. Things had to change.

It was around 1990–91 that Thompson started supporting good causes. He had always been one to attend smokers or social occasions but usually it would be boxing nights run by folk like his close friend the boxing promoter Alex Morrison or Spot Henry, the street player and brothel owner. His attendance with his entourage was in order that he was seen by other players as much as it was for the pleasure of watching the sport. But now, he was beginning to buy tables at dinners to raise money for children in need or other good causes and, as a result, was rubbing shoulders with TV celebrities, footballers, lawyers and journalists.

Slowly the view of Arthur Thompson as the old-time benign Godfather emerged. A mythical figure who was a hard man but who loved kids and puppy dogs and protected women and old folk. It was an image he deliberately helped to create, of course, and his continuing lack of charges and convictions went a long way to fostering it. It may have convinced the newspaper-reading public but it didn't fool the street players one bit.

After he had been run over, the cops found the car they believed had been involved in the hit. Paul Ferris and Tam Bagan were investigated as two young players who had ongoing disputes with Thompson. But Arthur didn't make a formal complaint and the cops couldn't find forensic evidence to link Ferris or Bagan with the crime scene that night. So no one was charged.

That Arthur Thompson knew who was in the car that night there is absolutely no doubt. According to the code of the street, the matter would be dealt with on the street. It would only be a matter of time before Thompson acted. Or so the faces expected.

One night, a few weeks after the hit-and-run, someone took a potshot at Tam Bagan as he drove in his Cavalier. Bagan was unhurt but a full forensic check of the bullet holes revealed something shocking. The gun was the one taken from

Thompson the night he was run over, the one the two young players had fired through the windscreen to give them the option of saying Thompson had shot at them first, the one that Thompson had then thrown into the long grass. It had been found by the cops and was revealed to have originated from MI5. How did Thompson come to have it in the first place? How did it fall back into the hands of a hit man? Who was the hit man? Was it Thompson or someone official? These questions have never been answered.

In spite of the hullabaloo he had created every day of his jail term, Fatboy had been moved from the grim environment of Peterhead Prison to an open jail, Noranside, near Brechin in Angus. The move was part of his preparation for release, the usual arrangements that had to be followed for someone who was serving a lengthy sentence. Fatboy was coming home.

Young Thompson obeyed all the rules expected of him and, according to prison staff, he progressed well. Having complied with the system, he was allowed weekend leave so he could gradually readjust to life back home. Well, that was the theory.

It seems strange that everyone knew Fatboy was still ranting on about his hit list of people who he would have killed as soon as he was at liberty and yet he was allowed to head back to freedom and Glasgow. By now, his list was only comprised of street players. At the top were Paul Ferris, Tam Bagan and anyone associated with them. What were the authorities doing? Watching and waiting to see if Fatboy would act on his boasts?

On 17 August 1991, Fatboy was enjoying his first spell of weekend leave, staying at his wing of The Ponderosa with his common-law wife Catherine. Of course, the proximity to his mother and father meant that he spent a great deal of time in the old man's company.

That first afternoon, you'd expect a man who'd been away for years to want some private, intimate time with his wife. Not young Thompson. Fatboy intended going to the Provanmill Inn for a few drinks. But, first, he stopped by Crocket's, the ironmonger's shop, where he bought the essential bits and bobs he needed to make a pistol. On his next trip home, he'd go to another store and buy the rest. Fatboy was back to his old tricks and he had plans.

In the Provanmill Inn, many of the regulars treated his homecoming as some cause for celebration and Fatboy was soaking up the attention. At one point, with the full attention of the bar, he unfolded several sheets of paper and treated everyone listening to the latest edition of his hit list. Paul Ferris, Tam Bagan, Jaimba McLean, Bobby Glover, Joe Hanlon . . .

According to Fatboy, in the years he had been in jail, nothing had changed. Maybe he hadn't been on the scene but now that was all going to be put right – in double-quick time. The Thompsons ruled Glasgow and now a few people were about to pay the ultimate price. The Godfather ruled Glasgow and he was The Godfather's son.

As in prison, as on the street, word spread fast. Fatboy Thompson was coming out and he was going to stir up some serious trouble. Something had to be done.

That night, Fatboy went with his parents to one of the top curry houses in Glasgow, the Café India at Charing Cross in the city centre. They served his favourite kind of food and their standards were high. It was an excellent supper. Not wanting to stay out late, they travelled home to The Ponderosa before it got too dark. It had been a relaxed day and a good night. Fatboy was looking forward to his final release date.

By 10 p.m., it was dark and the Thompson Family were locked up securely in the comfort of their homes for the night. Safe and sound. At the other side of Provanmill Road, about forty yards away, three pairs of eyes watched both wings of The Ponderosa. They were waiting for something to happen and they wouldn't have to wait for long. They knew that the Fatboy had paid his old man a visit. They knew everything the Thompsons had done that day.

A short while later, the front door of Arthur's house opened and out stepped Fatboy, just as The Apprentice knew he would. Quickly, noiselessly, The Apprentice slipped out of the bushes and headed across the street. Behind him, in their car, two Londoners slipped the safety catches off their guns and waited. The three had worked together before on jobs in London. All young, all good at what they did, they had realised they took all the risks but it was older people like Thompson who took the biggest cuts. Now they worked independently and sometimes, like that night, for nothing. Some things were worth doing for their own sakes.

The Apprentice slipped his .22 with the silencer out of his waistband and, holding it down by his side, headed towards Fatboy. This was the dangerous time – getting to him. Arthur Thompson might be getting old but he was a lethal man all the same. He would know that his oldest son was vulnerable on these visits home. Maybe he was sitting by his window watching the street from behind the curtains. You didn't survive to his age in this business without being alert. The Licensee thanked God that Thompson hadn't invested in all the security systems he had installed in his own house. If he had, this hit would not have been possible. Behind him, The Apprentice knew that one Londoner would have his long-range rifle trained on this scene. If Arthur Thompson charged out, he would be shot before he reached the pavement.

Fatboy was halfway to his own front door, only thirty yards away, when he spotted The Apprentice and froze. Now calm, slow and steady, the hit man walked towards his target, holding the gun in front of him with two hands. The long snout of the barrel and silencer looked deadly and pointed straight at Fatboy's head.

'You'd better get your father to get you out of this, you fat bastard,' cursed The Apprentice. On such jobs he had a rule never to speak – but this was personal and it was showing. He had to try to hold his discipline. Even in the weak, yellow, shimmering arch from a nearby streetlight, The Apprentice thought he saw Fatboy blanch.

'Just you wait here. I'm going to get my father,' spluttered Fatboy, starting to turn. Another time another night, The Apprentice would have gone for the old man too. But this was about the son and the son it would be. He fired at Fatboy's head.

When the first bullet hit Fatboy's cheek, he spun round and fell forward on to the ground. The wounded man scrambled to his knees and started crawling, crying out with high-pitched yelps. In his confusion, he was making towards his own house.

As the second bullet smashed through Fatboy's rib cage and punctured a lung, he collapsed face down on the pavement with a dull thump. He wasn't going anywhere now.

The Apprentice knew exactly where the third shot was going – up Fatboy's arse. This wasn't symbolic or carrying any meaning. The Apprentice was a professional and knew a bullet up the anus would undoubtedly destroy vital organs. In Fatboy's case, the slug went straight through his stomach and into his heart. One bullet to either could be fatal. He had hit two jackpots for the price of one.

Another bullet to the head would seal the deal. It was always good to make sure and The Apprentice considered stooping and firing at close range. But Fatboy was dying, that was obvious, and the silencer hadn't sounded as effective as it should have been in the empty night-time streets. Job done. Time to split.

Tracey Thompson had heard the shots. By the time she rushed out of the front door, The Apprentice and his London partners were well away. Spotting her brother lying on the ground, she screamed, 'What's happened?' Leaning down to him, she cradled his head.

'I've been shot, hen,' wheezed Fatboy. 'I think I'm going to collapse.'

In a flash, Arthur, Rita, Billy and the rest of the Thompson crew were out on the street. It was obvious Fatboy needed immediate hospital attention. No time to wait for an ambulance. Gun in hand, Arthur Thompson scoured the street, his teeth gritted, wishing that the gunman would come out of the shadows, gun blazing at him. He needed to hurt someone.

They carried Fatboy to his brother Billy's car and sped to the Royal Infirmary in convoy. At 00.18 on 18 August, forty minutes after his admission, the doctors declared that Fatboy Thompson was dead. Only then were the cops called and that was by the hospital staff, of course.

By then, The Apprentice and his team were well into their plan. Their car had been squashed in a scrapyard, the London men were on the M74 driving south and The Apprentice was in a taxi heading to where he had left his car primed to go. That night, he would drive to Manchester, catch a flight to Amsterdam and stay for a month or so. That would be no hardship – Amsterdam was one of his favourite cities.

Outside the Royal Infirmary, Arthur and Billy Thompson stood chatting and smoking. Their kith and kin lay dead inside, their women folk weeping and wailing. Yards away, at the hospital front door, two uniformed cops stood on guard in case the killer came calling again. Billy, in shock and trembling, spoke at great length over and over about what had happened and how it had been possible. Arthur said nothing, keeping his thoughts to himself. At last Billy raised his voice and shouted, 'I know who the fuck killed my brother.' The cops looked his way and he looked back as he continued, 'It must have been Paul Ferris.'

Arthur Thompson said nothing but just nodded his head.

Paul Ferris was travelling in a hackney cab through the east end. He'd flown up from London earlier that day for a bit of family business and to spend time with some friends. As the cab passed the Caravel, he couldn't ignore the crowd gathered outside it or the fact that it was crawling with cops. He told the driver to pull in so he could find out what the fuss was about.

'Have you heard the news?' asked one familiar face.

'No, what's happened?' asked Ferris.

'Arthur Thompson is dead.'

Ferris didn't know whether to laugh or cry. What he did know was that with all those bizzies swarming about the place, it wasn't safe for him to hang around. He also knew he was in big trouble. Just how big he would soon discover.

29

JUDAS IN A FROCK
1991

The morning after Fatboy's death, Paul Ferris was on the early shuttle back to London a lot sooner than he had planned. Now spending a great deal of his time working with the London teams, he had travelled up the day before to see to some business and spend time with his son, Paul Junior. Ferris and his boy's mother, Anne Marie, had separated but were still on good terms. Spending a few days in Glasgow was what he had planned but the murder of Fatboy had changed all of that.

The night before, when Ferris had stopped his cab outside the Caravel to see what the fuss was about, he discovered it was caused by another death. A soldier, Robert Mills, had been stabbed to death. By all accounts Mills was a Falklands veteran and a bit of a hero but few would recall his killing. All that folk could talk about was who killed Fatboy Thompson that same night and what his father, Arthur, would do now.

Later, Ferris would recount that, at first, he assumed Arthur Thompson Senior had been killed, believing Fatboy was still in jail. It was a perspective Glasgow cops had already dismissed without hearing it. They had Ferris's name at the top of their wanted list and that was that.

On the days after Fatboy's death, a stream of well-wishers turned up at The Ponderosa to pay their condolences to Arthur Thompson. Those in the know would have recognised many faces from the annals of crime, lower-level players who had worked with Thompson and even one or two from the C-list celebrity circuit in Scotland. Most folk wouldn't have recognised the tall, well-built man with short hair and immaculate black suit and black tie. The man was clearly upset and, as he left The Ponderosa, he wiped tears from his eyes. No problem there. Death is a time for tearful mourning. But this guy was a cop and, although lowly in rank, he was going to play a key role in the dramatic events that would unfold.

Two weeks later, Paul Ferris and Bobby Glover were arrested. Interrogated for hours about Fatboy's death and several other shootings, they were eventually thrown into the segregation unit at Barlinnie and charged with the knee-capping of a man called William Gillen. But it wasn't just that charge the cops had in mind when they jailed them. Both Ferris and Glover were designated as Category A prisoners which was unusual for men convicted of no offence. It meant that they were considered at risk of escaping and a potential danger to the general public. This was a strange call since they hadn't even been proven guilty of any misdemeanour.

A week later, they were taken to Kilmarnock Sheriff Court for a hearing. Gillen had been knee-capped in a lay-by near there so the offence fell under the jurisdiction of that court. Manhandled by the cops, deprived of cigarettes and having had some notes he had made for his court appearance confiscated, Ferris created a rumpus. In a separate cell, the more laid-back Bobby Glover tried to ease his good friend out of his anger by singing his favourite song, 'Mack the Knife'. Bobby had a rich baritone voice and sang the big band songs in pubs and clubs at the slightest opportunity. The ploy worked and the last Ferris heard was Bobby laughing and still singing as he was led away to the courtroom.

Bobby Glover was released that day on a Procurator Fiscal's decision. The PF is the prosecutor in Scottish courts and has the right to drop charges at any time – although offering a reason for doing so is not obligatory. In the face of how he was treated initially, it seemed a contradictory decision. Glover went from a maximum security risk prisoner under Category A and held in isolation in the most impregnable closed unit in Scotland one minute to free man the next. It was a huge leap and one that has never been publicly explained.

Ferris was sent back to the segregation unit at Barlinnie and the tongues started to wag. Did he or didn't he? If he did, why just kill Fatboy and not Arthur as well? If he didn't, who did? Who else had a reason for killing Fatboy? Those who thought they knew, but didn't, kept coming back to the answer – Ferris. Well, everyone knew he was capable of such a hit if he had wanted to do it. His reputation was well established. But street players knew better than to look at only one man. They knew the list of Arthur Thompson's enemies was endless. Then again, he had some unexpected friends as well.

Publicly, Arthur Thompson said nothing. Among his close associates, it was a different matter. Thompson was badly hurt by his son's murder. Not just because he was fond of all his kids but also that his elder boy was slaughtered practically at his front door, where he was meant to be safe. What did that tell the world?

With a few drinks in him, Thompson would tell close friends that he blamed Paul Ferris for the shooting. And, those days, wherever Paul Ferris went so too did Bobby Glover and Joe Hanlon. Arthur Thompson couldn't allow that to pass or he was finished. He was about to call on some weird allies.

William Lobban was a strange young man. Super-fit, he had a smooth, narrow-eyed faced. Some say he looked sexless, neutral. Others thought that some genetics had slipped. Lobban certainly had some interesting relatives. Lobban's mother's maiden name was Sylvia Manson – she was the sister of Billy Manson, a long-term associate of Arthur

Thompson. Billy Manson treated Lobban like a son and he reciprocated by doing anything the older man asked. Arthur Thompson asked him to oblige with some assistance in a little business and Manson never refused Thompson. William Lobban never refused Billy Manson. Arthur Thompson knew this fine well.

A year before, Lobban had been on the run from an English prison for a long time. At one time, he dressed up as a woman, a bit of a habit of his, to avoid detection. On another occasion, he donned women's gear yet again to carry out a robbery. The ploy earned him the nickname Tootsie in the media and on the street.

The year before, Lobban had arrived in Glasgow on the run and he needed shelter. Ferris and Glover were asked to help and, as is the expected code, immediately agreed even though they didn't know the young man. They gave Lobban a safe flat, an assumed name and made sure he had enough money. The two men didn't expect gratitude or thanks but neither did they expect moans or complaints. But that's what William Lobban gave them.

Almost immediately Lobban groaned and muttered about not getting out, about having spent all the cash they gave him and about being lonely. Although being in hiding can be mind-numbing, it is usually seen as a small price to pay to evade capture and jail. Lobban, it seems, had no patience or discipline at all.

No one would have blamed Ferris and Glover for writing off Lobban as an ungrateful sod and kicking him out of his free flat and subsidised existence. Instead, Bobby and his wife, Eileen, showed kindness above and beyond the call of any code. Lobban was invited to move in with the Glovers and their family – an offer he grabbed with two hands. For many months, he lived in the Glovers' home, sharing their food, their leisure, their time. He made only one small gesture of thanks to them by doing occasional babysitting. The

Glovers were happy to trust their young boy to his care and did so without looking for any recompense. They felt sorry for the young man and were glad to be able to help. It was typical of Bobby and Eileen Glover.

One night, three weeks after Fatboy's murder, the phone rang in the Glovers' home. Eileen answered and was greeted by the familiar voice of William Lobban who wanted to talk to Bobby. After being on the phone for a short time, Bobby told his wife he had to go out to a meeting. He didn't say who he was meeting or where and she did not ask. It wasn't the done thing.

Bobby's car was being held by the police in connection with the alleged knee-capping of William Gillen so he phoned his mate Joe Hanlon and asked if he would drive him. Of course, Joe would and he was soon at the front door in his blue Ford Orion.

With the murder of Fatboy and their friend Paul Ferris in jail, Eileen Glover was nervous and wary for her man – as any sensible person would be. But he would be in the best of hands with Joe, she reassured herself. Besides, they all knew that both Bobby and Joe were under twenty-four-hour police surveillance. The cops had hardly endeavoured to be discreet. By phoning Joe Hanlon for a lift, Bobby Glover was deliberately making no effort to conceal the meeting from his police tail. While the constantly hovering, snooping cops were an annoying irritation, Bobby and Joe thought at least it would keep them safe from attack.

Bobby and Joe were soon to find out that the Judas's work was done. What exactly happened next? You have a choice.

30

HOWL – ONE
1991

No one who was there that night is able or willing to talk. But there are those who heard the confidences of some and have shared their understanding of what happened. This is their account.

Bobby and Joe rolled up to the meeting place, a piece of rough ground at the rear of a well-known east-end pub. They were to meet William Lobban and Paul Hamilton but other, unexpected, company was also there – Frank McPhie, an infamous street player from Maryhill. McPhie was the one who was truly known as The Iceman and for two good reasons. Early on, he had realised the profit that could be made out of ice-cream vans serving the shop-starved schemes of Glasgow. But there was a more sinister reason – he was a cold-hearted, professional hit man.

McPhie was also a major drugs dealer, specialising in trade with the Irish gangs. A few years before, he had been arrested in possession of several kilos of cocaine and duly charged. Caught cold, it looked like he was going to go down for over ten years. Then he found a way out.

Thomas McGraw, The Licensee, had a wee arrangement with the cops that was to their mutual benefit. The chief constable of that time, Leslie Sharp, was keen on gun amnesties and pressurised his troops to get as many weapons handed in as possible. They duly obliged.

Through The Licensee, an individual could make a certain amount of illegal guns available to cops in exchange for charges being deleted. It was a simple trade-off and one nobody minded too much about. McPhie bought a stack of guns from a dealer and buried it at a specified gravestone in the cemetery near the Caravel. None of these arms had ever been used on the street, of course, and there was plenty more where they came from. But it made the cops look good and it got Frank McPhie off the drugs charges. But that put him in an even more dangerous position – in debt to The Licensee.

As Joe Hanlon drove his Ford Orion on to the waste ground, Bobby Glover nodded at Paul Hamilton and William Lobban who were standing there waiting, as arranged. Hamilton was a local player. He was independent although, along with many other street players, he sometimes worked for McGraw, The Licensee. As Hamilton opened the rear door and clambered in, Frank McPhie skipped round from the gable of the bar and into the car through the other rear door.

'How ye doing?' he asked, almost perkily, as he jabbed the barrel of a sawn-off shotgun at the two men.

'What the fuck?' Joe spun round in the seat, only to have the shotgun shoved close to his face.

'Time for a drive, boys,' said McPhie. 'Cracking day for a drive.'

Outside the car, William Lobban had turned, taken to his heels and sprinted away. Was he scared that Bobby Glover, who had shown him so much kindness, would look at him? Could he not face gentle Bobby's gaze? Did he suffer some guilt? Who knows? Who cares? The deed was done – the Judas kiss planted.

Bobby and Joe were unarmed. They couldn't be anything else while they were under such close police scrutiny. As

McPhie gave the directions, Joe drove and he would have been gripping the steering wheel and clenching his teeth. And it would have been his style to have turned and smashed McPhie in the face. He knew he could take him. All he needed was one chance.

Bobby would have been calmer – as if *he* was the one in control, not the guy in the back seat with the shooter. He could also have taken McPhie with ease. Later, Ferris would say that, while the world seemed to think he was the main man of that team, it was actually Bobby Glover. Not for nothing were the three amigos of Ferris, Glover and Hanlon so respected on the street.

Cool Bobby Glover would have reckoned that, any minute now, they'd be pulled in by the cops who were constantly tailing Joe and him.

'Silly fuckers,' he would have said to himself, referring to McPhie and Hamilton, 'you should have done your homework.' But there were no cops.

McPhie gave directions and they ended up on a country road to the north of Glasgow near Gartcosh. 'Pull in at this opening,' ordered McPhie. It was the wide entrance to a field, shielded from the quiet country lane by trees and bushes and nothing on the other side except long grass and distant hills. Forty yards into the field was an abandoned rust-red tractor that looked as if it hadn't seen service for decades. Next to it were some agricultural implements in the same colour scheme and behind them was a blue transit van. Paul Hamilton's van for the night.

Joe didn't like this one bit. Bobby had now realised that, for the first time in weeks, the cops weren't with them. But sitting in the front of a car, with a sawn-off pointing at you from the rear, was too weak a position. Any movement and you were a dead man. Paul Hamilton also had a gun, a pistol, trained on them. Bobby and Joe didn't think much of Hamilton but, when he was sitting behind them with a loaded gun, well, that was a different matter. A blind man could have killed them from there.

Eventually, a car pulled up. It was not one Bobby and Joe would have recognised but the driver was all too familiar. Arthur Thompson had arrived to take revenge for the killing of his boy.

Thompson looked his usual dapper self. A little bit paler and drawn about the face but still smart, well-groomed. Slowly, he got out of the driver's seat, stood erect, stretching his back and adjusting his suit jacket. Then he started to walk slowly towards the Ford Orion.

Joe had had enough. He yanked open his door and sprinted. Within seconds, Frank McPhie was out of the car and he blasted him in the back. One shot and Joe Hanlon fell. One of the toughest men on Glasgow's streets brought to earth by a single shot.

Now the team had to act quickly. They might have been in the country but someone might still have heard them. Frank McPhie was nothing if not professional. 'Out the car, you,' he barked at Bobby Glover, waving the gun in his direction. Bobby Glover wasn't scared of anything or anyone but, sitting there, he must have known what was coming. They couldn't shoot Joe without having to shoot him too because, as long as Bobby lived, they knew he would hunt them down for killing Joe. People who knew Bobby Glover well reckon that, although Bobby knew he was going to die and was, for once, totally helpless, he would have got out of that car with dignity. Joe was still alive. If his pal had uttered a noise, Bobby would have shouted out something reassuring, something positive. Glover had faced what seemed like certain death before. He had handled such situations in the same manner and won out. On those occasions, he had turned the tables and walked away, often with a wry smile. Why should he have seen this one as any different?

McPhie had ordered Bobby to walk so he chose to walk in Joe's direction. He didn't reach his mate. McPhie shot him in the back. The two men lay wounded, but alive and immobilised, yards from each other.

Then Arthur Thompson walked up. 'I killed your father,' he muttered to Joe, as he leaned over him. 'He took fucking ages to go. You should have heard him gurgle.' Joe's father had been choked to death, having had a fish supper, wrappings and all, stuck down his throat. Then, Thompson shot Joe in the head at close range.

'Your pal Ferris is next,' he said to Bobby. 'You're lucky – he's getting it slow.' Then he shot Bobby in the head at point blank range.

Beside the Ford Orion, Paul Hamilton, pistol still in one hand, his other on the car roof, leaned over and retched. Arthur Thompson, straight-faced as ever, looked at him with contempt and handed Frank McPhie the pistol.

'Make sure that cunt's fit to drive before you leave,' he told McPhie, nodding in Hamilton's direction. He then got into his own car. Opening the window and revving up the engine, he shouted to McPhie, 'Two down, one to go, Frank.' And he drove out of the field with a cheery wave.

The account makes sense. Those characters might well have been involved in such acts for Thompson. Some boasted about it later, others went into hiding. But, since this account has been published, objections have come from one place only – the police.

The Glasgow cops have made no official response, of course. That's not their way. Unofficial communication? Now that's a different matter.

One anonymous source claims that Thompson couldn't have been at the shooting since there was a twenty-four-hour guard on his house at that time. Two cops sat outside his front door and logged seeing him on at least seven different occasions through the evening.

But they either didn't know or chose to forget that Thompson had an escape route. An underground tunnel joined his house to Fatboy's. He could slip down, along to the other house, out the back and into a lane that in seconds would take him to another street. There a car would have been parked in advance. In he'd hop and off he'd go.

We don't know if he did that night, of course. But we do know that he'd used that escape route on many other occasions. The place it's alleged Bobby and Joe were led to in this account is a mere ten minutes' drive from The Ponderosa, if that. Thompson could have slipped out of his house, done the evil deed and be back home waving at the cops through his front window in less than half an hour.

So maybe that anonymous cop's objections are well meant but they don't dismiss this account. Yet any communication from the police about Bobby and Joe's murder should be treated seriously for one good reason – they were meant to be watching the pair that night. The cops should know what happened. Someone on the inside who agreed decided to share some key information. Their account follows.

31

HOWL – TWO
1991

Sketches were passed to certain parties. Sketches looking for all the world like artist's impressions – the way the police do when they have a witness account of a serious incident. Sketches that tell those in the know who, where and when. That tell you this:

Maybe William Lobban or his paymaster was lucky or clever. But when he made that call about some meeting and Bobby and Joe setting off, it was change-of-shift time for the cops. We can slag them off for leaving the two men at all. But, if this account is true, maybe previous suspicions that the cops deliberately turned a blind eye aren't accurate. Well, not on that night. Maybe the cops weren't corrupt, just incompetent. Was it that simple?

Bobby and Joe drove to some place in the east end where they were met by Lobban and his uncle, Billy Manson. Lobban and Manson got into the back of Joe's car and they drove on to a warehouse and yard in a small industrial estate. We do know that the guy who rented that warehouse had been warned at gunpoint to stay away and he had been forced to hand over his keys.

Once in the yard, Lobban locked the gates and the four sat in the car and chatted but not for long. Lobban and Manson pulled pistols. From behind, Bobby, in the passenger seat, got it first and then Joe.

Later, help arrived for Manson and Lobban but we don't know who from the drawings. What we do know is a van like one driven by Paul Hamilton was parked in the yard and the two pals' bodies were transferred to it.

We do know that the bodies were moved about the city that night in the back of the van. From the drawings, we can see that it wasn't a Ford Transit, as people have come to believe, but another model like a Mercedes. That has also been confirmed by the anonymous police contact.

Usually, in hits, the killing happens and the hit men get the hell away from the victims as fast as they can. This was different. All that driving around the city with two murder victims in the back took nerve, confidence, certainty that the cops weren't going to bother them. We have to ask why?

A few days later, the guy who hired the yard was given two options – leave town or kiss goodbye to life. He left town.

William Lobban also left Glasgow and fast, heading south as far as his Judas's pieces of silver would carry him. Billy Manson didn't go quite as far but took a wee holiday in a caravan owned by boxing promoter and good pal of Thompson, Alex Morrison. A holiday he told no one else about. Some call it hiding.

The guns were given to The Licensee to dispose of. As we'll find out later he didn't make too good a job of it.

This so-called official account of Bobby and Joe's murders makes sense. If the police know that much about the killings what else do they know that hasn't been leaked? What more do they know that they haven't told the Glover and Hanlon families? The full truth will one day emerge.

If this version is closer to what happened that night, did Arthur Thompson have anything to do with it? Didn't he always?

However the killings happened, two men were dead. Assassinated in revenge that very night for the killing of

Fatboy Thompson. In another part of the city, their best pal was having problems of his own.

In Barlinnie segregation unit, Paul Ferris was settling down to yet another night of disruptions. Screws in the employ of Arthur Thompson had been making his life hell. When he was reading, the lights were put out. When he was sleeping, the lights were switched on. Every fifteen minutes of every day, the spy hatch was rattled and the door booted. Burnt papers were stuck under his cell door, filling the airless box with rancid smoke.

Ferris cursed and swore but he was determined not to lose the place. He knew what this game was about. They were wearing him down, making him weak for his trial. He wasn't going to allow that to happen. Now he had been charged with the knee-capping and threatened with a stack of other charges, it was serious. Eventually, he fell asleep, thinking he had to keep strong because the trial was the most important challenge in his life.

Little did he know.

32

BLACK TIES AND BROWN
ENVELOPES
1991

It was early on the morning of Fatboy Thompson's funeral and Arthur Thompson was as happy as it is possible to be on such an occasion. His boy was dead – nothing would change that – but he'd drawn some retribution, some cold revenge, and he wasn't even finished.

There was going to be a grand show-up for the funeral – Arthur had seen to that. He'd made some calls to London, Liverpool, Manchester and Newcastle and other places too – wherever he had contacts and associates. He didn't ask them to come to the funeral, of course – that wouldn't be on. It was like when he phoned Bob Kelly, a well-known player from Newcastle. All he had said was that it might be to his benefit to be in Glasgow on that particular day. Kelly was going to bring Phillip Abbadon and a couple of Geordie mates who Arthur had never heard of. It didn't matter.

That group would add to the good show he reckoned his boy deserved. It would be worth Kelly's time. Arthur Thompson would slip him £500 for his attendance as he would numerous other faces who turned up on his invite. Thompson saw nothing wrong with paying folk to go to Fatboy's funeral. If he hadn't done so, it would have been a sparse showing. But Arthur had another surprise for the mourners. This was one they would enjoy, he was certain of that.

Eileen Glover was worried sick. Bobby had said he would be back in twenty minutes and he hadn't come home all night. It wasn't like him not to phone to let her know – not like him at all.

That's when Thomas McGraw, The Licensee, arrived at her door with bad news. 'Your man's dead,' said McGraw. 'He's lying in a car outside the Cottage Bar.'

The dread that had been hanging around Eileen like a bad taste all night suddenly kicked her in the stomach. She took off, speeding to the Cottage Bar as quickly as possible. Maybe there had been some mistake. Perhaps McGraw had got it wrong. She hadn't waited to ask him how he had heard about Bobby.

When Eileen arrived at the Cottage Bar, her worst fears seemed set to be confirmed. The place was crawling with police and their cars and a cordon of blue uniforms was holding back onlookers. Eileen pushed and shoved through the crowd and headed towards the blue Ford Orion when a policeman grabbed her by the shoulder.

'Let me through,' she pleaded, 'that's my man in that motor.'

'What's your man's name?' asked the cop, perplexed.

'Bobby. Bobby Glover,' she sobbed, now knowing the worst was bound to be true.

'You'll have to come with me,' said the cop, gently but insistently. It wasn't that he knew he was dealing with a widow. In fact, when Eileen Glover arrived at the Cottage Bar, the police had yet to identify the two dead men. They wanted to know how Eileen knew Bobby was dead before they did. She wanted to know how The Licensee had known even before that.

Eileen Glover wasn't allowed to grieve that day. She was taken to Shettleston Police Station and, for the next six hours, she was grilled about the death of her man. The cops were interviewing the wrong person.

The night Bobby and Joe were summarily executed, Arthur Thompson, arranged the destruction of a car at one of his own scrapyards. A strange thing to do the night before his son's funeral unless that was the car he had driven to the killings – or someone else had used in that connection. It was the night before his boy's funeral and he should spend time with Rita and the family but Billy Thompson wasn't going to be at home with them – he had an appointment.

Bobby and Joe's bodies were loaded into the back of the blue van and driven by Paul Hamilton to McGraw's pub, the Caravel. McPhie or Manson followed him in Joe's Ford Orion. It was late and the pub was closed except for a private wake. The two bodies were laid out and then The Licensee phoned The Ponderosa. A delegation, including Billy Thompson, attended so they too could see for themselves that the two men were dead.

After that disgusting ceremony, the bodies were loaded into the back of the blue van and driven to the yard of the warehouse and left overnight. We now know this to be true.

Before dawn, the van was driven to the Cottage Bar. There, on Darleith Street, the two men were dumped in Joe's Ford Orion. The spot was outside Bobby Glover's bar and directly on the route of Fatboy's funeral cortège. There was nothing accidental about where they had left the bodies.

Bobby was in a crumpled heap on the floor, wedged between the back and front seats. Joe's once-strong body was buckled in the footwells at the front. That's how they were discovered, early that morning, by Alan Cross, the charge-hand at the Cottage Bar.

Later that day, Paul Ferris was in his segregated cell, working through some legal papers. For once, the lights were on and he could see to read. Heavy footsteps outside stopped at his door. Ferris braced himself for some interruption or maybe sudden darkness. Instead, a newspaper was pushed under the cell door. At first he assumed it was just another sick joke. But he was bored so he lifted the paper and read . . . that his two best friends had been murdered.

Unashamedly, Ferris howled in grief, anger and guilt. Grief for his pals. Anger against the murderers. Guilt because he hadn't been there to help and protect them. He howled like a baby – except when the screws looked in. He would never weep in front of them.

All those years of paying backhanders to prison staff had served Arthur Thompson well. It helped his older boy when he was jailed and now it was tormenting Ferris, the man he believed killed his son. Worth every penny and he was only starting.

Fatboy's funeral was well enough attended and looked the part of a gangland gathering. Large black cars, full of heavy-set men with scarred faces and grim looks, rolled up to Riddrie Park Cemetery adjacent to The Ponderosa. The cops were on display big time and checked every individual seeking access to the burial ground.

Over fifty CID and 200 uniformed cops were investigating Fatboy's killing, making it one of the biggest investigations in Scottish history. This was being treated as deadly serious by the cops. With the hit on Fatboy and the murders of Bobby and Joe, the cops accepted that Glasgow was at war. The streets would burn – that was the prediction carried by most of the newspapers and the police didn't disagree.

The event passed without incident. The Great Train Robber Buster Edwards was there as was London face Ted Dennis, both close friends of Thompson. Messages of condolence were passed from the Kray Twins who were currently languishing in jail. Local players who had worked with Thompson were in attendance, as were younger blokes like Grant McIntosh from Paisley, Blind Jonah and Paul Hamilton as well as more senior Thompson regulars such as Frank Carberry and Billy Manson. Even Thomas McGraw, The Licensee, turned up with his usual entourage of heavies.

Afterwards, Arthur Thompson circulated among the mourners, shaking hands and handing out small envelopes. Bob Kelly wasn't the only one to get a £500 thank you from Thompson for attending. All the outside players did. It was a new slant on professional mourning.

As people still thronged around, they noticed Arthur Thompson go and chat to a policeman on duty. They seemed friendly, familiar, but, then, Thompson was always polite to the cops. No one thought anything of it till Thompson had to leave. As he walked past him, the cop took hold of his arm. 'Nice one last night, big man,' the cop smiled.

Thompson grinned back and nodded. That was a cop who should have been working the night before on the surveillance of Bobby Glover and Joe Hanlon – one of the cops who lost them and left them to be slaughtered.

Immediately, there was public panic about gangland Glasgow at war. Every day, the front pages of every newspaper were filled with new angles. It made the UK news and even the London-based broadsheets were reporting on the story. The cops were under tremendous public and political pressure to demonstrate they were in control – so they arranged a show.

Two days after Fatboy's funeral, the press were alerted to be on standby early the next morning. Hundreds of armed cops, several helicopters and armed response vehicles hit The Ponderosa just after dawn.

When Rita Thompson answered the door, she could see the sniper barrels trained on her, hear the Alsatian dogs barking round the corner and the buzz of the helicopter above. Was she overawed? Was she hell? As usual, she gave the cops a tongue-lashing extraordinaire and continued to do so till Arthur told her to be quiet. 'They're only doing their jobs, Rita,' he had said.

The search squad went through both wings of The Ponderosa carefully and efficiently. With all the talk that

Arthur Thompson had arranged for Bobby and Joe to be killed, top of the cops' search list was guns and ammunition.

In this, they were to be disappointed but not surprised. They had orchestrated the search as a publicity exercise rather than a top-secret operation. If Arthur Thompson hadn't known of the search in advance, then he would have wasted a lot of money over the years on brown envelopes to rogue cops and the occasional compromised journalist.

No guns were found but there was one discovery – the tunnel running from Arthur's wing of The Ponderosa to Fatboy's. Though it had been built years before, it was the first time the police had discovered that tunnel in spite of having searched The Ponderosa numerous times. How could they miss a tunnel? This time they were serious, then. Down there, they would normally have found a substantial arsenal and a load of drugs but all they discovered this time was a lonely bullet-proof vest and a small amount of cannabis – one perfectly legal, the other totally trivial. So little was found that no charges were made. That wasn't the point of the exercise.

Arthur Thompson's legal eagle, Joe Beltrami, went on to complain to Strathclyde Police about how certain aspects of the search were handled. No doubt Arthur was happy that the cops had no result but he was also very unhappy that his name and his house had ended up splattered all over the media again. As of now, he was going to stop being Mr Big. As he would say to the press at a later stage, 'Me? I'm more grandfather than godfather.' That's how Thompson wanted the world to see him from then on in. But there was a thorn in his side he had to finish off. Paul Ferris.

33

DIRTY TRICKS
1992

In spite of all predictions, the streets of Glasgow didn't explode after the deaths of Fatboy, Bobby and Joe. Arthur Thompson did his best to see that they wouldn't – it would've been bad for business. He had one major worry, though, and that was that Paul Ferris's popularity might screw up the court case. He'd have to fix that.

Thompson was determined that Ferris was going down for the murder of Fatboy and told his close associates so until they were sick to the back teeth of hearing it. This was his final step away from the old-time code of the street. If he thought Ferris had killed Fatboy, the code said that he should help Ferris walk free so that he could sort the issue out face to face – or, at least, nothing should be done to help get him convicted. But this gave Arthur Thompson a problem because he knew exactly how good Ferris was. That's why he had employed him and set him up for the cops. Too good.

If Ferris was sent down for life, he would enter the mainstream prison system instead of Barlinnie's segregation unit, where he had been jailed against his will since his arrest. Arthur Thompson could arrange for Ferris to be tormented by one or two guards in the segregation unit, but not harmed or killed as he could in a standard prison, where other inmates could get at him – inmates on Thompson's payroll.

Still only charged with the knee-capping of Gillen, some-how Ferris had won bail a while after Bobby and Joe had been killed. The polis then followed him about everywhere in cars, motorbikes and helicopters. Thompson couldn't get anyone near him without being surrounded by cops. In fact, the surveillance had been so heavy that Ferris himself had gone to a cop shop to complain. That's when the bizzies choked on their tea, pulled guns, arrested him for Fatboy's murder and stuck him back in segregation.

So Arthur Thompson didn't want Ferris free because he wasn't confident that his people could take him out. He knew Ferris would soon suss who was behind the killing of Bobby and Joe and, if the young man stuck to his usual MO, he'd come after Thompson. That's what Arthur expected him to do. There was only one place for Paul Ferris as far as Arthur Thompson was concerned – behind bars serving life for murder.

Thompson may have known Ferris's intelligence and lethal nature all too well but he had totally misjudged his popularity. What was it that he'd said so dismissively when Bagan and Ferris had left him? 'The Revolt of the Mice.' How wrong he had been.

Thompson now knew that Paul Ferris was seen as the new young hope among a whole generation of players. Many of the old school, like his great adversary Bobby 'The Devil' Dempster, had made it plain that they saw Ferris as a leader of the future and maybe that future was now. The McGovern Family supported him. The Daniel Brothers would work with him. Paisley players like Grant McIntosh wouldn't stand in his way. Even up-and-coming folk like the south side's Stewart 'Speccy' Boyd would put up no opposition, as long as they were left to their own business. And that was exactly Ferris's style. The only one that was out to get Ferris was McGraw, The Licensee, and Thompson didn't rate him, didn't rate him at all – except as a cop informant.

Ferris had become a sort of friend and hero to a whole host of individuals. Thompson's people had reported back to him numerous incidents where young guys had come in charging with blades because someone had been bad-mouthing Ferris. These were young guys who probably had never met the wee man. No, Thompson was sure that, if he was back on the street, a free man, Ferris could topple him and take what was The Godfather's at will. Thompson couldn't allow that to happen.

By greasing a few palms of minor bureaucrats in the justice system, through third parties, Thompson was well briefed on which witnesses were likely to be called for both the prosecution and the defence. The pen-pushers thought they were assisting some members of the press on the sly. Some were but some were helping The Godfather. It didn't cost him much and it paid dividends.

Trouble was that most of Ferris's witnesses would be staunch and moral. Usually, wee threateners, like sending bullets through the post, getting the Co-op funeral team to pay a visit with the hearse parked out on the street, torching their doors or leaving a slaughtered pig's head on their doorstep, did the trick. Not with this lot. They'd have to be convinced Ferris wasn't worth defending.

'Have a shufti at this.' Arthur Thompson waved a sheet of paper at Mick Healy. Healy was one of the keenest young players around. A skilled armed robber, he was on the run and deemed Britain's Most Wanted for a while.

'What is it?' Healy asked, not being used to Thompson showing him documents – unless they were the plans to some building he thought should be robbed.

'It's a letter from the Crown Office.'

'I can see that plain enough,' said Healy, referring to the heading.

'Read it,' said Thompson. 'Just read it.' Healy quietly scanned the few short paragraphs.

'Fuck sake! Is this right? Paul Ferris is a registered informant? Fuck sake. Where did you get this?'

'It "fell into my hands", you could say,' laughed Thompson. 'I was thinking of distributing it to Ferris's witnesses.' At that time, there was ill feeling between Mick Healy and Paul Ferris. Healy didn't care if Ferris went down or not but this was a serious allegation that would mean certain death for the bloke.

'Mind if I take this copy away, Arthur?' asked Healy. 'I want to show it to someone.'

'No problem, son, show it to anyone you like.'

Arthur Thompson was very happy with this little ploy. The letter was a fraud and it had cost him next to nothing to have it faked. In his line of business, it was easy to get his hands on paper that had a genuine Crown Office letterhead on it with the names of staff and so on. With a modern photocopier and the like, it was so easy to lay that letter out he didn't even bother going to one of the specialists – the guys who could do you a passport or even banknotes. It was only a letter after all.

What Arthur Thompson didn't know was that Mick Healy was taking the letter to a pal of his, a highly academic man who had numerous degrees in English. Healy wanted his mate's opinion on the authenticity of the letter.

'That's crap, Mick,' his friend had said, having read the letter once.

'How?' asked Mick, not being surprised but wanting details.

'It's full of spelling and grammatical errors. The Crown Office would never allow that to pass.'

'Do me a favour, eh?' asked Healy. 'Write down the mistakes, eh?'

With the dubious letter in his hand, Mick Healy went directly back to Arthur Thompson.

'You can't use that, Arthur, it's useless.'

'What the fuck do you mean?' Thompson rarely took such bad news well.

Healy showed him the letter where his friend had marked in pen where the mistakes were.

'Ach, there's only three.'

'Aye, but there's grammar mistakes as well and it's not laid out right. Don't pass it around, Arthur. No one will believe it.'

'I'm only sending it to Ferris's witnesses,' Thompson appealed, his hands open, eyebrows raised.

'And?' asked Healy, not getting the point he was trying to make.

'I've seen the list. Most of they cunts are lucky if they can read.'

Arthur Thompson did circulate the bogus letter to all of Ferris's defence witnesses. Then, he decided to circulate it even further – to pubs, clubs, drinking dens and at Shawfield, the dog track where a lot of players were in regular attendance. Why waste a good chance? And, if Ferris did get out, he might as well make sure the wee man had no support, no friends. But Thompson circulated too many copies.

What goes around comes around. Soon a copy of the fake letter was handed to Ferris in his cell in the Wendy House, the not-so-fond name Barlinnie prisoners had given to the segregation unit. He recognised the significance of the bogus letter right away and had his lawyer, Peter Forbes, get on to the case the very next day. Disproving the letter would be easy. The alleged author, Mr A. Vannet, had actually worked as a Deputy Crown Agent and was still around.

Getting the word and proof to Ferris's defence witnesses that the letter was a fabrication would be harder but at least his lawyers now knew there was a problem and could work on it. Not that they let on to anyone in the court system, of course. Thus, Arthur Thompson was totally oblivious that his plan had been blown. But still he was hatching other plots.

Ferris had another weakness – his family and, in particular, his mother and father, Jenny and Willie, who still lived round the corner from The Ponderosa. A year before, Willie Ferris, now getting on in years, had been run over by a lorry near the exit to the Fruit Market. Told he'd never walk again, Willie was a fighter, a small man with the heart of a lion. Now he could walk all right but only with the aid of a pair of sticks. That didn't stop Willie getting about as normal or from driving a car he got through the government's Motability scheme due to his disability.

Arthur Thompson discussed how to rattle Ferris with his close associates and Willie's name came up. They all shook their heads at the thought of anything happening to a man of his age and apparent frailty. But Billy Thompson was listening and he didn't give a toss about all that guff.

When Arthur Thompson heard that his son, Billy, had slashed the tyres of Willie Ferris's car, he said and did nothing. His associates expected him to lose the place. It wasn't right to treat an old guy like that, never mind if he was the father of an enemy. But Arthur Thompson didn't feel bad. Willie Ferris had given him the excuse he was looking for. Or so Thompson reasoned.

Being old school, Willie Ferris knew that what Thompson was expected to do was to ensure that Paul did not stand accused of Fatboy's murder. Willie was the type of man who would have pointed that out in no uncertain terms, whoever the parties were. That the man in the jail was his youngest son and the victim's father the most powerful gangster in Glasgow just made it more important he spoke his mind. And he did, straight to Thompson's face and in public. It was bad enough that the diminutive old man got the agreement of so many shared associates but what was worse was the direct manner of his approach. Willie Ferris took no prisoners in verbal exchanges.

So, when Billy Thompson moved on to pour acid over Willie Ferris's car, Arthur Thompson still said nothing and did less. Billy knew that meant he was getting his father's approval. If they thought that would shut Willie Ferris up, then Arthur Thompson must have forgotten all he had learned about the man. The two went back a few decades. The more they pushed, the more Willie Ferris stood up to them. That was his way.

When Billy Thompson and his team of young junkies – Billy never worked alone – beat Willie Ferris up, Arthur managed a smile. But, a few nights later, Willie Ferris got himself outside The Ponderosa and called, 'Thompson, you grass, come out and fight.' A small older man, who needed walking sticks, challenging a tall, younger and very strong top gangster in Glasgow to a duel? Sound farcical? But Willie Ferris was serious and some folk would have bet on him had the two had a fair square go.

Instead, Willie was met by Billy Thompson and his mates wielding baseball bats. They thumped and battered the old boy till he hit the deck but still he didn't shut up, calling out what he had always known about Thompson, the very advice he had given his son, 'What you working for him for? He's nothing but a fucking grass.'

Arthur Thompson considered himself to be reasonable. Had he not put up with Willie Ferris sherricking him publicly and calling him a grass and back-stabber? Had he not let that runt Billy play boys' games with the old bastard's car to teach him a lesson? Had he not stayed out of it? Till now.

Arthur Thompson cracked. He leapt from his favourite armchair, out the front door of The Ponderosa and, by the time he was on the pavement leaning over Willie Ferris, the open razor he always carried was in his hand. Religiously, Thompson sharpened that blade every week, sometimes more often. He stooped over and took the blade down the side of Willie Ferris's face just as the old man's hand found a walking stick and whacked The Godfather on the back.

'Get him the fuck out of here,' muttered Thompson, groaning and rubbing his back where the heavy stick had lashed him.

Before Thompson turned away, his son Billy and his mates were giving Willie Ferris a final kicking. But they needn't have bothered. That slashing had drawn almost all of the fight out of the old man just as it had drawn blood. They pulled him across the street and dumped him.

By the time Jenny Ferris was tending to her man, Arthur Thompson was sitting back in his favourite armchair, a large drink in his fist. He wasn't a heavy drinker but that quadruple measure went down fast. Sitting across from him Rita changed the TV channel, irritated that the ruckus had interrupted her night's viewing.

'Sorry, hen,' said Thompson, 'the old bastard went too far. But that'll be him shut up now.'

Two days later, Willie Ferris broke the principle of a lifetime. Speaking to the press about the attack on him, he sat with his shirt stripped off and posed for photographs. Even in the black and white photographs, the scar on his face looked long and livid, the bruises on his body deep and dark. But Willie Ferris was a fighter and he hadn't finished.

Alone in his cell in the Wendy House, Paul Ferris read the newspaper articles slipped under his cell door by friendly screws. At first, he cried for the pain etched all over his old man's body and face. Then he looked at the expression. It said, 'Come on, you bastards – I'm not beaten yet.'

Arthur Thompson sat in his favourite armchair and looked at the same picture. He knew what he would feel if that had been his father there. This fight wasn't won and that much he knew. But he was going to give it his best shot in a place he hadn't been for a while – the court. Willingly giving evidence for the prosecution was a new experience for him. And one he shouldn't be doing. But he was going to win this one – that was for sure and that meant that things had to change. But still he sat and worried and poured another drink.

Billy Thompson and his mates didn't read the newspapers. They hung out on the street in their baseball caps and tracksuits doing smack and speed. Billy was proud of himself. Time and again, he relived the beating of old Willie Ferris as if those listening hadn't been his partners in crime. For the last two days he had been carrying an old-fashioned razor just like his dad. Well that's what Godfathers did.

'See me,' he announced to his stoned buddies, 'one day all this will be mine.' He pointed at The Ponderosa then swung round, waving his arms in all directions of the city. 'One day soon, I'll be the man.'

Inside The Ponderosa, Arthur Thompson poured himself another drink and worried.

34

BACK TO THE WALL
1992

Arthur Thompson sat in his usual gunslinger's seat in the Provanmill Inn. With his back to the wall, at the end of the bar, he could see whoever was coming or going. Ordinary punters would say that they could see him noticing everything – he just had a wee sly glance, a slight movement of his eyes, but it was enough. But not that day. That day he seemed distracted. It was the day Paul Ferris's trial was due to end.

It had been a most unusual trial and Thompson knew that. Lasting fifty-four days and citing almost three hundred witnesses, it was the longest criminal trial in Scottish history to date and it was unique.

The cops had done him a good turn. Each morning and night a cavalcade of outriders, cars, armed cops and helicopters rushed Ferris between the jail and the court. It was always during the busy rush hours and disrupted so many commuters they couldn't help but pay attention. The TV cameras had caught it too. The message was clear – here is a dangerous man. A guilty man.

Every day in the witness stand, another face from the street appeared – gunmen, armed robbers, extortion racketeers and a clutch of young junkies. Thompson knew them for what they did and, often, he knew their fathers and uncles as well. There had been some sensational trials at Glasgow's High Court but nothing to match this.

Thompson was disappointed that his little fake letter scam wasn't more effective. Ferris's lawyer tracked down the so-called author, A. Vannet, and cited the bloke to court. The old gangster had heard about this before it was going to happen and had tried to intervene. Using the third parties who had managed to get information out of the court system for him, he attempted to get close to Mr A. Vannet. The man couldn't get paid a fortune working for the Crown, Thompson reckoned, so a little supplement would be tempting.

'No fucking chance,' his man had said, after a day or two of enquiries. 'The guy is so straight my contacts pissed themselves laughing when I suggested it.' Not one to give in, Thompson thought of arranging a wee accident for Vannet. But time was against him – and there was always the prospect of getting caught out. That would have totally blown his strategy.

So Vannet sat in the witness box and tore the letter alleging Ferris was a paid informant to shreds. Mick Healy's mate had picked up a number of the mistakes but Vannet added to them. The signature wasn't his, the layout was wrong and, by the way, he had never written to Paul Ferris ever. As damning evidence, the letter was ruined and Thompson knew that. But still he had a wry smile. He had had copies of the letter distributed everywhere, including London where Ferris had been spending a lot of time. How many of the southern faces had actually followed the media reports of the trial in great detail? Damn few was Thompson's reckoning so they would still see the letter as genuine. It hadn't been a total waste of his time.

At times, it had looked as if the trial was going totally against Ferris. Thompson had managed to lean on a local smackhead, Bernard Docherty, and the cops had done like-wise. The boy was denied his drug and told they'd let it be known that he had helped them in giving evidence against Ferris. Then, they told him that would mean he'd be taken out. What was it to be? With Thompson hovering in the background, Docherty swore that Ferris had offered him £30,000 to help in Fatboy's murder. Anybody who knew the street and Docherty knew this was preposterous but juries were a different matter. What did they know about the underworld?

A Blackhill guy, David Logue, had given evidence that he'd stolen a car for that night. It was clear from his statements that the jury should have been eyeing up the accused man, Paul Ferris. That was all right by Arthur Thompson even though he knew that the man who ordered the theft was William Lobban, Tootsie – the very man who'd made that Judas call to Bobby Glover the night he was killed.

Thompson had paid Lobban £10,000 to make that call. He had been willing to pay more but Lobban was desperate for cash. A mere ten grand to put a pal to their certain death. 'Who needs enemies with friends like Tootsie?' Thompson had asked some associates one night. But Tootsie wasn't going to open his trap. He was too scared of his uncle, Thompson's pal Billy Manson. And what if he had confessed to that call? He would suddenly be on the hit list of everyone who respected Glover and Hanlon. Not a good place to be. He was going to keep quiet.

Thompson had to laugh when the Crown called a witness named Dennis Woodman. One of his police contacts had visited him in a pub in the east end and told him, 'We've got something special planned, Arthur.'

'Never mind special – it better just nail the wee bastard.'

'We're bringing a bloke up from Dumfries Prison. He'll fix him.'

Dennis Woodman had been on remand facing charges of kidnapping a local farmer, his second such charge. As Thompson's cop pal explained to him, moving Woodman from a low-security prison to Barlinnie segregation unit took authority at the highest level.

'Pitt Street?' Thompson had asked, meaning the HQ of Strathclyde Police.

'Edinburgh,' the policemen had answered, meaning senior politicians and civil servants.

Arthur Thompson had laughed. So it wasn't just him who was out to get Ferris. He was team-handed with the powerful suits. The wee man was bound to go down. No way could he beat that lot.

Woodman swore that Ferris had confessed to the murder of Fatboy in the Wendy House.

'As if?' Thompson had snorted. 'Ferris owning up to a fucking stranger? Another prisoner he didn't know? No bloody chance.' But, as long as it helped convict Ferris, Thompson didn't care if it was true or not.

That's when Ferris's pals came into it again. A prisoner called Mark Leech recognised Woodman and passed a note to Ferris. A few days later a letter arrived from Mark Irvine, Woodman's brother-in-law. Seems that Woodman, or Wilkinson as he was sometimes known, had heard 'confessions' in jails all over England. Then the daft bugger started to take on Ferris's QC, the bold Donald Findlay. Findlay had one of the sharpest brains in any court circuit anywhere and here's this idiot having a go at him from the witness box. When Thompson heard that, he knew that Woodman was going to get a beating.

Sure enough, many hours into his evidence, Woodman swore on the graves of his two dead children. Then told his heart-rending tragic tale of how his kids had died. It was working. The jury felt for the pathetic bloke. Next day, Findlay was pointing out that his kids are alive and well thank you very much and Woodman was looking like the most callous liar in Glasgow. Game and set to Findlay.

All that was crucial to Arthur Thompson but still the most difficult part of the whole trial was when he was called to give evidence. For the first time in his life, Arthur Thompson was a willing prosecution witness. He had gone further and made a formal complaint to the cops that it was Paul Ferris who had tried to kill him by running over him repeatedly in that car.

'Better safe than sorry,' he had admitted to friends. 'The more Ferris is accused of, the more likely the jury will see him as a right bad bastard.' Ferris now faced charges of murder, two attempted murders, knee-capping and others. Thompson had seen it all before. If somehow he escaped the charge of killing his boy but got found guilty of one of the lesser charges, the court would give him maximum sentence. Thompson knew it shouldn't work that way but, this time, he was happy it did.

Heading towards the High Court to give evidence, Arthur Thompson was a worried man. It was one thing to plot Ferris's downfall but he couldn't be seen to be playing that game from the witness box. If he was going to pull it off it had to be the performance of a lifetime.

Every day the courtroom was packed to overflow and hundreds of people couldn't get in. Every day the newspapers and the TV and radio stations led with reports on how the trial was proceeding. For once, Arthur Thompson was going to have to play to the gallery and to the press. Most folk would believe how the media wrote up his performance. It was crucial he pulled the wool over their eyes.

Best suit, good shirt, neat knot in the tie and shoes polished and gleaming. He looked the part of the respectable businessman that he claimed to be. It wouldn't have taken much for Thompson to have arranged to be dropped off right at the front door of the court and to have slipped in quickly before any photographers noticed. But he decided to take a wee stroll. Let them see him and snap him. What did he look like? A middle-aged businessman, of course – just as he would insist he was to the world.

In the witness stand, Thompson kept his answers as short as he could. One liners was his way so this was the easy bit.

When they alleged that he was a gangster who earned £100,000 per week from loan-sharking alone, he had simply dismissed it, adding, 'It's just the press.' and giving a 'Who, me?' shrug towards the jury.

When they started referring to word of revenge hits on Bobby and Joe, Thompson was well prepared for that one since he knew it was coming. He said he bore no grudge against the boys Glover and Hanlon and that he didn't really know Glover very well. Then came the line he had prepared, the line that was true: 'The boy Hanlon I've known since he was three years old. I knew his father well.'

Hard man Shooders Hanlon choked to death on his own fish supper, wrappings and all. What is Thompson reported as saying as he leaned over Joe's gunshot-splattered body? 'I killed your father. He took fucking ages to go. You should have heard him gurgle.'

Arthur Thompson didn't blink. He had known Joe's father for a long time. He'd worked with him on different jobs and had become familiar with his family, including Joe. In the witness box, he was telling the truth – just not the whole truth, which, of course, was a regular state of affairs for Arthur Thompson.

Thompson was relieved. It looked like the ferocious probing of Donald Findlay was coming to an end. It was difficult to tell. Unlike most other briefs, Findlay didn't use notes. Didn't work through lists. Seemed to wander around and ask questions at random. Nothing was random, of course. The man was a fox of the courtroom and he wasn't to disappoint. Just as Arthur Thompson thought he was off the hook, Findlay asked one more question. Who did Arthur Thompson think had killed his son?

This caused Thompson most problems of all. In the courtroom, he looked placid, cool, contemptuous of the proceedings but, internally, he seethed with fury and a lust for revenge – just as he had since running out on to Provanmill

Road to see his boy's bleeding body. And now the man he blamed was just there, across the room from him. Everything in Thompson screamed at him to go for Ferris right there and then. Do him on the spot. That was Thompson's way. He took a deep breath, clenched his fists by his sides and said, 'We all know who shot him.' He hesitated and turned, staring directly at Paul Ferris, and continued, 'We think so.'

Perfect. Thompson had pulled it off exactly as he wanted to. No direct accusations. No name. No statement of blame. Just those words that would become part of the official record and of media reports. But, inside the courtroom, the jury watched and saw him turn and look at Ferris. They knew what he meant loud and clear.

Now it was all over. The lawyers had done their summing up, the judge had given his twopence worth and the jury were out, arguing in some room. Thompson had tried to knobble the jury with a few backhanders but his people couldn't get near them. Now he would just have to trust their judgement. It was a weak position and he didn't like it.

Thompson sat in the Provanmill Inn and waited for the result. Maybe it wouldn't come that day. But that would be hell for him. He just wanted it all over and Ferris in jail. He already had his plans set up. His hit men had been chosen and were ready in several jails – there was bound to be someone to cover whichever one Ferris was sent to. They wouldn't act right away. That would be too obvious. They'd be instructed to make sure Ferris had no trouble at all for a couple of months. If they started hassling the guy, the prison authorities would exclude him from the mainstream wings. His men would be told to let Ferris rule the roost. Take over the trading in tobacco and phone cards. Let him feel safe, powerful, relaxed – then they'd kill him.

A hit in a prison is usually cheap – costing the price of enough heroin and cannabis to last the sentence, a few grand when they came out. If they got caught, the same deal but money right away to their families. Cheap. But he'd have to pay extra for Ferris to get done. The wee bastard had too many friends and allies. Too many folk who would defend him or exact revenge. No matter, Thompson would pay what it took.

Then, the jury came out.

Paul Ferris had been found not guilty on all charges. Nobody could believe it. Well, nobody around Arthur Thompson that day admitted that they believed or welcomed it. Thompson said little and his face showed less. He just stayed at the bar for a while, drinking heavily. He didn't notice that drinkers were drifting away, slipping out of the door. No one wanted to be around Arthur Thompson that day.

At the High Court, Paul Ferris walked out the front door to a crowd of many hundreds cheering him on. They stretched from the front of the court right on to Glasgow Green. It was a hero's welcome that embarrassed Ferris. It was an outrage to Arthur Thompson. He was a very angry man.

After dark, Arthur Thompson made his unsteady way home up Provanmill Road. It was the very route he had taken thousands of times. The road he walked on the night they tried to kill him by a hit-and-run. Thompson was drunk and angry and almost wished they'd try it again that night. He'd be ready for them and he'd take no prisoners. When Arthur Thompson hurt, he had to hurt someone else. It had always been his way.

'Bad result the day, Arthur.' It was an old guy from nearby Riddrie. He had worked at the Fruit Market for years and was on his way back to the Budgie Bar near there to see some of his old mates. Occasionally he'd pop into the Provanmill Inn on the way. A familiar face and harmless.

'Whit?' Thompson stopped and turned, towering over the bloke.

'Said the result at the court, bad one, eh?' The old guy had stopped to pay his respects.

'What the fuck would you know about it, ye wee cunt?' Thompson took his open razor down both sides of the old man's face. When he crumpled to the ground, Thompson booted him on the side and the head and went on his way.

Some locals would say that was the very moment Arthur Thompson finally lost it.

35

THE PRICE OF PALS
1992–93

Glasgow spun round and round below him. Blood rushed to his brain and his heart thumped loudly in his chest keeping up a mad tempo with the ringing in his ears.

'You sure you don't know anything, ye prick?' The same question he had been asked so many times, this time from high above.

'No! No! I swear,' he shouted in reply.

'Aye, fucking right.'

'Aaaaaayyyy.' The street below jerked closer as his one of his feet kicked at plain air. John Masterton wasn't having a good day.

It had started the previous afternoon. There he was in London, in his home territory going about his business as usual. That was the problem – the 'as usual' bit. An old player like him should have known better but he thought he had retired from all that. Thought he didn't have to constantly look over his shoulder as he used to do every waking day of his life. But then he didn't think a lifelong friendship would come back and haunt him.

There he was just going about his business. He'd been to one of his shops to pick up some money and left about the usual time to go to his local for a drink. Life was good. Then they grabbed him.

There were no words, no warning, no questions. Three or four people had just lifted him off his feet, thrown a manky sack over his head and physically hoisted him into the back of some old van. All credit to those boys – they knew what they were doing. The transformation from his daily routine to hostage must have taken seconds.

After delivering a sharp crack to Masterton's skull, his captors tethered his wrists together and wrapped thick industrial tape round his ankles. Trussed up like a pig for the slaughter, the old street player lay there, knowing nothing would happen while the kidnappers drove through the busy London streets. Nothing would happen till the vehicle came to a halt – or so he thought. But he was right about one thing – he did have some time. So he lay there and tried to work out what the hell this was all about.

John Masterton was an old-time London face. Not one of the big boys whose names carried headlines but one of the second tier who did all the nasty work. He had survived a few decades in that business – an achievement in itself. And you didn't get through that time in London without making a lot of friends and some enemies as well.

The Kray Twins, the Richardsons, Frankie Fraser – he knew all the old-time teams. As he would tell people who would listen, he'd met the new teams too – the Adamses, the Arifs, Kenny Noye. In his opinion, the young faces were no match for the old boys. Now, that generation had been tough, really tough. Then the sack was roughly pulled off his head.

'You're no' sleeping, are ye?' the questioner was up so close, his spittle caught Masterton on the face. Worse, these guys weren't trying to conceal their identities. He'd recognise them all again – if they allowed him to leave alive. This was looking bad. 'There'll be no sleeping on this trip.' Then he battered Masterton on the side of the head with the barrel of a large, black pistol. It was just the start.

The three young men beat Masterton in the back of the van as it travelled at speed along a motorway. He could scream all he wanted, no one would hear a cheep. If Masterton hadn't been too busy trying to protect himself and work out what the hell this was all about, he might have admired the professionalism of the young men.

At first he thought the men were Irish. Southern Irish with thick impenetrable accents. They kept repeating the same question, 'Who killed Bobby and Joe?' He protested that he didn't have a clue who or what they were talking about. So they beat him again. And again, going on and on with the same question.

'How's the road behind us?' one of the men shouted to the driver.

'Clear,' was the response.

'Good 'cos I'm fucking fed up with this joker,' the other one said as he opened the van's doors and pushed Masterton out while still hanging on to his legs.

As the speeding tarmac of the motorway came closer and closer to his face, John Masterton thought he was a goner. All they'd have to do is let go of his arms. Or he might slip out of their grip and he'd be a dead man for sure.

At last they pulled him in.

'Look, we know you fucking know Thompson,' said one of his tormentors.

'Thompson? Arthur Thompson?' he asked.

'Well, it's no' fucking Daley Thompson we mean.'

Masterton had been one of Thompson's London contacts for more years than he cared to remember. He'd heard all about the shooting of Fatboy, of course, and the revenge killing of two boys. But Bobby and Joe? Their names meant nothing to him. And he knew nothing about their killings. Shame. So he paid the price of his silence all the way from London to Glasgow with more beatings, more dangling from the open back doors.

As the van approached the outskirts of Glasgow the sack was again thrown over Masterton's by-now battered head. Ten minutes later the van pulled to a stop, a knife sliced through the tape round his ankles and rough hands on both his arms yanked him to his feet hauling him inside the Red Road Flats on the city's north side. The Red Road Flats were infamous as a rough territory full of junkies, dealers and prostitutes. They were also the highest residential flats in Europe.

Inside the sack, Masterton could feel the jerk and fast upwards movement of a lift that seemed to go on forever. He didn't like this at all. When the sack was dragged off, he was inside a flat devoid of furnishings or furniture. It was a manky place that smelt of dust and disuse but, even in his distressed state, he could see that the panoramic view of the city at night was spectacular. It was a view he was going to get to know intimately.

Slamming the Londoner on to a hard, straight-backed chair, the team started on him again.

'Bobby and Joe.'

'Bobby and Joe.'

Eventually they held him down and stuck the long barrel of a pistol in his gob.

'Bobby and Joe.'

'Bobby and Joe.'

He said nothing as he knew nothing. Besides, if he tried to make something up and if these guys were conned that he did know something, he had no doubt that it would be his death knell. Then they pushed him out the window, holding him by his ankles, God knows how many floors up.

'Look, you can see old fucking Thompson's house from here,' said one of his captors. 'Maybe we should bell him and he can wave bye-bye to you as you head for the concrete.' They all found that funny. All except Masterton that is. The question started again.

'Bobby and Joe.'

'Bobby and Joe.'

Still nothing. They let go of one leg and made to let him slip. He was terrified all right and cried out but he stayed schtum as far as answers went.

They didn't say they believed him. They didn't apologise. They didn't say it was all over. They just pulled him into the flat, put the sack over his head again and bundled him down the lift and back into the van. 'This is it,' thought Masterton. 'They're going to take me some place and pop a bullet into my skull. No way they can let me go now.'

The van had only been on the move for a few minutes when the back doors were suddenly opened and Masterton was pushed out. He landed with a heavy crash on the street. Behind him, a car horn blared and brakes screeched. Standing up slowly and painfully, he pulled the sack from his head. He realised that the van had disappeared. He was on a main street and had been lucky not to have been run over when he hit the deck. As his eyes adjusted to the half light of dawn, he also realised they had dumped him at the doorway of a hospital. It was the Royal Infirmary where Fatboy Thompson had breathed his last.

Caring? Symbolic? John Masterton didn't waste any energy on such questions. Soon he was heading south to the safety of London. He'd never breathe a word about who his attackers had been or what they looked like. The best he'd say is, 'Young guys. Knew what they were doing. But I don't even know if they were Scottish or Irish.'

As some of Arthur Thompson's friends were about to find out, that wasn't such a stupid thing to say.

36

ENDGAME
1992–93

Arthur Thompson was losing friends fast and he didn't care. He was sixty-one years old and had survived a life as a street player but now he was tired. Tired and weary and he didn't care.

For two pins, Thompson would have moved to his house in Spain permanently. But Rita wasn't keen and, besides, too many semi-retired gangsters were getting picked off on the Costa del Sol and as word had it Scots guys were going across to do the deed. Thompson knew that he could never retire. As a top gangster, you have to keep going, keep the treadmill moving or, as soon as you stop, one of your many enemies or just a rookie gunslinger would have a pop.

At first, after the trial, he had been geared up for some sort of onslaught from Ferris. The world and his granny were predicting that he would take over Glasgow and Thompson fully expected him to do just that. But the onslaught never came. Ferris seemed too concerned with sorting out the affairs of his dead pals Glover and Hanlon and then spending most of his time in London and Manchester. Thompson thought the man was just playing a trick – pretending he wasn't interested. And, then, one night, he'd walk out of the shadows and come towards him, a blazing shooter in his hand. Thompson couldn't stand waiting.

The longer Ferris showed little interest in Glasgow, the less Thompson cared. That was the thing, he'd always cared before. No matter how bad things were, he cared enough to get a result, his result. Now, he didn't care.

Thompson was moving away from the street, creating a role for himself as businessman-cum-celebrity-gangster. The work he had started, attending functions that raised money for good causes, he extended now. It was the closest he would get to retirement, he reasoned. In the small goldfish bowl that is the spotlight in Scotland, he was obvious – in the public eye – and, therefore, safe. Who was going to put him down if he kept company with TV stars and entrepreneurs? He didn't need his old guard now so he abandoned them to their own devices. For some that was tragic.

Thompson's people had already been sent a warning card. Blind Jonah McKenzie was the first to fall. After being totally blinded, he became petrified. For a man who had led his life by his wits in the company of sharks, sudden blindness was a disability beyond compare. He couldn't adjust, couldn't adapt and he couldn't hide. Blind Jonah had the terrors that any minute someone would just pick him off. It was too much for him and he took to drugs big time.

Jonah fell into working with an east-end mob affiliated to McGraw, The Licensee. They had already had trouble in bringing in smack that was too pure and scores of Glasgow junkies died as a result. Not only was such carelessness likely to bring heat from the cops, it was also a waste of money. Properly cut, high-purity heroin brings in so much more profit than low-grade stuff. So they needed to test the gear. That's where Jonah came in.

Nothing scientific for this mob. No test tubes or chemical checks. Their test was easy. Jonah cooked up his works as per normal and took the golden needle. He told them if it was good or bad, if it could be cut more or if it had been cut too much. Blind Jonah's body was the living test tube.

One night, he was working as usual. The result came through that the smack was exceptionally pure. Not that Jonah told them as much. He just lay down on the bare floor and died.

The needle still dangling from a vein, Jonah was lifted out of that flat to a neighbouring close and dumped – a terrible, lonesome end and a waste.

Billy Manson had been a good friend to Arthur Thompson for many years. When he came out of his hiding place in Alex Morrison's caravan, someone had tried to kill him but had failed. He had gone to Thompson to seek his help. Manson was convinced that someone had sussed his role in the deaths of Bobby Glover and Joe Hanlon. Thompson dismissed his claim as 'overreacting' and did nothing.

One week later, Billy Manson was driving with his good friend Graham Scott when suddenly a car screeched to a halt in front of them and another one stopped at the rear. A team of masked men piled out of the cars and attacked Manson. The man was badly battered, broken and stabbed twenty times. Scott was left totally unharmed but had lost his voice. In spite of what they did to his friend, he saw nothing and knew nothing. He lived a quieter life after that. While Billy Manson survived, he was physically shattered and never active again.

Manson's nephew, William 'Tootsie' Lobban, who had made that fatal call to Bobby Glover, was finally arrested as an escaped prisoner. In Perth Jail, someone coshed Lobban with an iron bar only a few days after he arrived there. It almost killed him. Recovered but paranoid that they would come after him again, Lobban took a prison officer hostage then gave himself up, ensuring that he would be locked up in the protection of the isolation unit where it was safer.

Months later, Lobban was transferred to Shotts Prison and was only minutes from dying when the screws sussed that strychnine had been injected into his food. After that, he was transferred to a prison in England for his own protection.

Paul Hamilton made a fundamental error – he opened his mouth. Hamilton was boasting in pubs of having driven the blue van used to move Glover and Hanlon's bodies. That van had never been found, making the voluntary confessions even more ridiculous. It was no surprise when Hamilton was shot dead. His murder remains unsolved to this day.

The cops were suffering severe public embarrassment that they had lost Glover and Hanlon the night they had been murdered and were no closer to solving the case. Word got to them at the highest level that the two men's bodies had been in McGraw, The Licensee's pub, the Caravel, at one point. Warrants were obtained and a surprise raid planned.

McGraw's alliance with bent cops paid off. One warning phone call later, he was talking to an associate, Trevor Lawson, who ran a builders' company. That night, in the dark, Lawson moved in with his bulldozer and flattened the Caravel. By dawn, the site was cleared – nothing remained but wasteland.

Through all of this, Arthur Thompson remained aloof and continued with his new life. Even when the murder guns that killed Glover and Hanlon were discovered in a flat in Blackhill, Thompson didn't miss a beat and with good cause. The trail stopped with the guns. But how did the guns get there? In the so-called official version of events, it was Thomas McCraw, The Licensee's job to dispose of the weapons – a simple enough task for someone with access to scrapyards and incinerators. Yet there they were, less than a hundred yards from The Ponderosa.

The guns were found in a flat where an old couple lived. They had just been paid some money to look after a couple of bags with the small print that they never opened them. Good people and true. But someone had phoned the cops to say they should look there. There's no mystery about this. It's The Licensee's way. But, if he expected the link to be made to

Thompson, he was badly mistaken. The old couple never said a word. Nothing. Besides they really didn't know what was in the bags. A deal is a deal in their book. They were so professional they were not even charged, never mind Thompson.

Thompson had other matters to worry about – like his reputation. During Ferris's trial, the newspaper *Scotland on Sunday* had published a full investigative feature on the case. It made for juicy, exciting reading and featured characters everyone was interested in. Trouble was, the journalist went on to claim that Thompson had killed Bobby Glover and Joe Hanlon without backing it up with facts. The High Court found both the journalist, Ron McKay, and the editor, Andrew Jaspan, in breach and fined them substantial amounts. They were in good company since several media outlets were censured over that trial.

Most career criminals are told they have no reputation to defend so it would be a waste of their time pursuing a libel or defamation case. But Thompson decided to consult Martin Smith, one of the country's foremost libel lawyers. Smith took the view that Thompson had never been convicted of murder – OK, he'd been accused and tried many times but never found guilty. They sued *Scotland on Sunday* and won an undisclosed five-figure sum.

It put Thompson in an even better light with the media and the celeb circuit. Here was a man willing to defend his reputation and winning. When he donated every penny of his win to good causes, he moved further down the road to acceptance. It was the beginning of a remarkable turnaround from Mr Evil to Benign Godfather in the public eye. But that's not how the street viewed him.

Arthur Thompson was getting soft and careless. He had fallen into the habit of going to the same Bridgeton pub, at the same time, on the same night every week. It took an Irish team a few weeks to find what they were after – a time and place to kill Arthur Thompson.

First they had a courtesy call to make. They arranged a meeting in Baird's Bar in Bridgeton with Paul Ferris and, without revealing what was going down, strongly advised him to be in a very public place, in trustworthy company, on a certain night. They knew Ferris would get the blame if any harm befell Thompson and that wasn't on.

On the night in question, Ferris and his girlfriend were having dinner in his favourite restaurant with Jaimba McLean, a well-known Glasgow face, and his wife. Ferris knew that Joe Hanlon in particular had a lot of family and friends in Ireland who would want to seek revenge. But he also knew that the team he met weren't amateurs and they weren't gangsters. They were professionals.

Also, on the night in question, Arthur Thompson kept his appointment with death. Around the entrance to the pub there were five men with rifles and machine guns and two of them had grenades. Bang on time, up drove the red Vauxhall Cavalier Thompson used on these trips and the men tensed and readied themselves.

Change of plan. Tracey Thompson was driving. That was unusual but it was also fatal to their plans. They intended to kill one person only, Arthur Thompson, and wouldn't countenance any risk to another, especially not his innocent daughter.

The hit was postponed. They would get him again but, before they could, other threats intervened.

One night, a friendly face visited Arthur Thompson – a cop he had not seen in a couple of years. Although he was still phoning in information on players and the cops were still accommodating his illegal pursuits, the arrangement didn't have such urgency as it had done for many years.

'We think you should be getting out of Glasgow for a while,' said the cop, over a drink in The Ponderosa. 'You and Rita.'

The cop was being friendly. He was warning Thompson that they had picked up information that there was a hit contract out on him and they were taking it very seriously indeed.

'Right you are,' dismissed Thompson, 'so tell me something new.' For most of his life people had been talking about gunmen being paid to get him.

'Arthur, have I ever warned you off about this kind of business before?' asked the cop, knowing the answer.

'No, but . . .'

'But fuck all. Just listen to me, eh? You'll not even know the guy. You'll probably never even see him. This is a serious one, Arthur. Very serious.'

The police suggested the Thompsons head abroad but Arthur wouldn't have that. He knew too many ex-faces who had been taken out in Spain and he reasoned that he would actually be more vulnerable there. Rita wasn't fond of that prospect either but they did agree to go to their flat in Rothesay.

After a few weeks in Rothesay, Thompson got the all-clear from the cops. Two men had been arrested at Euston Station, their cases heavy with sniper rifles, £50,000 cash and pictures with Arthur Thompson's head circled.

It was a close call. Very close. But Thompson needed to get back to Glasgow. This was the longest he had ever been away and the street had picked up on that and the hit contract. Word was out that The Godfather was slipping, getting weak. He couldn't have that. Reputation was all. When you are The Godfather, losing face is a death sentence.

Arthur Thompson didn't care a hoot about his old associates who had fallen in the last year. But, when contracts were taken out on him, he had to respond. In spite of him hardly ever being in town, one name was still top of Thompson's hate list – Paul Ferris.

Arthur Thompson travelled to London to see an old friend. Lenny McLean is better known as The Governor of unlicensed, bare-knuckle boxing. But McLean was handy at any form of violence and scared of no one.

Arthur Thompson asked him to kill Paul Ferris and offered him £40,000. McLean accepted the job but refused the money. The Godfather was an old pal, The Governor would help him for free.

With a handshake, the deal was sealed. After another couple of drinks, Arthur Thompson headed back to Glasgow, happy in the belief that Paul Ferris would soon be dead and his troubles over.

A few days later, Thompson had a quiet day. He went to one of his businesses, watched TV with Rita and then had a couple of drinks at a local pub, before going to bed at a reasonable time. This quiet life was suiting him and soon he would be able to live without looking over his shoulder all the time. It had been a good day.

Arthur Thompson suffered a heart attack in his bed. A frantic Rita dialled 999 and an ambulance arrived at speed. Thompson was in agony, struggling for breath and the ambulance crew knew they had to act fast. But, when they applied the defibrillator to revive him, they discovered that the machine wasn't working. It was only a short journey to the hospital but the loss of those first minutes was vital. The next day, at the Royal Infirmary, Arthur Thompson was declared dead.

It was 13 March 1993. The Godfather's reign was over.

37

THE LAST OF THE GODFATHER

1993

'We should leave the phone call till the morning. That'll disrupt the old bastard's show.'

'Disrupt? Ha. It'll put it off for a day with the beauty we've planted.'

'Well, he bloody deserves it. Think he wouldn't hesitate to do it to us? Eh?' The other young player thought about that. He had come to hate Thompson – as many had. He had learned what the man said he stood for wasn't actually what he believed in or did. Now he was being told that he should behave as badly as Arthur Thompson – that couldn't be right. As much as he hated the old man, he had family who were just ordinary people. A wife he'd no grudge against. He got up and put on his jacket. 'Where you going?'

'To the phone box. I've a call to make.'

Within an hour, Riddrie Park Cemetery was surrounded by cops and the roads blocked off as the Bomb Squad edged a way through the ankle-length grass between the gravestones. Eventually they found it – gas canister, wires and a small flashing light with a timer – it looked like the real thing. Hours of careful manoeuvring later, they carried out a controlled explosion. It was a hoax.

As morning broke, they began to gather across Provanmill Road from The Ponderosa. Men in dark suits, black cashmere coats, wearing the scars of their world on their faces and carrying the gold of their success on their fingers, round their wrists and about their necks.

Above them, a police helicopter constantly hovered all day, returning to base four times for a refuel. Around them seemed to be gathered the full might of Strathclyde Police, one of the biggest forces in Europe, may of them with body armour and rifles. Nobody moved in or out without the cops' say-so. The scar-faced men gave them no problems.

Eulogies had been flowing since it was announced that The Godfather was dead. It was the celebrity Godfather they mourned. Nicholas Fairbairn QC, who had represented Thompson on more than one occasion, said, 'We won't miss him but he had great control and, without him, it might just break up into a criminal Bosnia.' Fairbairn was right about the potential for the Scottish crime scene to explode into warfare but he was also out of date. Thompson had relinquished control the day Paul Ferris walked free from court. The day he knew his son's murder would remain unsolved. The day he realised he didn't have the energy for that life any more. The day Arthur Thompson started waiting for the hit man to come for him. It was the waiting that killed him, some reckon.

But they came in their droves and no one had to pay them this time. Big players from the south, local hard men in their funeral and wedding suits, boxers and their promoters, footballers, lawyers, businessmen, Orange Lodge leaders, UDA officers, TV celebrities and more. There was a great deal of admiring, melancholic chat about Arthur. Soon word spread that he hadn't lost his touch. Why, just last week he had slashed someone. It was recounted again and again with admiration. But no one knew who he had slashed, when, where or why. Another Arthur Thompson myth was created even as he lay in his coffin.

As the mourners gathered, a tall, distinguished man visited The Ponderosa to pay his respects to the family. One more black suit in a day of black suits. As he left, he stopped and wiped tears from his eyes. An off-duty cop, one who knew Thompson well. The same one who was meant to be watching Bobby Glover and Joe Hanlon the night they were killed.

By the graveside, the mourners spread out around the plot, standing straight, silent, unmoved, the family close to the grave. As Thompson's coffin was lowered slowly into the pit, Rita howled in anguish and threw herself forward. Forget the tales of gore and street violence. This was just another woman who couldn't stand the loss of her man – whatever he was, whatever he did. Just in time, she was caught by her family and held. From then on in, as always, Rita would have to hold the family together.

The ceremony over, the mourners filed slowly away, sharing thoughts.

'He'll be missed . . .'

'. . . a one off.'

'Never again . . .'

'Things will be different now . . .'

They all agreed. They had come to mourn the man Arthur Thompson had allowed them to see, the man he made them believe in, the man who didn't exist, wasn't real. Elsewhere in the city, others knew the truth and smiled on the day of his burial. A few parties were held and many more quiet celebratory drinks shared. These others had a story or two to tell – ones that the mourners weren't ready to hear. Stories about the real Arthur Thompson. But there was no disagreement on the future. Things were going to be very different from now on in. No one person would rule Glasgow or any other city from now on. It was the modern way from now on. The business way, with as many groups as there are markets. A more uncertain way perhaps but then, again, no. Life on the street was always unpredictable. Always was. Always will be.

Another eulogy was delivered, this time from Leslie Payne, Ronnie Kray's personal adviser. 'There was as much violence done in a fortnight in Glasgow as both the Richardson and Kray gangs did in their entire careers.' It was meant as a compliment. To Arthur Thompson.

Some mourned, some celebrated but, in their own different ways, they had all said farewell to the Last Godfather.

38

THE AFTERMATH
1993–2006

She sits alone with her memories in a house that holds more than most. If walls could talk, the bricks and mortar of The Ponderosa would be cited to the High Court again and again and again. But, of course, being Arthur Thompson's house, they wouldn't say a word – unless it was personal. The same goes for his wife.

Life for Rita Thompson has been eventful, to say the least. What a story she could tell if she chose to. From the very first day Arthur Thompson courted her, she must have known that theirs would be a roller coaster of a relationship. But did she realise how much?

If she ever sits at her front window, she can see where three of her nearest and dearest perished: her mother in a car bomb designed for her husband; her son, Fatboy, shot down like a dog, his blood staining the pavement at her own front door; and, across the way, the house where her older daughter, Margaret, had died from a heroin overdose. Or had she?

If Margaret died of a simple overdose, just another sad junkie, why did the Glasgow cops pursue her boyfriend of the time, Gerry 'Cyclops' Carbin, as being responsible for her death? Margaret's death must have been at least suspicious in a way that the cops have not revealed to the public.

After the case against Cyclops was dropped, they pursued him as responsible for the death of another heroin addict,

John Sweeney, from Glasgow. That case failed too. But there must have been a pattern for the police to pay so much attention.

At the time of Margaret's death, word on the street was that significant amounts of heroin seized by the cops was being unofficially liberated and was finding its way to street players. They, of course, sold it on to addicts. Was Margaret Thompson killed by that liberated police heroin? Was that why they were so anxious to pin her death and those of other junkies on guys like Cyclops?

If Cyclops escaped prosecution for Margaret Thompson's death, he didn't get off scot free. After leading the cop forces of Europe a merry dance for years, he finally picked up the nerve to return to Glasgow in 2002. A relative of his, James 'The Iceman' Stevenson, was embroiled in a war with the McGovern family from Springburn and needed all the help he could get. The Carbins threw their weight behind him and Cyclops returned to Glasgow to make a point. Besides, Arthur Thompson was long dead by then and it was now safe for him to return. Or so he thought.

Cyclops had never kicked his heroin habit. A short while after his return to the city, he contracted the flesh-eating bug necrotising fasciitis and died a slow painful death. Just bad luck and the wrong type of bug getting into an open sore? Or the revenge of Arthur Thompson from beyond the grave?

Some believe the latter. Though it's not in the nature of this book or its author to accept such supernatural theories, it must be conceded that many of those who associated with Thompson, both for and against, have been hit with bad luck.

Billy Manson was first. The old Thompson loyal clearly played a part in the murders of Bobby Glover and Joe Hanlon. No matter that he hid, no matter that he had The Godfather's backing, a group of men tracked him down in his car, battering and knifing him to such an extent that he never recovered.

His nephew, William 'Tootsie' Lobban, was next. After escaping death by cosh and poison in his food in Scottish prisons, he was transferred down south. He very quickly realised he wasn't safe there either. With daily attempts on his life and his Judas money used up, he contacted Thompson asking for help. He never received a reply.

It took till 2004 for Lobban to pick up the nerve to return to Glasgow. Even then it was only on the guarantee from a Sunday tabloid that they would pay for his keep in a secret hotel and give him a few thousand pounds for his story. As the newspaper's photographer snapped away at pics for the story, Lobban requested a special pose. There he was bowing in front of The Godfather. Not Arthur Thompson but Marlon Brando in the film of the same name. If proof were ever needed that he had lost everything, that was it.

Paul Hamilton had made the mistake of thinking Thompson's power was infinite and all-reaching. The man openly boasted about driving Bobby Glover and Joe Hanlon's corpses in the back of his van. One night as he drove his car, another motor rammed him, and he was shot dead right there in the driver's seat.

Lenny 'The Governor' McLean was a close friend of Thompson's for years. He had promised The Godfather that he would kill Paul Ferris, the man he still blamed for shooting Fatboy. No sooner had McLean agreed than Thompson had died of a heart attack. 'A promise is a promise' was Lenny McLean's way and he would have attempted to follow through on his vow to his dead friend. Then suddenly McLean died too and of natural causes. Two hardmen nobody would have bet on dying in their beds.

Paddy Meehan, Thompson's old pal who had been wrongfully convicted of murdering Rachel Ross, fared no better. Officially Arthur Thompson had helped win a Royal Pardon for Meehan but privately Meehan was very angry and bitter towards his friend. Meehan knew about the influence

Thompson had had with the cops and questioned why he had let him be convicted in the first place.

The only answer he could come up with was self-interest. Thompson had been watching over his own contacts, especially top detective Charlie Craig. Meehan's view was that he would have been still rotting in jail had there been any chance that his freedom exposed Craig. He was right. But that didn't stop him dying a lonely and very bitter man, again of natural causes.

Frank McPhie, the man many street players believe pulled the trigger on Bobby Glover and Joe Hanlon, went from strength to strength during the 1990s, his rise mainly based on heroin and cocaine trafficking. McPhie was a sole operator who took sides with no one and owed nobody any favours. Then he started dealing with the Irish.

By the year 2000, gangs previously associated with the Loyalist movement broke away and went from political to criminal. McPhie was quite happy to use their transporting routes, bent officials and weapon power to do business with them. Then one night, another Glasgow face suddenly attacked McPhie mob-handed. Outnumbered, McPhie managed to get to his car and drove away at speed. As he drove, he called up some people, trying to muster a heavy team for when the mob came after him.

Arriving back at his flat in Maryhill, he paused at his doorstep just yards from his eleven-year-old son. That's when the sniper took him out. The shot had come from the top of an adjacent multi-storey car park. The killer fled immediately leaving the murder weapon behind. Of course there were no fingerprints, no forensics, no clues – a professional hit and clearly set up.

Word was put out that McPhie had cheated on the Irish. But had he or had those former Loyalists been told that he had worked with Arthur Thompson, the man who by then they would have discovered was a double agent working against them? Or was it some other Irish folk, relatives of Joe Hanlon exacting revenge?

Gordon Ross, the man who had tried to kidnap Billy Thompson, fared well for a while too, working with Thomas 'The Licensee' McGraw. Ross had gone from being a roofer to a crime millionaire. At his strongest when he should have been almost invincible, he stepped out of his own local pub in his own home patch one night when someone stabbed him. It was a scenario he had dealt with a hundred times before without mishap but for that night he died.

Even the man who took over Thompson's mantle as big-time police informant wasn't going to have it all plain sailing. Cops need information and will happily trade with gangsters to get it. With Thompson dead there was only one choice – the natural successor, The Licensee.

McGraw had his troubles with claims of police corruption and the threat of Paul Ferris taking over the city. But Ferris's lack of interest and McGraw's police minders took care of him – for a while. In the last couple of years, three of his top men have died violently and the other has been jailed big-time for drugs trafficking – some say set up by McGraw himself. Now no serious player will work with him.

His wife, Margaret 'The Jeweller', the brains of the operation, has left him. He's even lost his driving licence. It's been that way for McGraw lately – a multi-millionaire with few real friends, no home life and so paranoid about his own safety he can't sleep at night. With the death of Thompson, did he win out? What do you think?

Thompson's hex has reached his own surviving family as well. His brother died a sad man when he committed suicide. His younger daughter, Tracey, has tried and tried to make a straight life. She has the brains, the knowledge and the will but nothing seems to work for her. Then there's the youngest, Billy, the runt.

A drug addict from his teens, life hasn't got better for Billy

Thompson. For a few years after his father's death, he lived on his old man's reputation and his mother's money. But his drugs habit was running out of control and Rita must have put her foot down on the cash front. Otherwise why, in July 2000, did he try to demand a couple of quid from two local men? They didn't take kindly to his efforts at bullying and beat him up, badly. At one point, the youngest Thompson was lying unconscious on the ground and the men jumped two-footed on his skull. He was left brain damaged.

Even years after his father's death, the cops weren't taking any chances and they moved Billy from the top specialist neurology unit in Scotland, that happens to be in Glasgow, to another hospital in Edinburgh. Just for his own safety – in case anyone tried to finish him off.

Billy Thompson survived although he'd suffered physical and mental disabilities. Like his father before him, he signed up for the disability welfare benefits he qualified for and was even given a car from the government Motability scheme. But that was soon gone as the drugs habit kicked in again.

After a couple of years and in spite of his poor health, even his mother had had enough and kicked him out of the house. When he was last heard of, he had sold his story to a Sunday tabloid for a little bit of cash. It was the biggest waste of their funds as readers soon found out. Billy Thompson doesn't have a story except that he was his father's son.

Even Arthur Thompson's old HQ, the Provanmill Inn, didn't escape. Under new ownership, in 2004 someone torched the place badly but not badly enough. Two weeks later someone torched it again. This time there was nothing left standing.

Word was put out that the arson was over some business dispute. But was it? Say anything about Arthur Thompson and the Provanmill Inn follows soon after. They couldn't get at Arthur Thompson so did they get at his symbolic HQ?

No one is saying, least of all Rita Thompson. Loyal to the

last, she stays on in The Ponderosa and visits her husband in the cemetery that runs behind her home. She'll know the way to that grave blindfolded by now but, if you go looking for it, you might have a problem. The fiercest gangster Britain produced in the twentieth century lies in an unmarked grave.

It's not lack of money or respect. It's a real fear that someone will harm the grave, desecrate it, spoil it. Even after his death, people have old scores to settle with Arthur Thompson. After all, he was The Last Godfather.

WHERE ARE THEY NOW?

Here are the answers as of April 2006.

Adams Family
They are now widely accepted as the most powerful team in London.

Al Agha, Benjamin 'Ben'
Ben was recently tried on major smuggling charges but the trial collapsed. He lives openly in London and in several houses throughout Britain in spite of having had a deportation order hanging over his head for twenty years.

Apprentice, The
Still at large, he spends most of his time abroad.

Arifs
A major London team, they have been involved in drug trafficking, kidnappings and other aspects of organised crime.

Bagan, Tam
In 1995, he succeeded in forcing an inquiry into The Licensee's dealings with corrupt cops. The inquiry, by Glasgow's Procurator Fiscal Department, was inconclusive. Freed following a twelve-year sentence for armed robbery, he is now living peacefully and taken up painting.

Barlinnie Prison (aka BarL or The BarL)
In 2004, slopping-out ended at this jail.

Beltrami, Joe
After fifty years in the legal business, Beltrami is still practicing law and taking on high-profile cases.

Bible John
Even though a suspect's body was exhumed for DNA testing, the murders committed by Bible John remain unsolved.

Biggs, Ronnie
Having suffered many strokes, he returned from his exile in Brazil. Now very ill and frail, he is still locked up in the top security jail, Belmarsh Prison.

Blake, George
The MI6 spy was exposed as a double agent for the USSR and jailed for forty-two years in the UK. He escaped from Wormwood Scrubs in 1966 and fled to Moscow where, now aged eighty-three, he still lives.

Boyle, Jimmy 'Babyface'
Now a sculptor and wine dealer, Boyle splits his time between homes in France, where he has become something of a cult character, and Morocco. A French film on him is due for release in 2006.

Boyd, Stewart 'Speccy'
In Spain in 2003, he was killed in a mysterious car crash that is still being investigated by the authorities. His death has resulted in violent turf wars for control of the south side of Glasgow. Three years after his death, these turf wars have not been settled.

Brindles
This outfit is now one of the most senior gangs in London.

Budgie Bar
Still serving drink and food to the workers at Glasgow Fruit Market, this hostelry matches the workers' hours, making it just the place to go if you need alcohol for breakfast.

Campbell, Bobby
Having served ten years for an offence another man committed, he returned to his family to discover that former partners had cheated him out of money. He died of natural causes in the early 1960s.

Campbell, Thomas 'TC'
TC is free at last. In 2004, he successfully won his appeal against his conviction for the murder of the Doyle Family in 1984. His book Indictment reveals the horror of unjust conviction. He is currently fighting his case for compensation.

Caravel
Nothing of this remains but flattened earth.

Carbin, Gerry 'Cyclops'
He returned from his self-imposed exile in Spain to Glasgow in 2002 to take sides in a battle for the north side of the city. But, in 2003, broke and still hopelessly addicted to heroin, he contracted the flesh-eating bug necrotising fasciitis and died.

Cooney, Agnes
Her murder remains unsolved though police have announced that sophisticated DNA techniques have allowed them to link her death with those of five other women. Over a hundred former Strathclyde cops have been brought out of retirement to help in the investigation.

Cornell, George
In 1966, he was murdered in the Blind Beggar Pub by Ronnie Kray.

Cottage Bar
This pub is still open to the public.

Craig, Charlie
Retired from the police, he died of natural causes.

Dempster, Bobby 'The Devil' (aka The Quiet Man)
Still active on the Glasgow scene, he has major interests in the security sector. In 2002, a former associate of his, Lewis 'Scoobie' Rodden, was shot at point-blank range in Amsterdam but survived.

Dors, Diana
She married Alan Lake in 1968. Lake served one year in jail for a pub brawl and she joined a campaign for prisoners to be allowed to have sex with their partners. Dors died on 4 May 1984 of cancer.

Douglas, Wattie
Now known as 'Scarface' due to numerous plastic surgery operations to conceal his identity, he was last heard of in Amsterdam, Spain and Russia trafficking cannabis.

Edwards, Buster
After the Great Train Robbery, he escaped to Mexico where he lived for three years before giving himself up. He was the subject of the movie Buster, starring Phil Collins. Edwards ran a flower stall for many years but, in the late 1990s, he committed suicide.

Fairbairn, Nicholas, QC
He became Tory MP for Perth and Kinross from 1974 and was Solicitor General for Scotland from 1979 to 1982. He died in 1995 at the age of sixty-one.

Ferris, Billy
He was jailed for a second murder in 2004 but is currently preparing an appeal.

Ferris, Jenny
She has now moved out of Blackhill and away from Glasgow.

Ferris, Paul
Sentenced to seven years in prison at the Old Bailey in 1997 for gunrunning, he was liberated in January 2002, swearing to go straight, and he has been offence free since. He has had three books published and is busy working on other similar projects. He also runs a controversial website, www.ferriscon-spiracy.com.

Ferris, Willie
He died of natural causes in 1993, fighting all the way as usual.

Findlay, Donald, QC
Outspoken and controversial, he remains a top performer in court. He was a director of Rangers FC till a video of him singing sectarian songs was leaked and he resigned. But his clients don't care what religion he is or which football club he supports – it's his track record for getting not guilty and not proven verdicts that attracts them.

Forbes, Peter
He is still a successful lawyer.

Fraser, 'Mad' Frankie (aka The Dentist)
He has spent forty-two of his eighty-two years in prison. Now free, he spends his time writing books, running a website, www.madfrankiefraser.co.uk, occasionally starring in his own cabaret show and hosting guided tours of gangland London.

Fullerton, Billy (leader of the Billy Boys)
In 1962, he died of lung cancer.

Garland, Judy
By the time she was turning up at the Krays' Double R club, her life was already spiralling out of control. She died of drug addiction and illness on 22 June 1969, aged forty-seven.

Gentle, Andrew
Serving life for the murder of Ian Waddell and Josephine Chiperfield, he escaped from jail weeks before he was due for release. He predicted that, if he returned to jail, 'they' would get him. He was recaptured in 1996 and, three weeks after being sent back to jail, he was found hanging by the neck in his cell at Greenock Prison. His death has formally been recorded as suicide.

Gilmour, Raymond
He was released in 2002, pending appeal against his conviction for the murder of fifteen-year-old Pamela Hastie in 1981. At the time of writing, cops are investigating serial killer Robert Black for her murder.

Glover, Bobby
His murder remains unsolved.

Goldie, James
His murder remains unsolved.

Hall, Archibald (aka The Monster Butler)
He died of a stroke in Kingston Prison, Portsmouth, in October 2002.

Hamilton, Martin
In November 2000, he was jailed for life at the High Court, Inverness, having been found guilty of various charges to do with taking over the drugs trade in Broomhouse, Edinburgh. During the trial, tales of brutality and torture emerged and the media dubbed him the 'Blackhill Butcher'.

Hamilton, Paul
His murder remains unsolved.

Hanlon, Joe 'Bananas'
His murder remains unsolved.

Harrison, Margaret
see under Johnstone

Healy, Mick
He is now free, having served a long sentence for armed robbery in Torquay.

Hill, Billy
Having made a fortune out of the Second World War black market and raiding post offices, he lived in a baronial mansion in England. On his retirement in 1974, he moved to a large villa in Marbella. He died of lung cancer in 1984, aged seventy-three. His old partner Jack Spot called him 'the richest man in the graveyard'.

Jacobs, Gary
After a career at the top in boxing, he is now retired. In 2003, he was accused of dealing drugs but all charges were dropped.

Jaspan, Andrew

He went on to edit *The Observer* and the *Sunday Herald* and, in August 2004, he announced a move to edit *The Age*, a leading Australian newspaper.

Johnstone, Margaret (aka Harrison)

Her murder remains unsolved.

Kennedy, Ludovic

Now retired from TV, he continues to write books and give the occasional lecture.

Knight, Ronnie

Now free, he and his wife run a website – www.crooks-reunited.co.uk. Its aim is to help those who have been in jail, and their families, and who have lost touch with each other and bring them together.

Kray, Charlie

Aged seventy-three, he died of cancer in prison on the Isle of Wight on 4 April 2000. He was serving a twelve-year sentence for trafficking drugs.

Kray, Reg

At the age of sixty-six, he died on 1 October 2000. Shortly before his death the Home Secretary, Jack Straw, released him on compassionate leave on the grounds of his ill health. He had been serving thirty years for the murder of Jack 'The Hat' McVitie.

Kray, Ronnie

Aged sixty-one, he died of a heart attack in hospital on 17 March 1995, after collapsing in his cell in Broadmoor State Hospital. He was serving thirty years for shooting George Cornell in the Blind Beggar pub.

Lawson, Trevor

After demolishing the Caravel one night, to avoid a forensic check by the cops, Lawson suddenly obtained great wealth. He continued to work with the owner of the Caravel, Thomas McGraw, The Licensee. He was run over and killed in 2002 while crossing the M80 motorway to avoid a fight.

Leech, Mark

Having served sentences in many UK prisons, he reformed, qualified as a lawyer and is now a leading campaigner for prisoners' rights. Mark Leech has a lot of friends.

Leitch, Willie (aka 'The Saughton Harrier')

Free at last.

Liston, Sonny

The former world heavyweight-boxing champion was rumoured to have been linked to the Mafia and to have deliberately lost to Muhammad Ali on 25 May 1965 to allow Ali to win the world title. Aged thirty-eight, he died in mysterious circumstances on 30 December 1970. Officially, he had suffered a drug overdose but conspiracy theories abound – from being scared to death by the Nation of Islam to being killed by the Mob.

Lobban, William 'Tootsie'

In and out of English jails since 1991, he was most recently serving time in Perth Prison where he was asking for protection. From the money he received for setting up Bobby Glover and Joe Hanlon, all he has left is a watch which is why he was reduced to selling his story to a Sunday tabloid in 2005.

Malky or Malky Fraser

Rhyming slang for 'open razor', this one-time weapon of choice is now almost redundant, having been replaced by more efficient killing knives. The rumour is that it's making a comeback.

Morrison, Alex
Still promoting boxing.

McAulay, Hilda
Her murder remains unsolved though police have announced that sophisticated DNA techniques have now allowed them to link her death with five other women. Over a hundred former Strathclyde cops have been brought out of retirement to help in the investigation.

McCafferty, Anne Marie
Though separated from Paul Ferris, the two remain on good terms. She brought up their son, Paul Ferris Junior, remarkably free from any impact of the media coverage of his father.

McDonald, Blink and Alco
They continued with a career of crime but, since 2004, both have been at liberty.

McGraw, Margaret 'The Jeweller'
Now separated from her husband, The Licensee, she is spending an increasing amount of time in their house in Tenerife.

McGraw, Thomas 'The Licensee'
Now estimated to be worth £30 million, he is listed as one of the richest gangsters in the UK. Although he has many interests abroad, he is still active in Scotland. In 1998, he faced charges of major drugs trafficking but was acquitted. In 2002, along with one of his henchmen, Billy McPhee, he was involved in very publicly trying to kill TC Campbell. Early in 2004, he was at the Royal Oak bar in Glasgow when two of his associates, John McCartney and Craig Devlin, were gunned

down. He was declared bankrupt in September 2004 for not paying an income tax demand for under £13,000, a tiny percentage of his fortune. Since his separation from his wife, he has taken to heavy drinking and dating lap dancers.

McGraw, William 'Winky'
No longer addicted to heroin and now reconciled with his parents, he works in the family business overseeing their cartel of legitimate businesses. In 2002, he narrowly escaped when a gunman burst into the family home intent on killing his father. Luckily he had had no wish to kill the son.

McIntosh, Grant
Still active and based in Paisley, he has had no charges or convictions against him for a number of years. In 2005 his brother was killed in a bar room brawl.

McKay, Ron
He formed Arab TV (ATV) in 2003. He met with controversy when he rejected a tape with a message from Osama bin Laden and then broadcast an interview between Tony Benn MP and Saddam Hussein in which Saddam denied having weapons of mass destruction. The latter event had politicians describing the TV station as the dictator's mouthpiece. A close associate of 'Gorgeous' George Galloway the controversial MP who, in 2005 made an outspoken speech to the US Senate against the invasion of Iraq. In January 2006, Galloway entered the Celebrity Big Brother House as a contestant.

McLean, James 'Jaimba'
In 2002, he narrowly escaped death when he was shot in the chest. He suffers from long-term mental illness which, he claims, resulted from being drugged during an interview with MI5.

McLean, Lenny 'The Governor'

He has played roles in a number of films, including Barry the Baptist in *Lock, Stock and Two Smoking Barrels*. His autobiography, *The Guv'nor*, became an international best-seller. He admitted to agreeing to kill Paul Ferris on behalf of his long-term friend Arthur Thompson. McLean died of natural causes on 28 July 1998. Ferris is still very much alive.

McNee, Sir David

He went on to be the commissioner of the Metropolitan Police from 1977 to 1982 during which time he oversaw a period of race riots in Brixton and elsewhere. In 2002, he was involved in a company developing anti-terrorist computer software.

McPhee, Billy

In 1998, along with Thomas McGraw, The Licensee, he escaped conviction for drug trafficking. He and The Licensee were involved in a public attempt to murder TC Campbell in 2002. Later in 2002, McPhee survived being shot in the face at close range in Shettleston Juniors Social Club in Glasgow's east end. In March 2003, while watching a Scotland rugby international match on TV in the Springhill Tavern Brewer's Fayre in the east end, McPhee was stabbed twenty-seven times and died a short while later. A man, Mark Clinton, was charged with his murder but the trial collapsed after three hours, making it possibly the shortest murder trial in Scottish history where the defendant pled not guilty. McPhee's murder remains unsolved.

McPhie, Frank 'The Iceman'

Jailed for eight years in 1992 for drug trafficking, he became one of the major drug dealers in Scotland, linking with Irish teams. In 1997, the case against him for killing murderer William Toye in his cell at Perth Prison was found not proven.

In 1998, the jury at his trial for the murder of twenty-five-year-old bridegroom Christopher McGrory also returned a not proven verdict. McPhie had attended McGory's wedding two weeks before he was killed. On 10 May 2000, McPhie, aged fifty-one, was shot dead by a sniper outside his Maryhill flat within yards of his eleven-year-old son. His murder remains unsolved.

Norval, Walter
He is now at liberty and leading a peaceful life. In 2003, a biography about him, *Glasgow's Godfather*, written by Robert Jeffrey, became a best-seller. Now in his eighties, he is still strong, vibrant and full of charisma.

Noye, Kenny
Serving life imprisonment for a road-rage murder of a young man. Noye evaded capture for years by having plastic surgery to change his appearance and living abroad. He was eventually captured in a sting involving the victim's girlfriend who had witnessed the slaying.

Peterhead Prison
Now specialising in work with serious sex offenders, in 2002, it was almost closed down by the Scottish Executive before being reprieved by a public campaign backed by the media.

Ponderosa, The
Arthur and his wife Rita's home for many years, it is still occupied by Rita Thompson and some relatives and acts as a lasting monument to Arthur Thompson.

Preventive Detention
While long since fallen into disrepute, some say it has returned in the form of the new anti-terrorist legislation.

Provanmill Inn

The former Thompson HQ was badly damaged by fire in September 2004. It was later torched again and now there's nothing left of Arthur Thompson's symbolic HQ.

Pyle, Joey

He is seen by many as London's Don of Dons and the fact that he was told by the New York Mafia that he was the only player in the UK they'd deal with would tend to support this. He has now retired from his life of crime and is involved in legitimate business and promotional work.

Ramensky, Johnny

Awarded the Military Medal for his commando exploits in the Second World War, he returned to a life of crime. In 1972, he collapsed and died in Perth Prison, aged sixty-seven.

Reynolds, Bruce

The mastermind behind the Great Train Robbery of 1963, he was captured, penniless, after five years on the run and given twenty-five years in jail. Now aged seventy-one, Reynolds is involved in legitimate enterprises.

Richardson, Charlie

In 1966 in England, he was arrested and was heading towards the infamous Torture Trial. The proceedings were so significant that each jury member was given a personal bodyguard and the official papers remain sealed and banned to the public. Charlie Richardson was jailed for twenty-five years though many players reckon he took the rap as the leading member but others were actually more sadistic. The story was released as a film, *Charlie*, starring Luke Goss and Steven Berkoff, in 2004.

Richardson, Eddie

Along with Frankie Fraser, he was wounded in an infamous shoot-out in 1966. The showdown is now known as the Battle of Mr Smith's Club and it ended with many casualties and one death. While the reasons for the fight range from a take-over bid to fear of retribution by another guy for having an affair with the team's mechanic, it ended the Richardson Gang as an entity. Eddie went on to serve two lengthy prison sentences. Last heard of, he was on parole and spending his life painting, a discipline he had taught himself in jail.

Ross, Gordon

Along with Thomas McGraw, The Licensee, he escaped conviction for drug trafficking in 1998. He became increasingly unpopular among Glasgow street players because he chose to protect rather than punish a male relative who was known to have violently raped several women. In September 2002, outside The Sheiling Bar in the centre of his east-end territory, Gordon Ross was stabbed to death. For over an hour, his body lay ignored by the roadside till it was spotted by a passing police car. His murder remains unsolved.

Ross, Rachel and Abraham

Rachel Ross's murder remains unsolved. Abraham Ross is now deceased.

Shaw, 'Pretty Boy' Roy

Having spent decades in jail, he was deemed to be so uncontrollable that he was 'mentalled' and sent to Broadmoor. Eventually, he went on to prove his sanity and was released. He then entered the world of unlicensed boxing, promoted by Joey Pyle. He went on to become the undisputed champ and made an honest living from that and other legitimate businesses. See www.royprettyboyshaw.com for fuller biographical details.

Skibo Castle
It is now most famous for being the chosen venue for the wedding of Madonna and Guy Ritchie as well as a raft of other show-business celebrities.

Smith, Martin
This popular media lawyer – a tall and strongly built man – was often mistaken for a street player. This caused him and some of his clients, among them the most notorious men on Scotland's streets, some amusement. Unfortunately, after a short illness he died in 2004. The world's a sadder, more unjust place without him.

Spot, Jack
Once the undisputed king of crime in London, he died of natural causes in an old people's home on the south coast of England in 1996, a very old, forlorn and forgotten man.

Steele, Joe
Free at last: in 2004 he successfully won the appeal against his conviction for the murder of the Doyle Family in 1984. Currently fighting for compensation. As at the date of writing (Jan 2006) he has received nothing from the State and continues to live on welfare benefits.

Thompson, Arthur 'Fatboy'
His murder remains unsolved.

Thompson, Billy
The sole surviving male of the Thompson clan, he has not filled his father's shoes. With a well-established drug problem, his life is full of calamity. Armed police raided The Ponderosa in 1995 to find nothing more dangerous than a harpoon. Because it wasn't a gun, he was only sentenced to eighteen months. In 1999, while showing off a bullet-proof vest to

friends, he stabbed himself seriously in the chest when the blade of the knife he was using slipped through the reinforced slats. In 2000, while demanding £3.00 off some guys, he was beaten up and sustained serious brain injuries. He survived but suffers chronic disabilities. In 2005, his mother threw him out of The Ponderosa because she was fed up with his chronic drug problems. Last heard of, he was homeless and broke.

Thompson, Rita
Still living in The Ponderosa, she keeps a low profile and refuses to talk to outsiders.

Thompson, Tracey
She has made repeated attempts to break away from her family's association with crime. One such attempt involved her setting up legitimate businesses including a mobile phone shop, Communique, on Maryhill Road. In 1999, she was declared bankrupt over an unpaid VAT bill of only £3,718.

The Tuxedo Princess
This boat, which doubled as a venue for discos, has now sailed away into the sunset to party elsewhere . . . well, Newcastle actually.

Vannet, A.
Last heard of, he had transferred from the Crown Office to the Procurator Fiscal's Office in Glasgow and was then promoted to the post of Sheriff (a kind of judge in Scotland) in Airdrie, Lanarkshire.

Walker, Norrie, DI
A short while after having led the investigation leading to the conviction of TC Campbell and Joe Steele for the murder of the Doyle family in the so-called Ice-Cream Wars, he committed suicide. Since Campbell and Steele have been cleared by

appeal, family members are now saying that Walker did leave a suicide note – something the police denied at the time.

Watt, Mark
Jailed for nine and then ten years for drug dealing, in April 2000 he was involved in a car race along the M8, near Paisley, that resulted in the death of a six-month-old baby. Watt fled to Spain rather than face the court proceedings. Eventually, in December 2002, he appeared at the High Court, Glasgow, and was sentenced to five years.

Welsh Family
A spent force since the late 1980s, the surviving brothers were last heard of being involved in running saunas and the distribution of porn.

Wilson, Charlie
Sentenced to thirty years for his part in the Great Train Robbery, he is reputed to be the man who knew where most of the £2.5 million was stashed. In 1964, he escaped from Winson Green maximum-security prison and went to live on the outskirts of Montreal, Canada. His wife, making a mistake on the telephone, allowed British police to track him down and return him to jail. Having served his sentence, he became a drug trafficker on the Costa del Sol where, on 23 April 1990, as he was relaxing by his swimming pool, he was shot dead by a hit man.

World's End, The
This popular pub on Edinburgh's Royal Mile is still open for business.

World's End Murders, The
As this goes to print, a fifty-nine-year-old man is awaiting trial for the rape murders of teenagers Helen Scott and

Christine Eadie after they'd spent a night out at the World's End pub in Edinburgh in 1977. Advances in DNA technology led to the police tracking him down.

Zulu Stopper

This huge old type of revolver hasn't seen action on the streets of Glasgow since the demise of Fatboy Thompson.

BIBLIOGRAPHY

Campbell, T C and McKay, Reg, *Indictment – Trial by Fire* (Edinburgh: Canongate, 2001)

Campbell, T C and McKay, Reg, *The Wilderness Years* (Edinburgh: Canongate, 2002)

Davidson, Earl, *Joey Pyle – Notorious* (London: Virgin Books Ltd, 2003)

Ferris, Paul and McKay, Reg, *Vendetta* (Edinburgh: Black & White Publishing 2005)

Ferris, Paul and McKay, Reg, *The Ferris Conspiracy* (Edinburgh: Mainstream, 2001)

Forbes, George and Meehan, Paddy, *Such Bad Company* (Edinburgh: Paul Harris Publishing, 1982)

Fraser, Frankie, *Mad Frank – Memoirs of a Life of Crime* (London: Warner Books, 1995)

House, Jack, *Square Mile of Murder* (Glasgow: Richard Drew Publishing, 1984)

Jeffrey, Robert, *Gangland Glasgow* (Edinburgh: Black & White Publishing, 2002)

Jeffrey, Robert, *Glasgow's Hard Men* (Edinburgh: Black & White Publishing, 2002)

Kray, Reg, *Born Fighter* (London: Arrow Books, 1991)

Kray, Ron with Dinenage, Fred, *My Story* (London: Pan Books, 1993)

BIBLIOGRAPHY

Lucas, Norman and Davies, Phillip, *The Monster Butler* (London: Weidenfeld and Nicolson, 1990)

McLean, Lenny with Gerrard, Peter, *The Guv'nor* (London: Blake Publishing Ltd, 2003)

Morton, James, *Gangland 2 – The Underworld in Britain and Ireland* (London: Warner Books, 1995)

Richardson, Charlie, *My Manor* (London: Pan Books, 1992)

Shaw, Roy with Kray, Katie, *Pretty Boy* (London: Blake Publishing Ltd, 2003)

Skelton, Douglas, *Blood on the Thistle* (London: HarperCollins Publishers, 1994)

Skelton, Douglas, *No Final Solution* (Edinburgh: Mainstream Publishing, 1994)

INDEX

VENDETTA

PAUL FERRIS & REG McKAY

The Conspiracy Continues . . .

Paul Ferris ruled crime in Scotland. He had links to London firms, Manchester gangs and Liverpool faces. He'd been accused of murdering The Godfather's son, Fatboy, and found not guilty. Some cops talked of killing him. But, when he was released from prison in 2002, he told the world and the waiting press that he was walking away from his life of crime. But would they let him? As soon as his car sped away, the journalists were after him. And they weren't the only ones . . .

Vendetta tells the astonishing inside story of what happened next to Paul Ferris. And it's a story of international gangsters, hit contracts, murders, bank scams, Essex-boy torturers, corrupt politics, crack-head hit men, knife duels, Securi-wars, drugs, guns, Yardies, terrorists and more. In *Vendetta*, Paul Ferris slashes open the underbelly of Britain's streets and exposes the dark forces that police them as well as revealing the truth about what really happened to him and about the conspiracies and corruption that won't leave him alone.

For years, new enemies and old foes have tried to silence Paul Ferris. But it's Ferris who's here to tell the tale while many of them are not. And some tale it is.

£9.99 PAPERBACK (ISBN 1-84502-061-8)

*Available from all good bookshops
or, to order direct from our distributor,
call Book Source on 0870 240 2182*

MURDER CAPITAL

LIFE AND DEATH ON
THE STREETS OF GLASGOW

REG McKAY

A new Glasgow true-crime book from Reg McKay,
the undisputed master of the genre

A warm welcome or a blade in the guts – it's the contradiction that makes Glasgow unique. Tourists and natives alike love Glasgow's people, the social scene, the music. Millions of visitors come to the city every year and most feel safe. Yet you're twice as likely to be murdered in Glasgow as you are in London and more likely to die violently there than in Belfast, Paris or Berlin. In *Murder Capital*, Reg McKay, who loves the city and knows about crime from the inside, offers up forty modern murder cases. This collection of tales, all bloody, all violent and all true, graphically explores how the city has earned its unenviable title of Murder Capital of Europe.

There are deadly honey traps, a politician whose daughter is doped and slain, bodies disposed of in council incinerators, deaths that have been treated as suicides in the full knowledge that they are in fact murder victims and drunken and drug-fuelled fights that end in death. Some of the names of those involved will be familiar but many will be a surprise.

PUBLISHED JUNE 2006
£9.99 PAPERBACK (ISBN 1-84502-093-6)